DIETARY SUPPLEMENTS AND NUTRACEUTICALS

SCIENTIFIC PRINCIPLES AND HEALTH BENEFITS

PROF. V. GIRIJA SASTRY, DR. N. SIVA KUMAR,
MS.Y. ACHYUTHA VALLI DEVI

Made with ♥ on the Notion Press Platform
www.notionpress.com

Contents

Dietary Supplements And Nutraceuticals

Scientific Principles and Health Benefits

AUTHORS
Prof. Girija Sastry Vedula
Professor,
A.U. College of Pharmaceutical Sciences,
Andhra University,
Visakhapatnam, Andhra Pradesh, India
Dr. Siva Kumar Nemala
Associate Professor,
Sri Vasavi Institute of Pharmaceutical Sciences,
Pedatadepalli, Tadepalligudem,
West Godavari (Dist.), Andhra Pradesh, India
Ms. Achyutha Valli Devi Yerra
Research Scholar,
A.U. College of Pharmaceutical Sciences,
Andhra University,
Visakhapatnam, Andhra Pradesh, India

Editor
Dr. A. Muralidhar Rao, M.Pharm., PhD., FISCA., FICPHS
Principal,
St. Mary's College of Pharmacy,
Secunderabad, Telangana, India
Published by Notion Press
Notion Press, Inc.
800, West El Camino Real #180,
California, USA 94040
Notion Press Media Pvt Ltd
#7, Red Cross Road,
Egmore, Chennai, Tamil Nadu 600008
Email ID: publish@notionpress.com
Phone Number: +91 44 46315631

Preface

The growing interest in dietary supplements and nutraceuticals has led to a dynamic intersection of nutrition, medicine, and pharmaceutical sciences. Over the past few decades, an increasing body of scientific evidence has highlighted the significant role of bioactive compounds in promoting health, preventing diseases, and complementing conventional therapeutic approaches. This book, **"Dietary Supplements and Nutraceuticals: Scientific Principles and Health Benefits,"** aims to provide a comprehensive and evidence-based resource for students, researchers, healthcare professionals, and industry experts seeking a deeper understanding of the science and applications of nutraceuticals.

This book is structured to cover the **fundamental principles, biochemical mechanisms, and health implications** of dietary supplements and nutraceuticals. It begins by defining key concepts and classifications, distinguishing between dietary supplements, functional foods, and pharmaceuticals. The discussion extends to the bioactive components found in plant, animal, and microbial sources, including vitamins, minerals, polyphenols, flavonoids, carotenoids, probiotics, and prebiotics. Their mechanisms of action, efficacy in disease prevention, and potential therapeutic roles are explored through recent scientific studies and clinical research.

A significant emphasis is placed on **the role of nutraceuticals in managing chronic diseases**, such as cardiovascular disorders, diabetes, cancer, neurodegenerative conditions, and metabolic syndromes. Each chapter presents the latest research findings on how these bioactive compounds influence biological pathways, reduce oxidative stress, modulate immune responses, and support overall well-being. The **safety, toxicity, dosage considerations, and regulatory aspects** of dietary supplements are also thoroughly discussed, providing clarity on international guidelines set by regulatory authorities such as the **Food and Drug Administration (FDA), European Food Safety Authority (EFSA), Codex Alimentarius, and Good Manufacturing Practices (GMPs).**

In an era where **evidence-based nutrition and personalized healthcare** are gaining prominence, this book serves as a valuable academic reference by bridging the gap between **traditional knowledge and modern scientific advancements**. We hope this book will contribute to a **deeper**

appreciation of the scientific foundations of nutraceuticals and encourage further research into their potential in promoting global health.

We extend our sincere gratitude to our colleagues, students, and researchers whose valuable insights and contributions have shaped this work. We also acknowledge the dedication of scientists and healthcare professionals working to advance nutraceutical science, making significant strides in improving health and wellness worldwide.

We hope this book provides a **meaningful resource for academicians, industry professionals, and students** interested in the field of **nutraceuticals and dietary supplements**.

AUTHORS

Prof. V. Girija Sastry, Dr. N. Siva Kumar, Ms. Y. Achyutha Valli Devi

CHAPTER ONE

Introduction to Nutraceuticals and Functional Foods

1.1.1.1 Functional Foods

Functional foods are defined as foods that provide benefits beyond basic nutrition due to the presence of bioactive compounds that can help improve health and reduce the risk of disease. These foods have characteristics that include a rich content of vitamins, minerals, antioxidants, and other phytochemicals that play important roles in maintaining the normal function of the body. For example, foods such as tomatoes contain lycopene, a powerful antioxidant that can be present in amounts ranging from 3 to 7 mg per 100 grams, while green tea contains catechins which may vary from 100 to 200 mg per serving. These values indicate the significant nutritional components that help in neutralising free radicals and protecting cellular integrity. Functional foods often include whole grains, fruits, vegetables, nuts, and seeds that have not only essential macronutrients such as carbohydrates, proteins, and fats but also micronutrients that support metabolism, immune function, and hormonal balance. Their characteristics also extend to their ability to provide bioactive compounds that influence metabolic pathways; for instance, the presence of omega-3 fatty acids in fish and flaxseeds helps to lower blood cholesterol levels and improve cardiovascular function.

Examples of functional foods include foods like oats that are high in soluble fibre, which can lower low-density lipoprotein cholesterol by 5 to

10% when consumed regularly, and fermented foods such as yogurt, which contain live cultures like Lactobacillus species that can enhance gut health. The nutritional significance of these foods is evident from studies showing that diets rich in fruits, vegetables, and whole grains can lower the incidence of chronic diseases such as diabetes, cancer, and heart disease by 20 to 30% compared to diets lacking in these foods. This significance is also supported by data from dietary surveys where populations consuming a higher proportion of functional foods report better overall health outcomes.

The role of functional foods in health promotion and disease prevention is based on their ability to provide natural bioactive compounds that improve the body's defence mechanisms. These foods work by enhancing the body's antioxidant capacity, reducing inflammation, and modulating the immune response. They can also regulate metabolic pathways, which is crucial for preventing lifestyle-related disorders such as obesity and type 2 diabetes. For example, regular consumption of foods high in polyphenols, such as berries, is associated with improved insulin sensitivity and a lower risk of developing type 2 diabetes. In addition, the inclusion of functional foods in the diet supports cardiovascular health by preventing the oxidation of low-density lipoproteins and by promoting a healthy lipid profile. Research has shown that a daily intake of functional foods can improve cardiovascular parameters by reducing blood pressure and improving endothelial function. Overall, functional foods play an essential role in promoting long-term health by providing a combination of essential nutrients and bioactive compounds that help in maintaining physiological balance and protecting against chronic diseases.

1.1.1.2 Nutraceuticals

Definition and Scope

Nutraceuticals are defined as food-derived products that offer health benefits beyond the provision of basic nutritional value. They include substances that are extracted from natural sources and are used to promote overall well-being, prevent chronic diseases, and support the management of existing conditions. Nutraceuticals encompass a broad range of products, from isolated nutrients and dietary supplements to herbal extracts and fortified foods. For instance, the use of omega-3 fatty acids derived from fish oil, which are often present at dosages ranging from 300 to 1000 mg per capsule, exemplifies how these products provide specific health benefits such as improving cardiovascular function and reducing inflammation. The scope of nutraceuticals extends into preventive healthcare, where these products are incorporated into daily diets to support the immune system, regulate metabolic processes, and enhance the body's natural defence mechanisms. Nutraceuticals serve a dual purpose by not only supplying essential nutrients but also by offering additional bioactive compounds that exert pharmacological effects, such as reducing oxidative stress or modulating hormone levels, which are crucial for maintaining optimal health in both preventive and therapeutic settings.

Differentiation from Conventional Food and Pharmaceuticals

Nutraceuticals differ from conventional foods in that conventional foods primarily focus on basic sustenance and energy provision, while nutraceuticals are formulated to deliver extra health benefits through concentrated doses of bioactive compounds. Unlike conventional foods, which provide nutrients in amounts determined by their natural composition, nutraceuticals often contain enriched levels of vitamins, minerals, or phytochemicals that have been isolated and standardised to ensure consistent efficacy. This standardisation can involve precise measurements; for example, a nutraceutical product might contain 500 mg of a specific polyphenol per serving, a concentration that is unlikely to be achieved through a regular diet. In comparison to pharmaceuticals, nutraceuticals are derived from natural sources and are used primarily to support health rather than to treat or cure specific diseases. Pharmaceuticals undergo rigorous clinical trials and are regulated strictly as drugs, with defined therapeutic dosages and mechanisms of action. Nutraceuticals, on the other hand, typically face a different regulatory framework and are often marketed with claims related to wellness and health maintenance. They are not intended to replace prescription medications but to complement a healthy lifestyle by providing additional nutritional support, thereby bridging the gap between food and medicine in a manner that is accessible and safe for long-term use.

Categories and Types Based on Source and Composition

Nutraceuticals can be categorised based on both their source and their chemical composition, resulting in several distinct types. One important category includes vitamins and minerals, which are essential micronutrients required in small amounts for numerous biochemical processes; examples include vitamin D for bone health and iron for oxygen transport, often available in dosages that meet or exceed the Recommended Dietary Allowance (RDA). Another category comprises bioactive compounds derived from plants, such as polyphenols, flavonoids, and carotenoids. These compounds are usually extracted from fruits, vegetables, herbs, and spices, and their concentration in nutraceutical products is standardised to provide consistent benefits; for instance, resveratrol supplements may contain between 100 and 500 mg per day, a level supported by various studies for their antioxidant and cardioprotective properties. Nutraceuticals also include functional proteins, such as those derived from soy or whey, which are used not only to supply amino acids but also to enhance muscle maintenance and metabolic functions. In addition, probiotic nutraceuticals consist of live microorganisms like Lactobacillus species, which are administered at levels typically ranging from 10^7 to 10^9 colony-forming units (CFU) per serving to support gut health and improve digestion. This classification based on source and composition allows for a detailed understanding of the specific components and their roles in health promotion, ensuring that each nutraceutical product delivers targeted benefits while being derived from natural and scientifically validated sources.

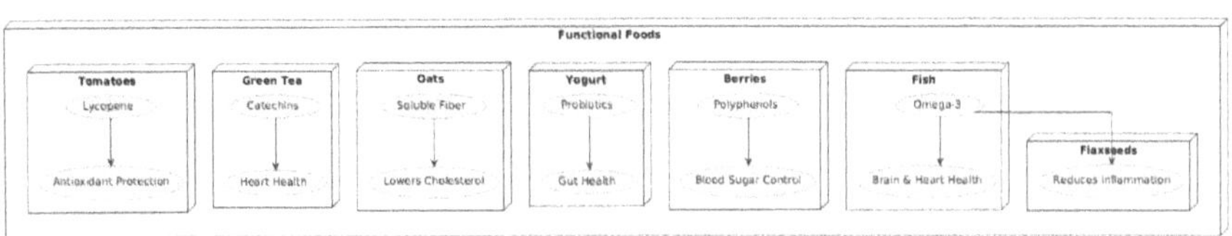

Functional Foods: Nutrition and Health Benefits

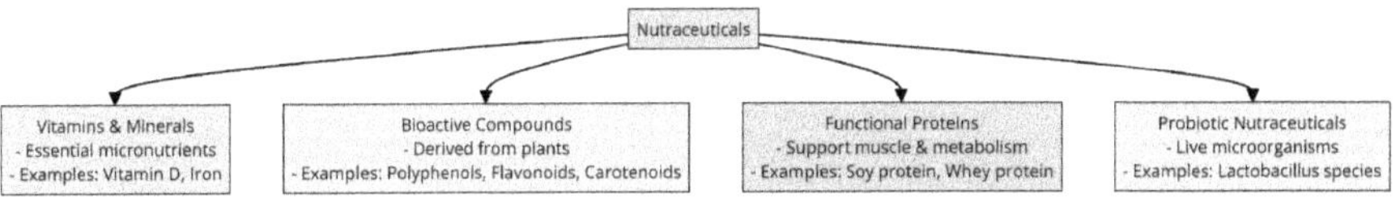

Categories of Nutraceuticals

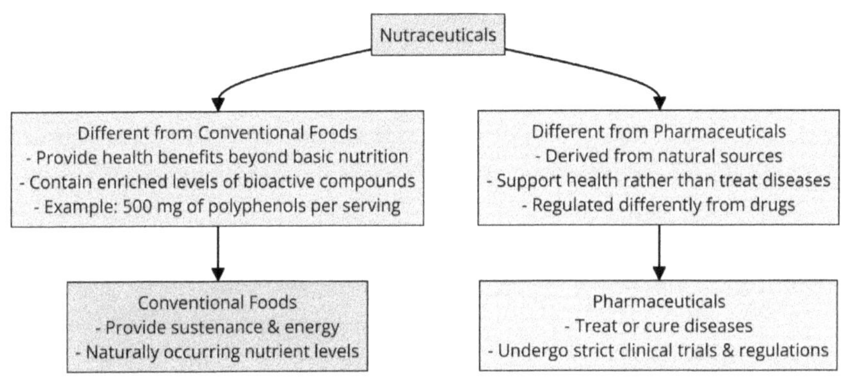

Differentiation of Nutraceuticals from Conventional Food and Pharmaceuticals

1.1.1.3 Dietary Supplements

Definition and Regulatory Aspects

Dietary supplements are defined as products intended to supplement the diet that contain one or more dietary ingredients such as vitamins, minerals, herbs or other botanicals, amino acids, enzymes, or a combination of these substances. They are designed to be taken by mouth in the form of capsules, tablets, powders, liquids, or other forms, and they aim to support overall health by providing nutrients that may not be consumed in sufficient quantities through a regular diet. Regulatory aspects of dietary supplements vary by country, but in many regions, such as India and the United States, these products are subject to specific guidelines that ensure their safety, quality, and accurate labelling. In India, the Food Safety and Standards Authority of India (FSSAI) oversees the regulation of dietary supplements and has established standards regarding the permissible levels of active ingredients, quality control measures, and labelling requirements. For example, dietary supplements that claim to provide vitamin D must clearly indicate the dosage, which often ranges from 400 to 1000 International Units (IU) per serving, while ensuring that the product does not exceed levels considered safe for long-term consumption. The regulatory framework is intended to protect consumers by requiring manufacturers to provide evidence of the purity and potency of the ingredients used, along with clear instructions for use and any potential health warnings. This regulatory oversight distinguishes dietary supplements from conventional foods and pharmaceuticals by ensuring that these products meet standards of efficacy and safety while being marketed for general health support rather than as treatments for specific diseases.

Forms (Capsules, Powders, Tablets, Liquids)

Dietary supplements are available in a variety of forms to cater to the different preferences and needs of consumers. Capsules are one of the most common forms and typically contain powdered or liquid ingredients enclosed in a gelatin or vegetarian capsule. This form allows for precise dosing, with many supplements providing specific amounts such as 500 mg per capsule of herbal extracts or 1000 IU per capsule of vitamin D. Tablets are another widely used form that offer convenience and portability; they are produced by compressing the active ingredients along with excipients and are designed to be swallowed whole. The dosage in tablets is carefully controlled, with examples including calcium tablets that may contain 500 mg of elemental calcium per tablet. Powders offer a flexible alternative, allowing consumers to mix the supplement with water, milk, or smoothies; they are particularly useful for athletes or individuals who require larger doses, such as protein powders where the serving size may be 20 to 30 grams of protein. Liquids are also popular, especially for individuals who have difficulty swallowing solid forms; liquid supplements such as vitamin B12 solutions or herbal tinctures are often formulated to deliver active ingredients in measured drops or millilitres, ensuring accurate dosing. Each form is developed with consideration for the stability and bioavailability of the active ingredients, ensuring that the intended health benefits are delivered effectively to the consumer.

Examples of Common Dietary Supplements and Their Active Ingredients

There are several common dietary supplements that have gained popularity due to their well-documented health benefits and scientifically validated active ingredients. For instance, vitamin C supplements, which are available in both tablet and capsule forms, typically provide dosages ranging from 500 to 1000 mg per serving; these supplements are known for their antioxidant properties and role in supporting the immune system. Another example is vitamin D supplements, which commonly offer 400 to 1000 IU per dose, and are essential for calcium absorption and bone health; studies have indicated that adequate vitamin D intake can reduce the risk of osteoporosis and support immune function. Calcium supplements, often provided in tablet or chewable forms, generally supply 500 mg to 600 mg of elemental calcium per serving, aiding in the maintenance of strong bones and teeth. Omega-3 fatty acid supplements, derived from fish oil, are typically available in softgel capsules and provide between 300 to 1000 mg of eicosapentaenoic acid (EPA) and docosahexaenoic acid (DHA) per serving, which are beneficial for cardiovascular health and reducing inflammation. Additionally, herbal supplements such as those containing turmeric extract are standardised to include 95% curcuminoids, with dosages commonly around 500 mg per capsule, and are recognised for their anti-inflammatory and antioxidant effects. Probiotic supplements, containing live microorganisms such as Lactobacillus acidophilus, are formulated to deliver between 10^7 to 10^9 colony forming units (CFU) per serving, thereby supporting gut health and the balance of intestinal flora. These examples illustrate how dietary supplements are specifically designed to deliver targeted health benefits by providing precise amounts of active ingredients, and their widespread use is supported by regulatory measures that ensure quality, safety, and accurate labelling.

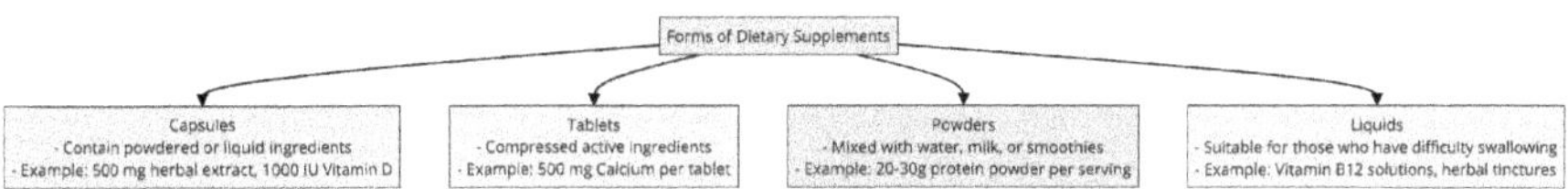

Forms of Dietary Supplements

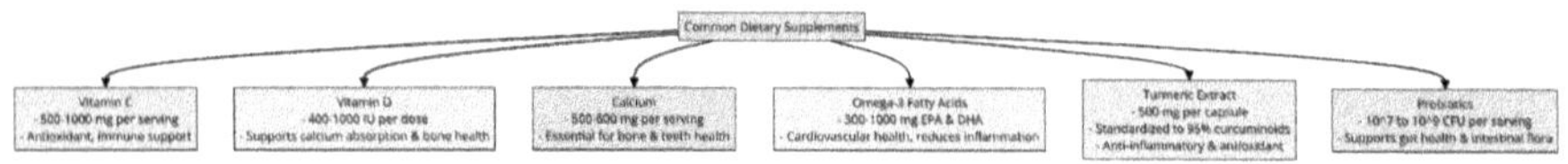

Common Dietary Supplements and Their Benefits

1.1.2 Historical Perspective and Evolution

1.1.2.1 Development of Nutraceuticals in Public Health

In ancient civilizations, people recognized that certain foods had properties that contributed to health and well-being. Long before modern science was established, communities in India, Egypt, China, and Greece used natural food components to prevent and treat common ailments. Ancient Ayurvedic texts, for example, describe the use of herbs, spices, and natural extracts in daily diets to improve digestion, boost immunity, and enhance longevity. In these early practices, the emphasis was on whole foods that naturally contained vitamins, minerals, and bioactive compounds. Traditional diets that incorporated a variety of fruits, vegetables, grains, and spices provided not only essential nutrition but also bioactive substances that modern research now recognises as beneficial in reducing the risk of diseases.

The discovery of vitamins, minerals, and other bioactive compounds marked significant milestones in the evolution of nutraceuticals. In the early twentieth century, scientists began to isolate and identify substances such as vitamin C, vitamin D, and vitamin E, which are now known to have specific roles in maintaining health. Researchers observed that populations suffering from vitamin deficiencies often experienced severe health problems, which led to controlled studies that established the importance of these micronutrients. The scientific identification of these compounds allowed for the formulation of fortified foods and dietary supplements. For instance, the fortification of milk with vitamin D began in the 1930s to help prevent rickets in children, a condition that had been common in many parts of the world. This period witnessed a surge in research focusing on the protective effects of bioactive compounds, and the data gathered from these studies provided evidence that the integration of these compounds into the diet could have a measurable impact on public health.

With advances in nutrition science and technology, nutraceuticals were integrated into modern public health initiatives as a strategy to combat chronic diseases and improve overall population health. Health authorities and government agencies started promoting dietary guidelines that encouraged the consumption of foods rich in bioactive compounds. Large-scale public health campaigns were initiated to address issues like malnutrition, vitamin deficiencies, and the rising incidence of lifestyle-related disorders such as cardiovascular diseases and diabetes. These initiatives led to the development of policies that supported food fortification and the use of nutraceuticals as a complement to conventional medical treatments. Over the past several decades, clinical trials and epidemiological studies have reinforced the concept that nutraceuticals can play a vital role in disease prevention and health maintenance. As a result, modern public health programs now include strategies for the regular consumption of nutraceuticals, which have been shown to improve immune function, regulate metabolic processes, and reduce the risk of chronic diseases by up to 20 to 30% in various populations. This integration of traditional wisdom with modern science has established nutraceuticals as an important tool in promoting long-term health and preventing disease.

1.1.2.2 Transition from Traditional Medicine to Modern Dietary Supplements

Traditional medicine has a long history that spans thousands of years in many cultures, including Indian, Chinese, and Mediterranean civilizations. These practices relied on natural remedies and the use of herbs, spices, and other natural substances that were believed to restore balance in the body and prevent illness. Ancient practitioners used formulations that included turmeric, ginger, garlic, and various herbal extracts to treat common ailments such as digestive disorders, respiratory problems, and inflammatory conditions. These remedies were developed based on observation and the collective experience of generations, with the emphasis on using whole plant materials and naturally occurring compounds. Traditional medical systems, such as Ayurveda and Traditional Chinese Medicine, provided detailed accounts of natural ingredients, their preparation methods, and dosages, which were passed down orally and through ancient texts. The use of these natural remedies was deeply integrated into daily life, with food and medicine often overlapping as part of a holistic approach to health.

Over time, the empirical use of natural remedies evolved into scientifically validated products as modern research began to investigate the active components of traditional medicines. In the early 20th century, scientific advancements led to the isolation and identification of key bioactive compounds such as curcumin from turmeric, allicin from garlic, and various flavonoids from fruits and vegetables. These discoveries were supported by controlled laboratory studies and clinical trials that quantified the benefits of these compounds using standard measurements and assays. For instance, the antioxidant activity of curcumin was measured using techniques such as the oxygen radical absorbance capacity (ORAC), which provided numerical values that validated its effectiveness in neutralizing free radicals. The evolution from empirical knowledge to scientific validation involved the application of modern analytical techniques including high-performance liquid chromatography (HPLC) and mass spectrometry, which enabled precise measurement of the concentration and purity of these bioactive substances. This scientific approach established the safety and efficacy of compounds that had been used traditionally, thereby bridging the gap between traditional knowledge and modern health science.

The emergence of standardized dietary supplements in clinical practice marks a significant milestone in the evolution of natural remedies. As the scientific community recognized the potential of these bioactive compounds, manufacturers began to develop formulations that offered precise dosages and consistent quality. Standardization involves the rigorous control of factors such as extraction methods, purity of active ingredients, and stability of the final product. For example, a standardized curcumin supplement may contain 95% curcuminoids and be produced in capsules delivering a fixed dose of 500 mg per serving, which is supported by clinical studies that have demonstrated improvements in inflammatory markers and joint health. Similarly, vitamin supplements are now produced to meet the Recommended Dietary Allowances (RDAs) and are subject to quality control measures set by regulatory authorities such as the Food Safety and Standards Authority of India (FSSAI). The development of standardized dietary supplements has allowed these products to be integrated into modern clinical practice as adjuncts to conventional therapy, with many health professionals recommending them to support overall well-being, manage specific conditions, and address nutritional deficiencies. This transition reflects a journey from traditional empirical use to a modern, evidence-based approach that ensures reliability, safety, and effectiveness in the promotion of health through natural products.

1.2 Classification of Nutraceuticals

1.2.1 Categories and Types

1.2.1.1 Based on Chemical Composition

Nutraceuticals can be classified according to their chemical composition, which helps in understanding the specific components responsible for their health benefits. One important category under this classification is vitamins. Vitamins such as vitamin C and vitamin E are essential micronutrients that play vital roles in various metabolic processes. Vitamin C, known for its antioxidant properties, is crucial for collagen synthesis and immune function and is typically found in amounts ranging from 50 to 90 mg per day in a balanced diet. Vitamin E, which acts as a fat-soluble antioxidant, protects cell membranes from oxidative damage and is often present in doses of around 15 mg per day in recommended dietary allowances. The precise chemical structures of these vitamins, such as the ascorbic acid structure of vitamin C and the tocopherol structure of vitamin E, determine their solubility and mode of action in the human body.

Another significant category is minerals, which are inorganic elements required in small amounts for maintaining the structure and function of the body. Calcium and iron serve as prime examples in this group. Calcium is vital for bone health, muscle function, and nerve transmission, and is commonly found in dairy products and green leafy vegetables with recommended intakes of around 1000 mg per day for adults. Iron, essential for the transport of oxygen in the blood via hemoglobin, is typically recommended at 18 mg per day for women of reproductive age and 8 mg per day for adult men. The chemical nature of these minerals, often present as salts or complexes, allows them to participate in enzymatic reactions and structural functions, thereby contributing significantly to overall physiological health.

In addition to vitamins and minerals, nutraceuticals also include bioactive compounds such as polyphenols, carotenoids, and flavonoids. Polyphenols, which are abundant in fruits, vegetables, tea, and wine, have a complex chemical structure that includes multiple phenol units and contribute to the prevention of oxidative stress and inflammation.

Carotenoids, which include compounds such as beta-carotene and lycopene, are responsible for the vibrant colors in many fruits and vegetables and play a role in reducing the risk of certain cancers and eye diseases; for example, beta-carotene can be converted into vitamin A in the body, with conversion ratios that may vary depending on dietary intake and individual metabolism. Flavonoids are a diverse group of phytonutrients with a characteristic flavone backbone that can modulate inflammatory pathways and act as antioxidants; they are found in foods like citrus fruits, berries, and green tea, and their consumption has been associated with improved cardiovascular health. Together, these bioactive compounds, present in nutraceutical products, enhance the value of foods by providing additional health benefits that go beyond basic nutrition.

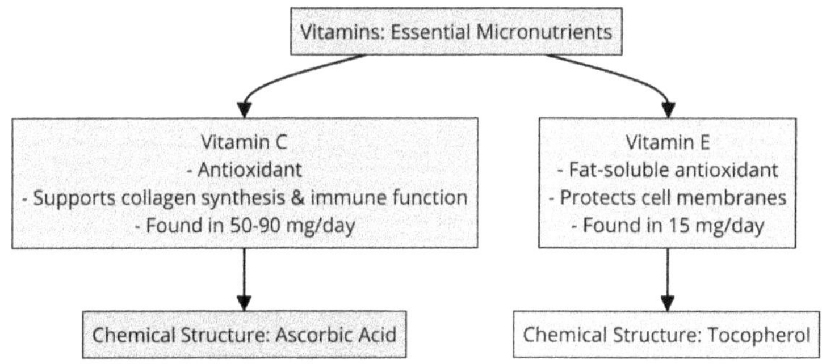

Roles of Vitamin C and Vitamin E

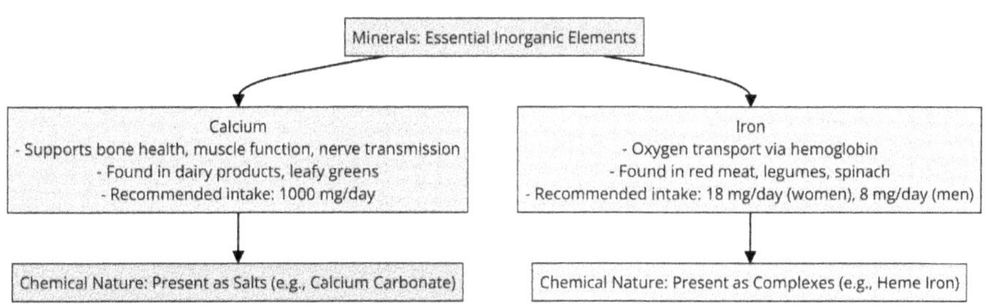

Roles of Calcium and Iron

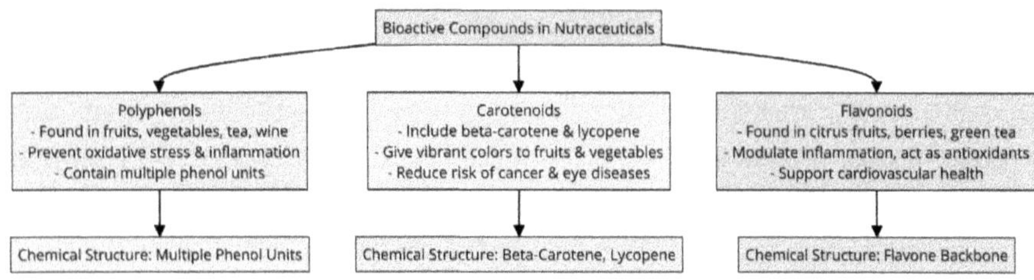

Bioactive Compounds in Nutraceuticals

1.2.1.2 Functional Classifications

Preventive Nutraceuticals

Preventive nutraceuticals are designed to maintain overall health and to reduce the risk of developing chronic diseases by providing essential bioactive compounds as part of the daily diet. These nutraceuticals are incorporated into foods or taken as supplements with the primary aim of strengthening the body's natural defence mechanisms, boosting the immune system, and maintaining optimal physiological function. For example, omega-3 fatty acids derived from fish oil, which are often included in preventive formulations, have been shown to lower blood triglyceride levels by 10 to 15% and improve heart health when consumed regularly at doses of 300 to 1000 mg per day. Similarly, dietary polyphenols, found in fruits such as blueberries and green tea extracts, contribute to the prevention of oxidative stress by neutralising free radicals; laboratory assays such as the ORAC test have demonstrated that high-polyphenol diets can increase antioxidant capacity by measurable values that correlate with reduced inflammation and improved vascular function. These preventive nutraceuticals are not intended to cure diseases but to create an internal environment where the body is less susceptible to the onset of conditions such as cardiovascular diseases, type 2 diabetes, and certain cancers. Their usage is supported by epidemiological studies and clinical trials, which have provided evidence that populations with higher intakes of preventive nutraceuticals experience a reduction in the incidence of chronic illnesses by significant percentages, sometimes up to 20 to 30% compared to populations with lower intake. The integration of preventive nutraceuticals into regular dietary patterns serves as an effective strategy for long-term health maintenance and disease prevention.

Therapeutic Nutraceuticals

Therapeutic nutraceuticals are used as adjuncts to conventional treatments to manage or treat specific health conditions, and they are designed to provide targeted benefits beyond basic nutritional support. These nutraceuticals are formulated with concentrated doses of active ingredients that have been scientifically validated for their therapeutic effects. For instance, curcumin, extracted from turmeric and standardised to contain 95% curcuminoids, is often used in therapeutic applications to reduce inflammation and support joint health, with typical dosages of 500 mg to 1000 mg per day being recommended in clinical studies. Similarly, therapeutic formulations of probiotics, containing strains such as Lactobacillus acidophilus at levels ranging from 10^7 to 10^9 colony forming units (CFU) per serving, have been shown to restore healthy gut flora and alleviate symptoms of gastrointestinal disorders. These products are often used in combination with standard medical treatments, helping to enhance the overall therapeutic outcome by addressing underlying nutritional deficiencies, reducing systemic inflammation, and improving metabolic functions. The role of therapeutic nutraceuticals is particularly evident in conditions such as metabolic syndrome, where supplementation with ingredients like omega-3 fatty acids, antioxidants, and fiber can improve insulin sensitivity and reduce the risk of cardiovascular events. The efficacy of these nutraceuticals is supported by numerous clinical trials and research studies that provide quantitative data on their ability to modulate disease markers and improve patient outcomes. By complementing traditional pharmaceutical interventions, therapeutic nutraceuticals offer an additional layer of support that can contribute to more effective management of chronic diseases and improved quality of life.

1.2.2 Health Problems Addressed

1.2.2.1 Weight Control

Weight control is a significant health concern in modern society, and nutraceuticals offer a range of mechanisms that aid in the regulation of metabolism and maintenance of a healthy body weight. Nutraceuticals designed for weight control work by modulating metabolic pathways involved in energy expenditure and fat storage. They often contain bioactive compounds such as conjugated linoleic acid (CLA), green tea catechins, and fibers that enhance satiety and boost metabolic rate. For instance, studies have reported that the regular intake of green tea extract, rich in catechins and caffeine, can increase energy expenditure by approximately 4 to 5% and fat oxidation by 10 to 17% over a period of several weeks. These bioactive compounds improve insulin sensitivity and promote the oxidation of fatty acids, leading to a reduction in adipose tissue. In addition, dietary fibers from fruits and whole grains delay gastric emptying and improve satiety, which further aids in weight control by reducing overall calorie intake. The combined effects of these nutraceuticals on metabolic regulation contribute to maintaining a healthy body mass index (BMI) and reducing the risk of obesity-related complications. Regular consumption of these nutraceuticals, when combined with a balanced diet and physical activity, has been associated with modest yet significant reductions in body weight and fat mass, highlighting their potential as a preventive strategy against obesity and its related disorders.

1.2.2.2 Diabetes

Diabetes is a chronic condition that affects the body's ability to regulate blood glucose levels, and nutraceuticals play a pivotal role in managing glycaemic control and enhancing insulin sensitivity. Specific nutraceuticals, such as cinnamon extract, alpha-lipoic acid, and chromium supplements, have been studied for their capacity to improve glucose metabolism. Cinnamon, for example, contains bioactive compounds that have been observed to reduce fasting blood glucose levels by 10 to 20% in some clinical trials by enhancing insulin receptor activity and facilitating the uptake of glucose into cells. Alpha-lipoic acid, an antioxidant, supports the regeneration of other antioxidants and improves insulin sensitivity, thereby reducing the risk of diabetic complications such as neuropathy. Chromium, a trace mineral, assists in the potentiation of insulin action and has been shown to improve glycaemic control in patients with type 2 diabetes when administered at doses ranging from 200 to 1000 micrograms per day. These nutraceutical interventions work through multiple pathways by reducing oxidative stress, modulating inflammatory responses, and improving the overall function of insulin receptors. Consequently, they serve not only as a preventive measure but also as a supportive therapy alongside conventional antidiabetic medications, contributing to better blood glucose regulation and a lower risk of long-term diabetic complications.

1.2.2.3 Cancer

The role of nutraceuticals in cancer prevention and supportive therapy is an area of significant research interest, as many bioactive compounds found in nutraceuticals possess potent anticancer properties. Nutraceuticals such as resveratrol, curcumin, and sulforaphane have been extensively studied for their ability to interfere with the molecular pathways that lead to cancer development. These compounds function by inducing apoptosis in abnormal cells, inhibiting angiogenesis, and modulating the cell cycle. For example, curcumin, derived from turmeric, has been shown to inhibit the activation of nuclear factor-kappa B (NF-κB), a key regulator of inflammation and cell proliferation, thereby reducing the risk of tumor growth. Similarly, sulforaphane, a compound present in cruciferous vegetables like broccoli, induces the activity of phase II detoxification enzymes, which enhance the elimination of potential carcinogens from the body. Resveratrol, a polyphenolic compound found in grapes and red wine, acts as a powerful antioxidant and has been associated with reduced risks of cancers such as breast and prostate cancer. These nutraceuticals not only serve preventive functions by reducing oxidative DNA damage and mutagenesis but also provide supportive therapy by enhancing the efficacy of conventional cancer treatments and reducing side effects. Clinical studies have shown that individuals who consume diets rich in these bioactive compounds have a 10 to 20% lower risk of developing certain types of cancer, underlining the importance of nutraceuticals in the integrated approach to cancer prevention and management.

1.2.2.4 Other Lifestyle-Related Disorders

In addition to weight control, diabetes, and cancer, nutraceuticals play an important role in addressing a variety of other lifestyle-related disorders, including cardiovascular diseases, osteoporosis, and neurodegenerative disorders. Cardiovascular diseases benefit from nutraceuticals such as omega-3 fatty acids, which are known to reduce triglyceride levels and improve overall heart health by enhancing endothelial function. Regular intake of omega-3 fatty acids, typically at doses of 300 to 1000 mg per day, has been associated with a 10 to 15% reduction in cardiovascular events, as these fatty acids reduce inflammation and inhibit the formation of arterial plaques. Osteoporosis, a condition marked by decreased bone density and increased fracture risk, can be managed with nutraceuticals like calcium, vitamin D, and isoflavones. Calcium supplements, when combined with vitamin D, ensure better absorption and maintenance of bone mineral density, with recommended dosages of 1000 mg of calcium and 400 to 800 IU of vitamin D per day for most adults. Isoflavones, particularly from soy, contribute to bone health by mimicking the effects of estrogen, which is important for maintaining bone density, especially in postmenopausal women. Neurodegenerative disorders, such as Alzheimer's and Parkinson's diseases, also see potential benefits from nutraceuticals like antioxidants and omega-3 fatty acids, which protect neuronal cells from oxidative stress and inflammation. Studies have shown that diets rich in antioxidants and omega-3 fatty acids may slow the progression of cognitive decline and improve neuronal function, offering a complementary approach to traditional therapies. These examples illustrate how nutraceuticals, by addressing key metabolic and physiological processes, serve as a comprehensive strategy for preventing and managing a range of lifestyle-related disorders, thereby contributing to overall health and improved quality of life.

1.3.1.1 Prevention of Disease

Nutraceuticals prevent disease through a variety of biochemical and molecular mechanisms that work in tandem to maintain cellular homeostasis and reduce the risk of chronic conditions. One primary mechanism is the antioxidant activity of nutraceuticals, which involves the neutralisation of free radicals and reactive oxygen species that are generated during normal cellular metabolism or due to external stressors. For instance, bioactive compounds such as vitamin C and vitamin E scavenge free radicals by donating electrons, a process that can be represented by the reaction where ascorbic acid ($C_6H_8O_6$) donates an electron to neutralise a hydroxyl radical (•OH), thereby converting into a relatively stable ascorbate radical. Vitamin E, present as α-tocopherol, plays a crucial role by reacting with lipid radicals in cell membranes, interrupting the chain reaction of lipid peroxidation and thus protecting the structural integrity of the membranes. Studies have demonstrated that diets rich in these antioxidants can lower oxidative stress markers by up to 20 to 30 percent, which is significant in preventing cellular damage. In addition to the direct scavenging of free radicals, nutraceuticals modulate inflammatory pathways by influencing enzyme systems and cytokine production. Many nutraceuticals inhibit key enzymes such as cyclooxygenase (COX) and lipoxygenase (LOX), thereby reducing the synthesis of pro-inflammatory mediators like prostaglandins and leukotrienes. Curcumin, a bioactive compound found in turmeric, has been shown to inhibit the activation of nuclear factor kappa B (NF-κB), a transcription factor that regulates inflammatory responses, resulting in a reduction of inflammatory cytokines such as interleukin-6 (IL-6) and tumor necrosis factor alpha (TNF-α) by as much as 25 to 40 percent in controlled studies. This dual action of reducing oxidative stress and controlling inflammation plays a vital role in preventing diseases such as cardiovascular disorders, diabetes, and cancer. Moreover, the enhancement of the body's endogenous antioxidant systems is another important aspect, where nutraceuticals stimulate the activity of enzymes like superoxide dismutase (SOD) and catalase, thereby further reinforcing the natural defence mechanisms against oxidative damage. Overall, the antioxidant properties combined with the modulation of inflammatory pathways underscore the preventive potential of nutraceuticals, offering a scientifically substantiated approach to reducing the incidence of chronic diseases and supporting long-term health.

1.3.1.2 Therapeutic Effects

Nutraceuticals offer therapeutic effects by enhancing cellular repair mechanisms that support the recovery and maintenance of normal cell function. Many bioactive compounds found in nutraceuticals help stimulate the repair of damaged cellular structures, including the repair of DNA and the restoration of mitochondrial function. For example, certain polyphenols and antioxidants such as resveratrol and curcumin have been shown to activate specific signalling pathways that trigger the repair of oxidised proteins and lipids. These compounds also enhance the activity of enzymes involved in DNA repair processes, such as the activation of poly (ADP-ribose) polymerase (PARP), which plays a crucial role in detecting and repairing single-strand DNA breaks. Studies have demonstrated that regular intake of these nutraceuticals can lead to a measurable increase in the activity of endogenous repair enzymes, thereby reducing the accumulation of cellular damage over time. This improved cellular repair capability helps to slow down the progression of chronic diseases and supports the body's natural ability to recover from oxidative stress and inflammation. In many experimental models, the supplementation of bioactive compounds has resulted in improvements in cell viability and a reduction in markers of cellular damage by up to 20 to 30 percent, which underscores their importance in therapeutic interventions.

In addition to enhancing cellular repair, nutraceuticals can act in synergy with conventional therapies to improve overall treatment outcomes. When used as adjuncts to standard medical treatments, these bioactive compounds can help to reduce the side effects of pharmaceutical drugs and boost their efficacy. For instance, in cancer therapy, the combination of nutraceuticals such as curcumin with chemotherapy agents has been observed to improve the sensitivity of cancer cells to treatment while protecting normal cells from the toxic effects of the drugs. This synergistic effect is achieved by nutraceuticals modulating various molecular pathways that are also targeted by conventional treatments. They help in downregulating inflammatory cytokines, reducing oxidative stress, and inhibiting pathways that lead to drug resistance. As a result, patients often experience better clinical outcomes and an improved quality of life when nutraceuticals are incorporated into their treatment regimen. Clinical trials have reported that the combined use of nutraceuticals with conventional therapy can lead to enhancements in treatment response rates, with improvements in certain biomarkers of disease progression noted in several studies. Overall, the therapeutic effects of nutraceuticals not only support cellular repair mechanisms but also work in tandem with established medical treatments, providing a complementary approach that can lead to more effective management of chronic diseases.

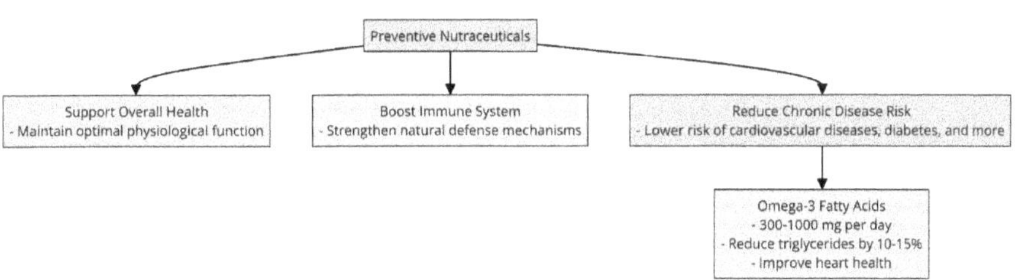

Preventive Nutraceuticals and Their Benefits

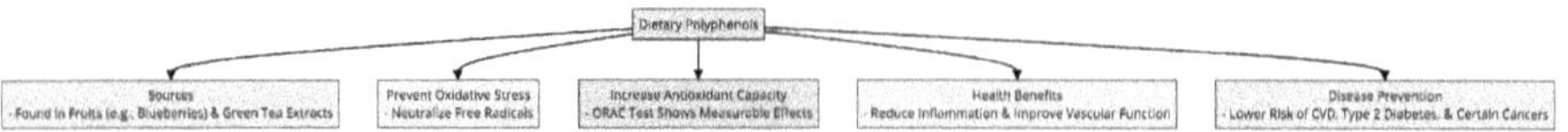

Role of Dietary Polyphenols in Disease Prevention

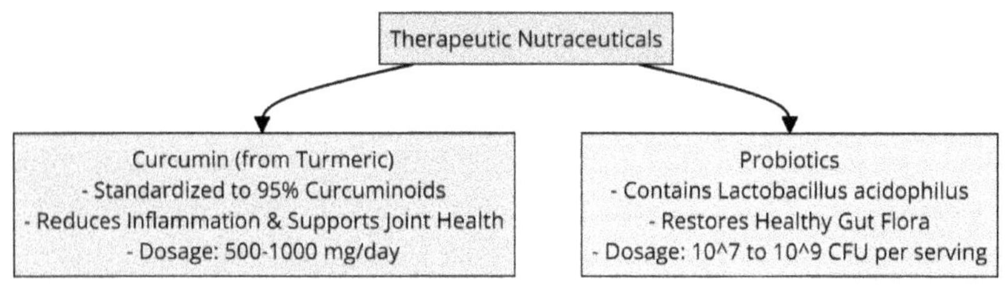

Therapeutic Nutraceuticals: Curcumin and Probiotics

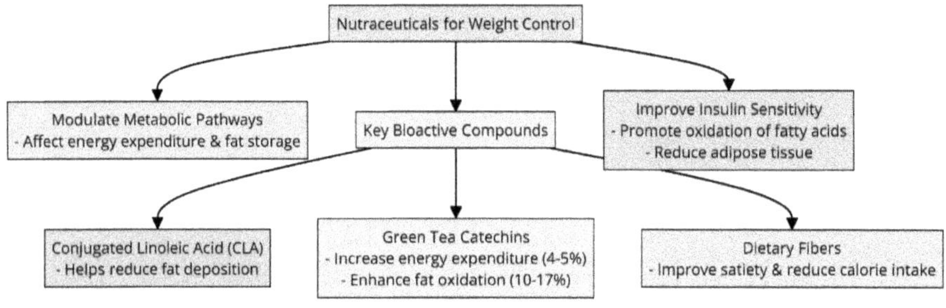

Nutraceuticals for Weight Control

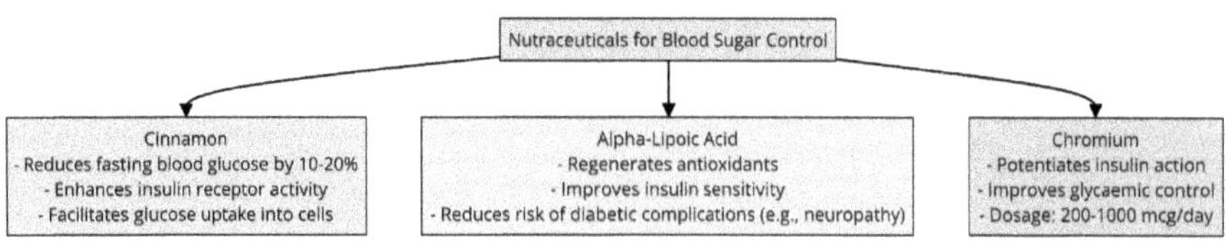

Nutraceuticals for Blood Sugar Control

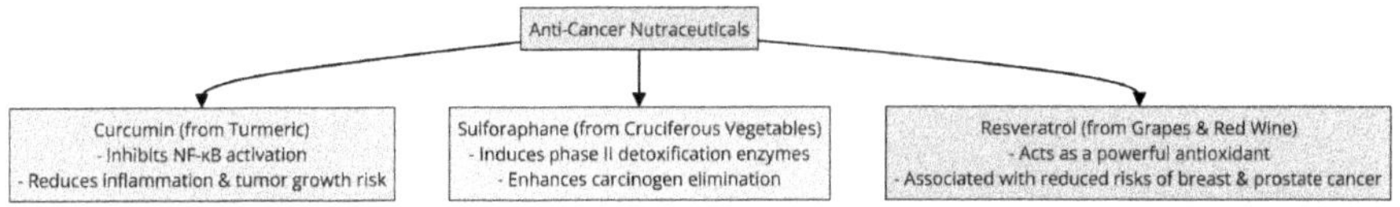

Anti-Cancer Nutraceuticals

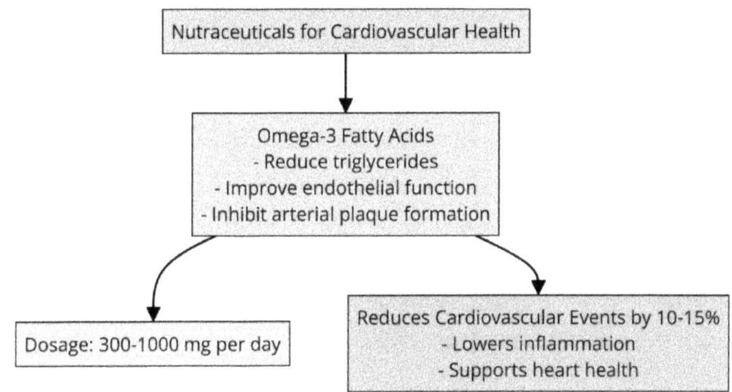

Nutraceuticals for Cardiovascular Health

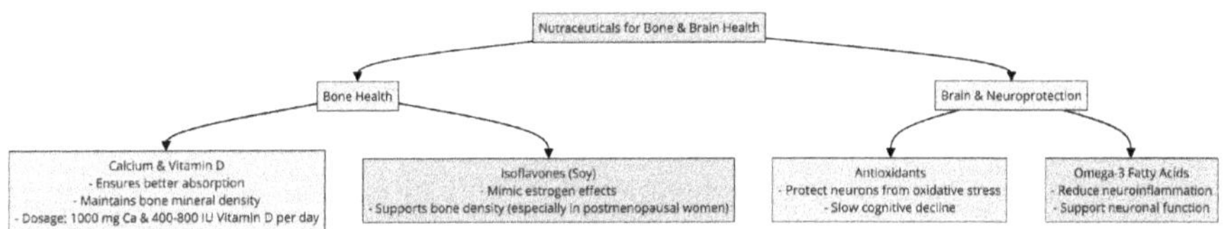

Nutraceuticals for Bone & Brain Health

1.3.2 Epidemiological Evidence

1.3.2.1 Clinical Trials and Studies

Numerous clinical trials and epidemiological studies have established the beneficial effects of nutraceuticals on human health, providing quantitative data that support their use in both disease prevention and therapeutic interventions. Landmark studies have investigated the role of various nutraceutical compounds in reducing the risk of chronic conditions such as cardiovascular diseases, diabetes, and cancer. For instance, large-scale trials on omega-3 fatty acids have shown that supplementation with fish oil, often providing doses of 300 to 1000 mg per day, can lower triglyceride levels by 15 to 20 percent and reduce the incidence of major cardiac events by approximately 10 percent in high-risk populations. These studies have involved thousands of participants over extended periods, thereby offering robust evidence of the cardioprotective benefits of omega-3 fatty acids when included as part of a comprehensive dietary strategy.

Other landmark studies have focused on polyphenolic compounds such as resveratrol and curcumin, which have been evaluated for their antioxidant and anti-inflammatory properties. Clinical trials involving resveratrol have demonstrated improvements in endothelial function and reductions in inflammatory markers such as C-reactive protein by up to 25 percent in patients with metabolic syndrome. Similarly, curcumin has been the subject of multiple randomised controlled trials where its use as an adjunct therapy in inflammatory conditions resulted in significant decreases in interleukin-6 (IL-6) and tumor necrosis factor-alpha (TNF-α) levels, with some studies reporting a reduction of these markers by as much as 30 to 40 percent. These trials provide quantitative data that underscore the potential of these compounds to modulate key pathways involved in chronic disease progression.

Further evidence from epidemiological studies highlights the long-term health benefits of nutraceutical-rich diets. Populations that consume diets high in fruits, vegetables, and whole grains, which naturally contain a range of vitamins, minerals, and bioactive compounds, exhibit a 20 to 30 percent lower incidence of certain cancers and cardiovascular diseases compared to populations with lower intake levels. This correlation is supported by data from cohort studies and meta-analyses, where increased consumption of nutraceuticals is consistently associated with improved health outcomes and a reduction in overall mortality rates. The quantitative data from these studies not only confirm the efficacy of nutraceuticals but also provide a scientific basis for their inclusion in public health guidelines and dietary recommendations. Collectively, the evidence from clinical trials and epidemiological studies forms a strong foundation for the role of nutraceuticals in health promotion and disease prevention, reinforcing the concept that these compounds can serve as effective tools in the maintenance of long-term health.

1.3.2.2 Population-Based Evidence

Correlations between Dietary Patterns and Reduced Disease Incidence

Population-based studies have provided substantial evidence linking dietary patterns rich in nutraceuticals with reduced incidence of various chronic diseases. Large-scale epidemiological surveys conducted in different regions of India and globally have consistently shown that individuals consuming diets abundant in fruits, vegetables, whole grains, and other functional foods exhibit lower rates of cardiovascular diseases, diabetes, and certain types of cancer. For instance, studies have reported that populations with high intakes of antioxidant-rich foods experience a 20 to 30 percent reduction in the risk of coronary heart disease compared to those whose diets lack these bioactive compounds. Data from national nutrition surveys indicate that individuals who include at least five servings of fruits and vegetables daily tend to have lower blood pressure and improved lipid profiles, which are key indicators of cardiovascular health. In addition, diets that emphasize whole grains and plant-based proteins contribute to better glycaemic control and a lower prevalence of type 2 diabetes. These correlations are derived from longitudinal studies that follow thousands of participants over extended periods, allowing researchers to identify statistically significant associations between healthy dietary patterns and reduced disease risk. The strength of these associations is often expressed in relative risk reductions or hazard ratios, where a relative risk value less than 1.0 signifies a protective effect of the diet against disease occurrence.

Meta-analyses and Systematic Reviews Highlighting Efficacy

Meta-analyses and systematic reviews further reinforce the efficacy of nutraceutical-rich diets in preventing chronic diseases by aggregating data from multiple studies to provide a more comprehensive analysis. These reviews have examined diverse populations and employed rigorous statistical methods to pool results from individual studies, thereby enhancing the reliability of the conclusions. One meta-analysis investigating the impact of dietary polyphenols on cardiovascular health reported an average reduction in cardiovascular events by approximately 15 to 20 percent among individuals with high polyphenol consumption. Similarly, systematic reviews focusing on the role of omega-3 fatty acids in metabolic health have demonstrated improvements in lipid profiles and insulin sensitivity, with quantitative estimates showing a decrease in triglyceride levels by 10 to 15 percent. Reviews on the intake of soy isoflavones have also noted a significant reduction in the risk of hormone-related cancers, with some studies indicating a risk reduction of up to 20 percent in populations that consume soy-based products regularly. These aggregated analyses provide strong evidence that the consistent consumption of nutraceuticals is associated with measurable health benefits. The conclusions drawn from these meta-analyses and systematic reviews contribute to the development of dietary guidelines and public health policies that advocate for diets rich in nutraceuticals as a cost-effective strategy to reduce the burden of chronic diseases in the community.

1.4 Emerging Trends in Nutraceuticals

1.4.1 Innovations in Nutraceutical Formulations

Recent advances in formulation technology have led to the development of novel nutraceutical products with enhanced bioavailability and targeted delivery systems. Innovations include the use of nanoemulsions, liposomes, and encapsulation techniques to protect sensitive bioactive compounds from degradation and improve their absorption. These techniques not only increase the efficacy of the nutraceuticals but also allow for controlled release, ensuring a sustained supply of active ingredients to the body. Additionally, the integration of natural carriers and biodegradable polymers in formulations is paving the way for safer and more efficient nutraceutical products. Research in this area focuses on optimizing particle size, surface charge, and encapsulation efficiency to tailor products for specific health outcomes.

1.4.2 Personalised Nutrition and Nutraceuticals

The concept of personalised nutrition is rapidly gaining importance in the nutraceutical industry, driven by advances in genomics, metabolomics, and nutrigenomics. Personalised nutraceuticals are designed based on an individual's genetic makeup, lifestyle, and health status, offering tailored solutions that can more effectively prevent or manage diseases. This approach involves identifying biomarkers and genetic polymorphisms that influence nutrient metabolism and the body's response to specific bioactive compounds. By customising nutrient intake and supplement recommendations, personalised nutraceuticals aim to improve health outcomes and mitigate the risk of chronic diseases. Ongoing research and the development of diagnostic tools are critical for translating this personalized approach into practical dietary strategies and consumer products.

1.4.3 Technological Advances in Nutraceutical Production

Technological advancements are transforming the production of nutraceuticals, making processes more efficient, sustainable, and scalable. Modern extraction techniques, such as supercritical fluid extraction and ultrasound-assisted extraction, allow for higher yields and purer extracts from plant and microbial sources. These technologies minimise the use of harsh chemicals and reduce energy consumption, thereby contributing to environmentally friendly production methods. Furthermore, the use of advanced analytical tools, including high-performance liquid chromatography (HPLC) and gas chromatography-mass spectrometry (GC-MS), has improved the accuracy of quality control measures. The integration of automation and digital monitoring systems in manufacturing facilities also enhances consistency, reduces human error, and ensures that products comply with stringent regulatory standards. As these technologies continue to evolve, they are expected to drive innovation and growth in the nutraceutical market.

1.5 Challenges and Opportunities in Nutraceutical Research

1.5.1 Regulatory and Quality Assurance Challenges

Despite the growing popularity of nutraceuticals, the industry faces several regulatory and quality assurance challenges. Establishing uniform standards across different countries and regions remains a significant hurdle, as varying regulatory frameworks can affect market access and consumer trust. Ensuring that nutraceutical products are free from contaminants and accurately labelled requires robust quality control measures and adherence to Good Manufacturing Practices (GMPs). Moreover, the scientific substantiation of health claims often involves complex clinical trials, which can be resource-intensive and time-consuming. These challenges underscore the need for harmonised regulations and collaborative efforts between industry stakeholders and regulatory bodies to maintain high-quality standards and protect public health.

1.5.2 Scientific and Clinical Research Opportunities

There is considerable scope for advancing the scientific and clinical research of nutraceuticals. Opportunities lie in further elucidating the molecular mechanisms through which bioactive compounds exert their health benefits, as well as in exploring the synergistic effects of combined nutraceutical ingredients. Clinical trials with larger sample sizes and long-term follow-up are essential to establish efficacy and safety profiles for various nutraceuticals. Additionally, emerging fields such as nutrigenomics offer exciting prospects for understanding individual responses to dietary components, paving the way for personalised nutraceutical interventions. Collaborative research initiatives and cross-disciplinary studies can help bridge the gap between laboratory findings and clinical applications, ultimately leading to more effective and targeted nutraceutical therapies.

1.5.3 Market Trends and Consumer Acceptance

The nutraceutical market is experiencing rapid growth, driven by increasing consumer awareness of the benefits of a healthy diet and preventive healthcare. Consumers are increasingly seeking products that are natural, scientifically validated, and capable of addressing specific health concerns. This shift in consumer preference has opened up new opportunities for product innovation and market expansion. However, maintaining transparency in advertising and ensuring ethical marketing practices are critical for sustaining consumer trust. Market trends also indicate a rising demand for personalised nutraceutical solutions and functional foods tailored to individual health needs. As consumer education improves and technology advances, the industry is likely to see further diversification of products, more stringent quality standards, and greater integration of digital platforms for health monitoring and personalised recommendations. These factors together contribute to a dynamic market environment, offering both challenges and opportunities for researchers and manufacturers in the nutraceutical sector.

Review questions

1. What are functional foods, and what are the key characteristics that distinguish them from conventional foods?
2. Can you provide examples of functional foods and explain their nutritional significance in a balanced diet?
3. How do functional foods contribute to health promotion and the prevention of diseases?
4. Define nutraceuticals and discuss the scope of these products in the context of health and wellness.
5. In what ways do nutraceuticals differ from conventional foods and pharmaceuticals in terms of composition and intended use?
6. Describe the various categories of nutraceuticals based on their chemical composition, including examples such as vitamins, minerals, and bioactive compounds.
7. What are dietary supplements, and what are the regulatory aspects that govern their production and labelling?
8. List the different forms of dietary supplements and provide examples of common active ingredients found in each form.
9. How were natural food components used in ancient civilizations, and why are these early practices important for understanding modern nutraceuticals?
10. Identify and explain the key milestones in the discovery of vitamins, minerals, and bioactive compounds that have influenced nutraceutical development.
11. How have nutraceuticals been integrated into modern public health initiatives, and what impact has this integration had on disease prevention?
12. Describe the role of traditional medicine practices and natural remedies in the early use of nutraceuticals.
13. Explain how the evolution from empirical use of natural remedies to scientifically validated products has shaped the nutraceutical industry.
14. What factors contributed to the emergence of standardized dietary supplements in clinical practice?

MCQS

1. Which of the following best defines functional foods?
   A. Foods that provide only basic nutrition
   B. Foods that contain added chemicals for preservation
   C. Foods that provide additional health benefits beyond basic nutrition
   D. Foods that are exclusively processed
   Correct Answer: C
2. Which example is commonly cited as a functional food?
   A. White bread made solely of refined flour
   B. Carrots, which are high in beta-carotene
   C. Sugary soft drinks
   D. Salted snacks
   Correct Answer: B
3. Nutraceuticals are best described as:
   A. Synthetic chemicals used to treat diseases
   B. Food-derived products that offer extra health benefits
   C. Processed foods with no health impact
   D. Drugs that replace conventional food
   Correct Answer: B
4. How do nutraceuticals differ from conventional foods?
   A. They are always synthetic and artificial
   B. They provide health benefits beyond basic nutrition
   C. They are only used in pharmaceuticals
   D. They lack bioactive compounds
   Correct Answer: B
5. Which of the following is NOT considered a dietary supplement form?
   A. Capsules
   B. Powders
   C. Tablets
   D. Raw fruits
   Correct Answer: D
6. Dietary supplements are regulated primarily as:
   A. Pharmaceuticals
   B. Foods
   C. Cosmetics

D. Over-the-counter drugs

Correct Answer: B

7. Which nutrient is often highlighted as a key bioactive compound in functional foods?

   A. Saturated fat

   B. Beta-carotene

   C. Simple sugars

   D. Trans-fats

   Correct Answer: B

8. The early use of natural food components in ancient civilizations primarily served to:

   A. Enhance processing speed

   B. Treat acute infections only

   C. Promote health and prevent nutritional deficiencies

   D. Replace traditional medicine entirely

   Correct Answer: C

9. One milestone in the discovery of vitamins was the identification of:

   A. Vitamin K only

   B. Vitamin C as the anti-scurvy agent

   C. The concept of trans-fats

   D. Artificial food dyes

   Correct Answer: B

10. Which statement best describes the integration of nutraceuticals into modern public health initiatives?

    A. Nutraceuticals have replaced all conventional medicines

    B. They are used solely for weight loss

    C. They complement conventional medical treatments and promote preventive health

    D. They have no role in managing chronic diseases

    Correct Answer: C

11. Traditional medicine practices often relied on:

    A. Synthetic chemicals

    B. Natural remedies and whole foods

    C. Exclusive use of processed supplements

    D. Only animal-derived products

    Correct Answer: B

12. The transition from traditional medicine to modern dietary supplements involved:

A. A complete rejection of ancient practices
B. The use of empirical evidence only
C. Scientific validation of natural remedies and standardisation of dosage
D. Decreasing the bioavailability of active ingredients
Correct Answer: C

13. Which of the following is an example of a nutrient used in nutraceuticals based on chemical composition?
A. Artificial flavoring
B. Vitamin E
C. Preservative chemicals
D. Synthetic dyes
Correct Answer: B

14. Preventive nutraceuticals are primarily designed to:
A. Cure diseases immediately
B. Enhance basic taste without health benefits
C. Maintain health and reduce disease risk
D. Replace prescription medication entirely
Correct Answer: C

15. Therapeutic nutraceuticals are best used as:
A. Standalone treatments with no conventional therapy
B. Adjuncts to help manage or treat diseases
C. Products with no scientific evidence
D. Items that only provide energy
Correct Answer: B

16. In the context of weight control, nutraceuticals work by:
A. Increasing appetite significantly
B. Modulating metabolic regulation and promoting fat oxidation
C. Replacing all dietary calories with supplements
D. Blocking nutrient absorption completely
Correct Answer: B

17. Nutraceuticals can play a role in managing diabetes by:
A. Eliminating insulin production
B. Impairing glycaemic control
C. Improving insulin sensitivity and glycaemic control
D. Increasing blood glucose levels
Correct Answer: C

18. Which bioactive component in nutraceuticals is linked with cancer prevention?

A. Refined carbohydrates
B. Polyphenols
C. Saturated fats
D. High-fructose corn syrup
Correct Answer: B

19. Epidemiological studies in nutraceutical research have shown that diets rich in bioactive compounds are correlated with:
A. Increased risk of chronic diseases
B. No change in disease incidence
C. Reduced incidence of chronic diseases
D. Only short-term health benefits
Correct Answer: C

20. The concept of nutraceuticals has evolved to include both:
A. Only traditional herbal remedies
B. Only synthetic drugs
C. Both traditional natural remedies and scientifically validated dietary supplements
D. Only genetically modified ingredients
Correct Answer: C

CHAPTER TWO

Nutraceutical Sources and Their Marker Compounds

2.1.1.1 Importance of Natural Sources in Functional Foods

Plant- and microbe-derived nutraceuticals are an essential component of functional foods and offer distinct advantages that support health and wellness. Natural sources from plants provide a rich array of bioactive compounds, such as vitamins, minerals, polyphenols, carotenoids, and flavonoids, which contribute not only to basic nutrition but also to disease prevention and the enhancement of overall health. These compounds are present in their natural form, allowing them to interact synergistically with other nutrients in the diet. For example, the naturally occurring antioxidants in fruits and vegetables work together to neutralise free radicals and reduce oxidative stress, which is a major contributing factor in chronic diseases. The complex mixtures of phytochemicals in plants have been developed over centuries through natural selection and evolution, and their structures are optimised for bioavailability and effective metabolic interactions within the human body.

Microbes also play a vital role in producing bioactive substances that are used in functional foods. Certain bacteria, such as Lactobacillus and Bifidobacterium species, are employed as probiotics to enhance gut health by restoring the balance of intestinal flora. These microorganisms are not only involved in the fermentation process that produces foods like yogurt, kefir, and traditional fermented beverages, but they also generate metabolites such as short-chain fatty acids during fermentation. These metabolites are important for maintaining the integrity of the gut lining and have been shown to modulate the immune response. In addition, microbes are used in biotechnological processes to produce enzymes, vitamins, and even bioactive peptides that are subsequently incorporated into dietary supplements and functional foods, thereby extending the benefits of natural sources.

Examples from traditional and modern diets further illustrate the importance of natural sources in functional foods. Traditional diets in many parts of India have long relied on a variety of plants and fermented foods that are rich in nutraceuticals. For instance, traditional Ayurvedic practices emphasize the use of turmeric, amla, and garlic for their health-promoting properties, a practice that is now supported by modern scientific research. Similarly, in modern diets, the inclusion of foods such as berries, green tea, whole grains, and fermented dairy products is encouraged due to their high content of antioxidants and probiotics. These natural sources are now recognized not only for their nutritional value but also for their ability to help manage lifestyle-related diseases such as cardiovascular conditions, diabetes, and obesity. The integration of these natural compounds into everyday diets exemplifies the bridge between traditional knowledge and contemporary nutritional science, offering a comprehensive approach to health maintenance and disease prevention through functional foods.

2.2.1 Spirulina

2.2.1.1 Source, Marker Compounds, Chemical Nature

Spirulina is a blue-green microalga that grows in both fresh and saline water environments and is celebrated for its high nutritional value and bioactive composition. This microalga has been cultivated widely in open ponds and closed photobioreactors under controlled conditions to ensure its purity and consistency. Spirulina appears as a filamentous, spiral-shaped organism that is rich in proteins and pigments. It serves as a natural source of essential nutrients and is recognised for its vibrant blue-green colour, which is primarily due to the presence of the pigment phycocyanin. Phycocyanin is one of the key marker compounds in Spirulina, and it functions not only as a pigment but also exhibits strong antioxidant and anti-inflammatory properties. Alongside phycocyanin, Spirulina contains chlorophyll-a, which contributes to its green colour and is important in photosynthesis, helping the microalga to convert sunlight into chemical energy. Another significant marker compound is beta-carotene, a provitamin A carotenoid that plays a critical role in maintaining vision and immune function. In addition to these pigments, Spirulina is a rich source of high-quality proteins, which typically constitute between 60 to 70 percent of its dry weight. These proteins include all essential amino acids required for human health, making Spirulina a valuable dietary supplement for vegetarians and those with protein deficiencies. The microalga also provides essential fatty acids, including gamma-linolenic acid (GLA), which contributes to anti-inflammatory responses and supports cardiovascular health.

Spirulina

The chemical composition of Spirulina reflects its status as a nutrient-dense superfood. It contains a balanced mix of vitamins, such as the B-complex group, vitamin E, and small amounts of vitamin C, alongside minerals including iron, magnesium, and potassium. The mineral content is particularly noteworthy, with iron levels reaching up to 25 mg per 100 grams of dried Spirulina, which is significant for supporting healthy blood production and preventing iron deficiency. In terms of its lipid profile,

Spirulina is low in saturated fats and rich in polyunsaturated fatty acids, which are beneficial for maintaining healthy cholesterol levels. The carbohydrate content in Spirulina is minimal, making it a favourable option for low-carbohydrate diets, while the dietary fibre present, though in small amounts, aids in digestive health. Overall, the nutritional values of Spirulina are impressive, with high levels of bioavailable proteins, antioxidants, and essential fatty acids, which together contribute to its wide range of health benefits. The natural balance of these components makes Spirulina an important functional food, supporting immune function, reducing oxidative stress, and providing the necessary building blocks for cellular repair and energy production.

2.2.1.2 Medicinal Uses and Health Benefits

Spirulina is well-known for its robust antioxidant, anti-inflammatory, and immune-modulating effects, which together contribute significantly to its medicinal uses. The antioxidant properties of Spirulina are largely attributed to its rich content of phycocyanin, beta-carotene, and chlorophyll-a. These compounds help neutralise free radicals generated during normal metabolic processes and due to environmental stress, thereby reducing oxidative damage to cells and tissues. For example, studies have demonstrated that regular intake of Spirulina can lower markers of oxidative stress by approximately 20 to 30 percent in experimental models. In addition, its anti-inflammatory effects are realised through the inhibition of pro-inflammatory cytokines and enzymes such as cyclooxygenase, which are often elevated in chronic inflammatory conditions. By reducing inflammation at the cellular level, Spirulina can help alleviate symptoms associated with conditions like arthritis and other inflammatory disorders. The immune-modulating properties of Spirulina also play a crucial role in its medicinal applications. It enhances the activity of natural killer cells and macrophages, thus improving the body's ability to fight off infections and support overall immune function. This immune support is particularly beneficial for individuals with compromised immune systems or those recovering from illnesses.

Spirulina has also been shown to improve lipid profiles and support detoxification processes in the body. The bioactive compounds in Spirulina contribute to lowering low-density lipoprotein (LDL) cholesterol levels and increasing high-density lipoprotein (HDL) cholesterol, thereby promoting cardiovascular health. Clinical studies have reported that supplementation with Spirulina, typically in doses ranging from 2 to 8 grams per day, can lead to a reduction in LDL cholesterol by about 10 to 15 percent. Furthermore, Spirulina aids in detoxification by binding to heavy metals and facilitating their elimination from the body. This detoxifying effect is particularly important in reducing the burden of environmental toxins, which are known to contribute to oxidative stress and various chronic diseases.

Clinical evidence supporting the use of Spirulina is substantial and comes from both laboratory research and human trials. Multiple clinical studies have documented improvements in metabolic parameters, immune function, and oxidative stress markers with regular Spirulina supplementation. In one controlled trial, participants who consumed Spirulina daily for several weeks showed significant improvements in lipid profiles and a reduction in markers of inflammation compared to those in the placebo group. Other studies have highlighted its benefits in enhancing overall physical performance and endurance, particularly among athletes and individuals undergoing rehabilitation. The consistent findings from these studies reinforce the role of Spirulina as a valuable nutraceutical with multifaceted health benefits. The combination of antioxidant activity, anti-inflammatory effects, and immune modulation, along with its ability to improve lipid metabolism and assist in detoxification, makes Spirulina a potent functional food that supports long-term health and aids in the management of various chronic conditions.

2.2.2.1 Marker Compounds and Chemical Properties

Soya bean, known botanically as Glycine max, is widely recognised for its rich composition of bioactive compounds that make it a valuable nutraceutical ingredient. It is particularly noted for its high content of isoflavones, with genistein and daidzein being the primary components. These isoflavones have a chemical structure that closely resembles human estrogen, which allows them to interact with estrogen receptors and modulate hormonal activity. The concentration of isoflavones in soya bean can vary from 1 to 3 mg per gram of dry weight, depending on the variety and processing methods, and they are credited with contributing to reduced risks of hormone-dependent conditions such as certain cancers and osteoporosis. Alongside isoflavones, soya bean is a rich source of high-quality proteins, constituting about 36 to 40 percent of its dry weight.

These proteins provide all the essential amino acids required for human nutrition, making them particularly beneficial for vegetarians and those seeking plant-based protein alternatives. In addition to these, soya bean contains saponins, which are glycosides known for their cholesterol-lowering effects and immune-modulating properties, and these compounds also support the overall health of the cardiovascular system.

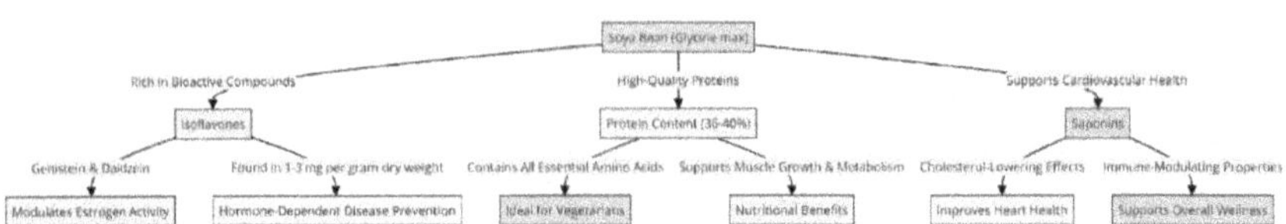

Bioactive Components of Soya Bean

Furthermore, the lipid fraction of soya bean is notable for its high concentration of polyunsaturated fatty acids. Soya bean oil typically comprises about 50 to 60 percent polyunsaturated fats, including linoleic acid and alpha-linolenic acid, which are essential for maintaining healthy lipid profiles and reducing inflammation. These fatty acids play a critical role in modulating cell membrane fluidity and can help in the prevention of heart disease by lowering low-density lipoprotein (LDL) cholesterol and promoting a favourable balance with high-density lipoprotein (HDL) cholesterol. The overall chemical composition of soya bean is complemented by a range of other nutrients, including dietary fibre, vitamins from the B-complex group, and essential minerals such as calcium, iron, and magnesium. These components not only contribute to the overall nutritional profile of soya bean but also enhance its therapeutic potential in supporting metabolic processes and maintaining overall health. The unique combination of isoflavones, high-quality proteins, saponins, and beneficial fatty acids makes soya bean a comprehensive source of nutraceuticals, which is utilised both in traditional diets and modern food products aimed at promoting health and preventing disease.

2.2.2.2 Role in Disease Prevention and Health Improvement

Soya bean plays a significant role in disease prevention and the improvement of overall health due to its rich composition of bioactive compounds, which have been extensively studied for their beneficial effects on various body systems. One of the key areas where soya bean demonstrates its potential is in the prevention of hormone-related cancers. The isoflavones, particularly genistein and daidzein, found in soya bean are structurally similar to human estrogen, allowing them to bind to estrogen receptors and modulate hormonal activity. This binding can result in a balancing effect that may reduce the risk of cancers such as breast and prostate cancer, conditions that are influenced by estrogen levels. Epidemiological studies have reported that populations consuming higher amounts of soya bean products tend to have a lower incidence of these cancers, with some studies indicating a risk reduction of up to 20 percent when compared with populations that have a low soya intake. In addition, soya bean supports cardiovascular health through its positive impact on cholesterol levels. The polyunsaturated fatty acids present in soya bean oil, including linoleic acid and alpha-linolenic acid, help to lower low-density lipoprotein (LDL) cholesterol while promoting high-density lipoprotein (HDL) cholesterol. Clinical trials have shown that regular consumption of soya protein can lead to a decrease in LDL cholesterol levels by approximately 5 to 10 percent, which is significant for reducing the risk of atherosclerosis and other cardiovascular disorders.

Soya bean also contributes to bone health, particularly in postmenopausal women, through the estrogen-like effects of its isoflavones. The phytoestrogens in soya can help maintain bone density by mimicking the effects of natural estrogen, which is critical in preventing osteoporosis. Studies have documented that soya isoflavone supplementation may improve bone mineral density and reduce bone resorption, contributing to stronger bones and a lower risk of fractures. The integration of soya bean in the diet has been associated with improvements in various markers of bone health, making it a useful dietary component in managing age-related bone loss. Epidemiological data and clinical trials support these health benefits, with research showing that diets rich in soya products correlate with improved cardiovascular parameters and bone density. Longitudinal studies and systematic reviews have further reinforced these findings by demonstrating that regular soya consumption is linked to lower incidences of hormone-related cancers, better lipid profiles, and improved skeletal health. Collectively, the diverse components of soya bean and their synergistic effects provide a comprehensive approach to disease prevention and health improvement, making soya bean an essential component of a balanced and health-promoting diet.

2.2.3 Ginseng

2.2.3.1 Active Constituents and Mechanisms of Action

Ginseng is a well-known herb that has been used in traditional medicine for centuries, and its therapeutic properties are largely attributed to a group of active compounds known as ginsenosides. Ginsenosides are a class of steroidal saponins that are divided into two main groups based on their chemical structures: protopanaxadiols and protopanaxatriols. Protopanaxadiols include compounds such as Rb1, Rb2, Rc, and Rd, while protopanaxatriols comprise Rg1, Re, and Rf. These compounds possess a dammarane skeleton with varying numbers and positions of sugar moieties attached to them, which influences their solubility, bioavailability, and biological activity. Research has shown that the total ginsenoside content in ginseng roots generally ranges from 2 to 5 percent of the dry weight, although this value can vary depending on the species, cultivation practices, and age of the plant.

Ginseng

The mechanisms of action of ginseng are complex and involve multiple biochemical pathways. Ginsenosides modulate the activity of several cell signalling pathways, including the mitogen-activated protein kinase (MAPK) pathway and the nuclear factor-kappa B (NF-κB) pathway. For example, the inhibition of NF-κB by ginsenosides leads to a reduction in the production of pro-inflammatory cytokines such as interleukin-6 and tumor necrosis factor-alpha, which are often elevated during inflammatory responses. In addition, ginsenosides are known to influence the AMP-activated protein kinase (AMPK) pathway, which plays a critical role in cellular energy homeostasis and has implications for improving insulin sensitivity and metabolic regulation. This modulation of biochemical pathways contributes to the herb's antioxidant, anti-inflammatory, and immunomodulatory effects, making ginseng useful in managing stress, improving cognitive function, and supporting overall vitality.

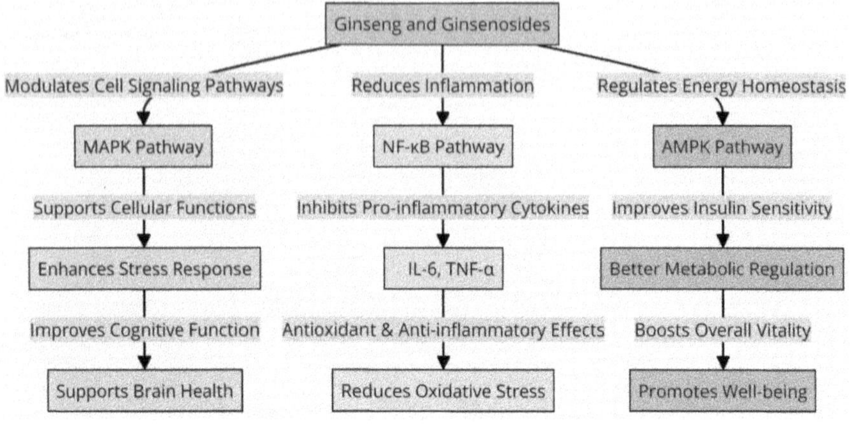

Mechanisms of Action of Ginseng

Quantitative data on ginsenoside content is important for standardising ginseng products and ensuring their efficacy. Standardised extracts typically contain a minimum of 2 percent total ginsenosides, although premium products may offer up to 5 percent or more. Analytical techniques such as high-performance liquid chromatography (HPLC) are used to measure the individual ginsenoside content, providing precise data that can be correlated with specific health benefits. In many clinical studies, doses ranging from 200 to 400 mg of standardized ginseng extract per day have been used to evaluate improvements in physical performance and cognitive function. The consistent presence of these bioactive compounds and the ability to quantify them accurately contribute to the scientific validation of ginseng as a potent nutraceutical with a broad spectrum of health benefits.

2.2.3.2 Traditional and Modern Medicinal Applications

Historical Use in Traditional Chinese and Korean Medicine

Ginseng has been esteemed for centuries in traditional Chinese and Korean medicine as a vital herb for promoting longevity, enhancing vitality, and restoring balance in the body. In ancient texts and traditional herbal formularies, ginseng was revered for its ability to boost energy, support the immune system, and improve overall well-being. Historical practices emphasised the use of ginseng roots in tonics and decoctions, with practitioners recommending its use to combat fatigue, enhance physical endurance, and promote mental clarity. Traditional healers believed that the complex blend of bioactive compounds in ginseng, primarily the ginsenosides, was responsible for its restorative properties and its capacity to harmonise the body's internal energies. In these traditional systems, ginseng was often administered as a daily tonic in the form of soups, teas, or powdered supplements, with the dosage and duration of use tailored to the individual's constitution and specific health needs. The historical use of ginseng was rooted in empirical observations and accumulated wisdom, where its benefits were passed down through generations as an essential remedy for various ailments, from digestive disorders to chronic fatigue.

Modern Clinical Applications: Cognitive Enhancement, Stress Reduction, and Metabolic Benefits

In modern clinical practice, the applications of ginseng have been validated through rigorous scientific research and controlled clinical trials. Recent studies have shown that ginseng supplementation can lead to improvements in cognitive function, particularly in the areas of memory, attention, and processing speed. Clinical trials using standardised ginseng extracts, typically in doses of 200 to 400 mg per day, have reported enhancements in mental performance, especially among older adults and individuals experiencing mild cognitive impairment. Alongside its cognitive benefits, ginseng is also recognised for its role in stress reduction. The adaptogenic properties of ginseng help the body to manage physical and emotional stress by modulating the hypothalamic-pituitary-adrenal (HPA) axis and reducing the secretion of stress hormones such as cortisol. This effect is particularly valuable in modern lifestyles where stress-related disorders are prevalent. Furthermore, ginseng has been shown to exert metabolic benefits by improving insulin sensitivity and enhancing lipid metabolism. Studies indicate that regular consumption of ginseng can lead to a reduction in fasting blood glucose levels and improved overall energy regulation, which is crucial in managing conditions like type 2 diabetes and metabolic syndrome. The modern clinical applications of ginseng underscore its potential to serve as a complementary therapy that supports cognitive health, alleviates stress, and optimises metabolic functions in diverse populations.

Comparative Analysis of Traditional Use versus Modern Evidence

When comparing traditional use with modern evidence, it becomes apparent that the benefits attributed to ginseng in ancient practices find substantial support in contemporary scientific research. Traditional medicine described ginseng as a potent tonic that rejuvenates the body and mind, a view that is now corroborated by clinical studies demonstrating its efficacy in enhancing cognitive performance and reducing stress-related symptoms. Modern research has elucidated the biochemical mechanisms underlying these effects, particularly through the action of ginsenosides on key cellular signalling pathways such as MAPK and NF-κB, which are involved in inflammation and cell repair. While traditional usage relied on observational and experiential knowledge, modern evidence provides quantitative data that validate these historical claims. For instance, improvements in cognitive function and metabolic regulation observed in clinical trials offer measurable benefits, such as an increase in cognitive test scores by a significant margin and reductions in fasting blood glucose levels by 10 to 15 percent. This comparative analysis highlights that the long-held beliefs in the restorative properties of ginseng are not only rooted in ancient wisdom but are also supported by contemporary scientific findings, thereby bridging the gap between traditional medicine and modern therapeutics. The convergence of historical knowledge with modern clinical validation has established ginseng as a multifaceted nutraceutical that continues to play an important role in both preventive health strategies and therapeutic applications in today's healthcare landscape.

2.2.4.1 Key Sulfur-Containing Compounds

Garlic is renowned for its distinctive aroma and potent biological effects, which are primarily attributed to its rich content of sulfur-containing compounds. In its fresh state, garlic stores a precursor molecule called alliin (chemical formula $C_6H_{11}NO_3S$) in the intact cells, isolated from the enzyme alliinase by compartmentalisation. When garlic is chopped, crushed, or otherwise mechanically disrupted, alliinase is released and catalyses the conversion of alliin into allicin (diallyl thiosulfinate, chemical formula $C_6H_{10}OS_2$). Allicin is responsible for the characteristic pungent aroma of fresh garlic and serves as a reactive intermediate that exhibits strong antimicrobial and antioxidant properties. However, allicin is unstable and undergoes rapid chemical transformations to yield a variety of secondary sulfur compounds such as diallyl sulfide and allyltrisulfide, among others. The conversion of allicin into diallyl sulfide ($C_6H_1\ {}^0S$) and allyltrisulfide is part of a complex cascade of reactions that occur either during storage or processing, and these compounds contribute significantly to the overall bioactivity of garlic.

The chemical transformations in garlic are highly dependent on the method of processing and storage. In fresh garlic, the intact cell structure ensures that alliin and alliinase remain separated until the garlic is physically disturbed, resulting in a sudden burst of allicin production. Once formed, allicin begins to decompose, and its rate of decomposition increases with factors such as temperature and time. For example, when garlic is exposed to heat during cooking, allicin degrades rapidly into a mixture of organosulfur compounds, including diallyl sulfide and allyltrisulfide, which may also include minor amounts of diallyl disulfide. The transformation is influenced by the pH and moisture content of the garlic, with freshly crushed garlic showing higher concentrations of allicin—estimates suggest that one typical garlic clove may produce between 5 and 9 mg of allicin—while processed or cooked garlic tends to contain lower levels of allicin but a higher proportion of its decomposition products.

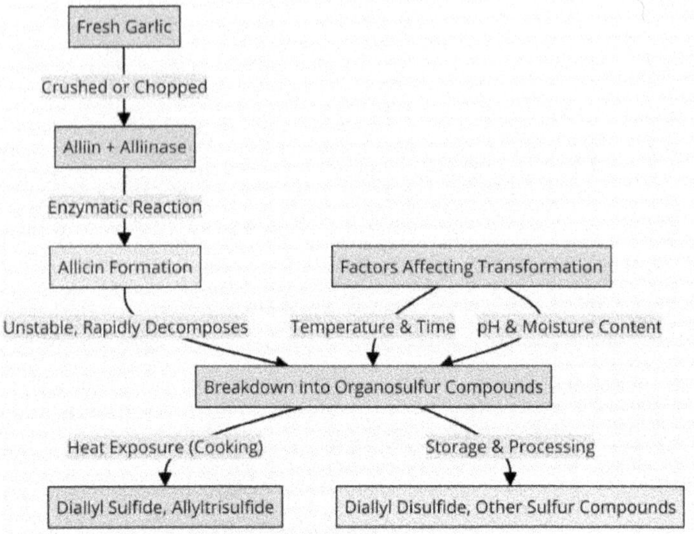

Chemical Transformations in Garlic

In terms of concentration, fresh garlic generally contains significant levels of alliin, which can vary from 3 to 14 mg per gram of fresh weight, depending on the garlic variety and cultivation conditions. After processing, the concentration of allicin formed can be quite variable, as it is subject to rapid degradation; however, controlled processing methods are designed to optimise allicin yield before it transforms into diallyl sulfide and allyltrisulfide. These secondary compounds are present in measurable amounts in garlic extracts and are believed to account for many of the health benefits associated with garlic consumption, including cardiovascular protection and antimicrobial effects. The specific concentration levels and ratios of these sulfur-containing compounds are critical for standardising garlic supplements and functional foods, ensuring that the bioactivity is consistent and effective in promoting health.

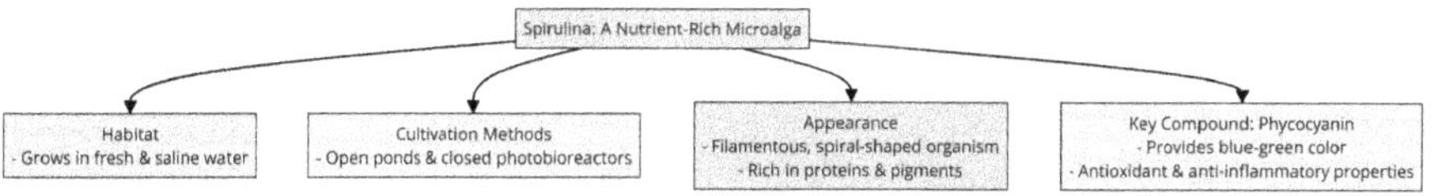

Spirulina: A Nutrient-Rich Microalga

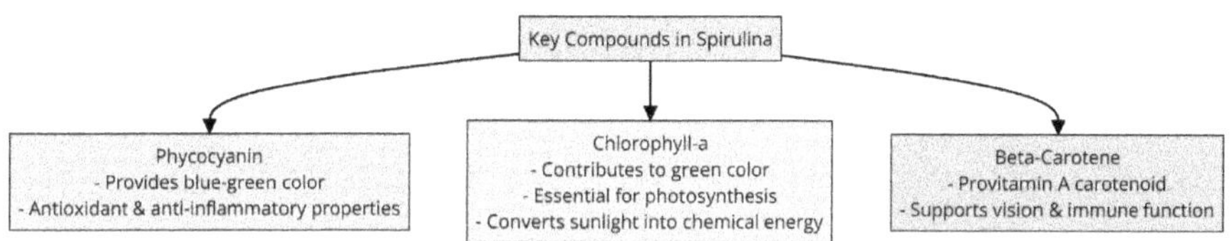

Key Compounds in Spirulina

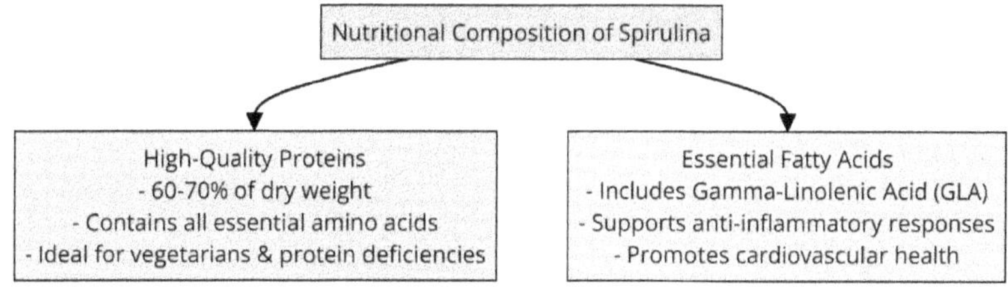

Chemical Composition of Spirulina

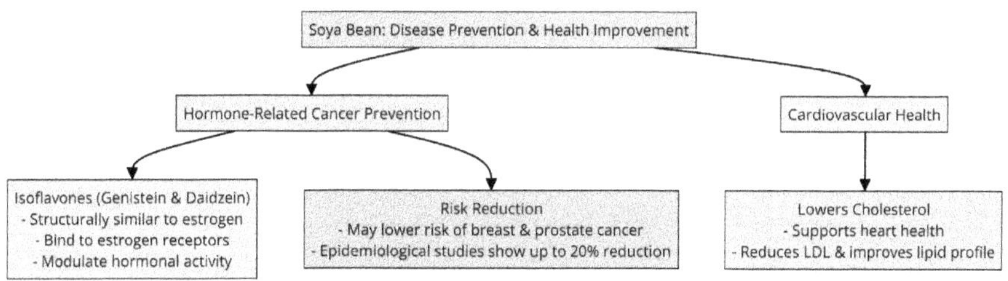

Role of Soya Bean in Disease Prevention and Health Improvement

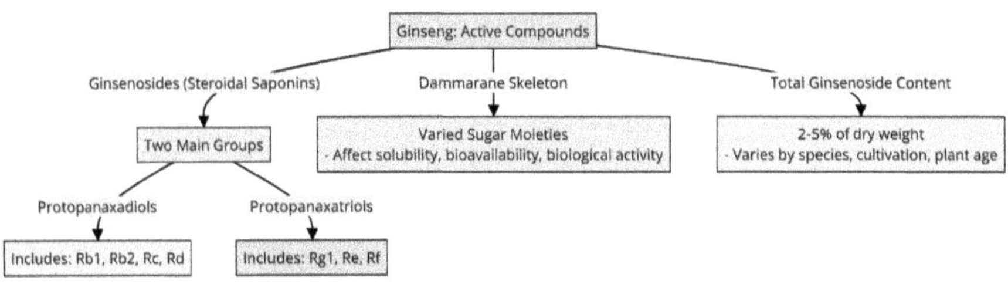

Ginsenosides in Ginseng

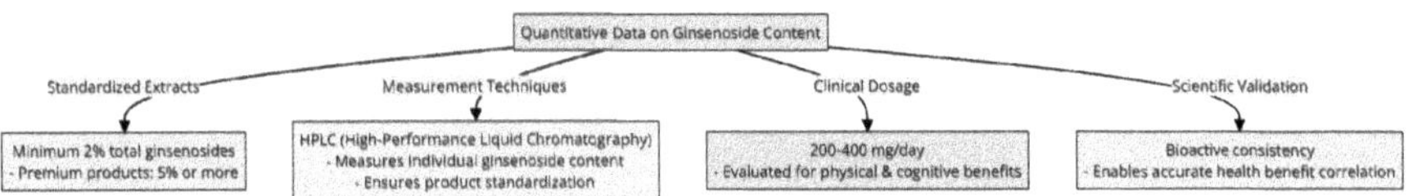

Quantitative Data on Ginsenoside Content

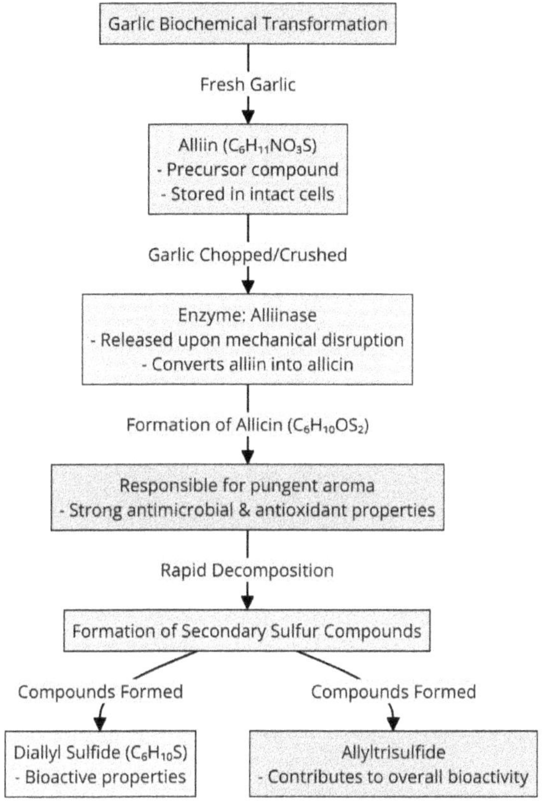

Biochemical Transformation of Garlic Compounds

2.2.4.2 Health Benefits and Anti-Disease Properties

Cardiovascular Benefits: Blood Pressure and Cholesterol Modulation

Garlic exhibits a significant impact on cardiovascular health by modulating blood pressure and improving cholesterol profiles. The organosulfur compounds derived from garlic, such as allicin and its subsequent breakdown products like diallyl sulfide and allyltrisulfide, have been shown to promote vasodilation through the stimulation of nitric oxide production. This process helps in relaxing the smooth muscles of blood vessels, which leads to a reduction in blood pressure. Clinical studies indicate that regular consumption of garlic supplements, typically in the range of 600 to 1200 mg per day, can result in a decrease in systolic blood pressure by approximately 8 to 12 mm Hg and diastolic blood pressure by 5 to 8 mm Hg in individuals with hypertension. In addition, garlic has a beneficial effect on cholesterol levels. The bioactive sulfur compounds in garlic inhibit the synthesis of cholesterol in the liver, thereby reducing low-density lipoprotein (LDL) cholesterol and raising high-density lipoprotein (HDL) cholesterol levels. Several controlled studies report that garlic supplementation can lower LDL cholesterol by up to 10 to 15 percent, which plays a crucial role in reducing the risk of atherosclerosis and other cardiovascular disorders.

Antimicrobial, Anti-Inflammatory, and Anticancer Properties

Garlic is well recognised for its broad-spectrum antimicrobial effects, which help in combating bacteria, viruses, and fungi. The compound allicin, which forms when garlic is crushed or chopped, has demonstrated the ability to disrupt the cell membranes of various pathogens, leading to a reduction in microbial viability. Laboratory experiments have shown that allicin can inhibit the growth of common bacterial strains such as Escherichia coli and Staphylococcus aureus, with effective concentrations often observed in the low milligram range. In addition to its antimicrobial action, garlic exhibits potent anti-inflammatory properties by suppressing the activity of inflammatory mediators such as prostaglandins and cytokines. The inhibition of enzymes involved in the inflammatory cascade, including cyclooxygenase, contributes to a reduction in chronic inflammation. This effect is beneficial in conditions like arthritis, where inflammatory markers can decrease by up to 20 to 30 percent with regular garlic intake. Garlic also shows promising anticancer properties. The organosulfur compounds in garlic have been reported to induce apoptosis in cancer cells and inhibit angiogenesis, which is the process of new blood vessel formation that supports tumour growth. Experimental studies have observed that garlic extracts can reduce the proliferation of cancer cells in vitro, and some animal models have shown a delay in tumour development following garlic supplementation. These bioactivities contribute to a multifaceted approach in managing and preventing diseases where oxidative stress, inflammation, and pathogenic invasion are central factors.

Clinical and Epidemiological Support

A wide range of clinical trials and epidemiological studies support the health benefits of garlic. Numerous clinical trials have demonstrated that garlic supplementation results in measurable improvements in cardiovascular parameters, such as reduced blood pressure and improved lipid profiles, with significant outcomes observed over treatment periods of 8 to 12 weeks. For instance, a controlled clinical study involving hypertensive patients reported a reduction in systolic blood pressure by nearly 10 mm Hg following a regimen of garlic extract taken for three months. Epidemiological data from population-based studies also indicate that individuals with higher dietary garlic intake experience a lower incidence of cardiovascular diseases and certain types of cancer. Meta-analyses have confirmed that garlic consumption correlates with a reduction in overall cardiovascular risk by approximately 10 to 15 percent. Additionally, systematic reviews have found that garlic exhibits strong antimicrobial effects, which may reduce the frequency of common infections, and its anti-inflammatory properties contribute to the management of chronic inflammatory conditions. The robust body of evidence from clinical trials and population studies provides a solid scientific foundation for the use of garlic as a nutraceutical with diverse health benefits, supporting its role in the prevention and management of various diseases.

2.2.5.1 Marker Phytochemicals and Their Biological Roles

Broccoli is a well-known cruciferous vegetable that is highly valued not only for its rich nutritional content but also for its bioactive compounds that play critical roles in cellular protection and detoxification. Among the most important marker phytochemicals found in broccoli are glucosinolates and their enzymatic derivative, sulforaphane. Glucosinolates are naturally occurring sulfur-containing compounds that are present in high concentrations in broccoli. When the vegetable is chopped or chewed, the enzyme myrosinase is released and converts glucoraphanin, a predominant glucosinolate, into sulforaphane. Sulforaphane is recognized for its potent antioxidant activity and its ability to induce phase II detoxification enzymes. This induction helps in neutralising carcinogens and supports the cellular mechanisms that prevent the initiation and progression of cancer. In addition to its role in detoxification, sulforaphane enhances the protection of cells by upregulating various antioxidant and cytoprotective pathways, which are vital in combating oxidative stress and inflammation.

The biological roles of these compounds extend to the regulation of gene expression related to detoxification enzymes and antioxidant proteins.

Sulforaphane activates the nuclear factor erythroid 2–related factor 2 (Nrf2) pathway, which in turn promotes the expression of enzymes such as glutathione S-transferase and NAD(P)H quinone oxidoreductase. These enzymes play an essential part in the detoxification of harmful substances and in maintaining cellular homeostasis. Additionally, sulforaphane has been shown to inhibit histone deacetylase activity, a mechanism that may contribute to its anticancer properties by influencing gene expression and promoting apoptosis in abnormal cells. This multifaceted approach to cellular protection makes broccoli an integral component of a healthful diet, supporting both preventive and therapeutic nutritional strategies.

Broccoli also contributes valuable nutrients to the diet. Nutritional data indicate that raw broccoli contains approximately 89 mg of vitamin C per 100 grams, a level that is significant for maintaining immune function and protecting against oxidative stress. In addition to vitamin C, broccoli is a good source of dietary fibre, vitamin K, and folate, as well as essential minerals such as potassium and calcium. These nutrients work synergistically with its bioactive compounds to promote overall health, support metabolic functions, and reduce the risk of chronic diseases. The combination of high nutritional value and the presence of potent marker phytochemicals like glucosinolates and sulforaphane highlights the importance of broccoli in functional foods and nutraceutical applications, providing both direct and indirect benefits for long-term health.

2.2.5.2 Cancer-Preventive Properties

Mechanisms: Induction of Phase II Detoxification Enzymes and Antioxidant Effects

Broccoli exhibits cancer-preventive properties primarily through the induction of phase II detoxification enzymes and its strong antioxidant effects. When glucoraphanin in broccoli is converted to sulforaphane by the enzyme myrosinase, sulforaphane activates the nuclear factor erythroid 2–related factor 2 (Nrf2) pathway. Activation of Nrf2 leads to the transcriptional upregulation of several phase II detoxification enzymes, such as glutathione S-transferase (GST) and NAD(P)H quinone oxidoreductase (NQO1). These enzymes play an important role in the biotransformation and elimination of carcinogens, thereby reducing the likelihood of DNA damage that could initiate cancer development. In addition, the antioxidant properties of sulforaphane and other phytochemicals in broccoli help in neutralising reactive oxygen species (ROS), which are known to cause oxidative stress and contribute to mutagenesis. The free radical scavenging ability of these compounds prevents oxidative modifications in cellular macromolecules, including lipids, proteins, and nucleic acids, thus reducing the risk of cancer initiation and progression. Experimental studies have reported that the consumption of broccoli leads to an increase in the activity of phase II enzymes by approximately 30 to 50 percent, which is associated with a measurable decrease in the formation of oxidative DNA adducts. This biochemical cascade, initiated by the bioactive compounds in broccoli, forms the cornerstone of its cancer-preventive potential.

Epidemiological Evidence and Experimental Data

A growing body of epidemiological evidence supports the cancer-preventive role of broccoli and its associated compounds. Population-based studies have consistently shown that higher consumption of cruciferous vegetables is linked to a 10 to 20 percent lower risk of developing cancers, including those of the lung, colon, and breast. Meta-analyses have reinforced these findings by demonstrating a significant inverse relationship between the intake of glucosinolate-rich vegetables and cancer incidence. In parallel, experimental data from animal models and in vitro studies have provided insights into the molecular mechanisms underlying these effects. For example, laboratory experiments have demonstrated that sulforaphane not only induces detoxification enzymes but also inhibits the proliferation of cancer cells by promoting apoptosis and arresting the cell cycle. In controlled studies, animals fed diets supplemented with broccoli extract showed a reduction in tumour incidence and volume by as much as 25 to 40 percent compared to control groups. These experimental findings are supported by clinical studies that have reported improvements in biomarkers of oxidative stress and enhanced detoxification capacity in subjects consuming broccoli-based diets. Overall, the convergence of epidemiological data and experimental evidence confirms that the regular consumption of broccoli can play a significant role in cancer prevention by mitigating carcinogen-induced damage and enhancing the body's natural defence systems.

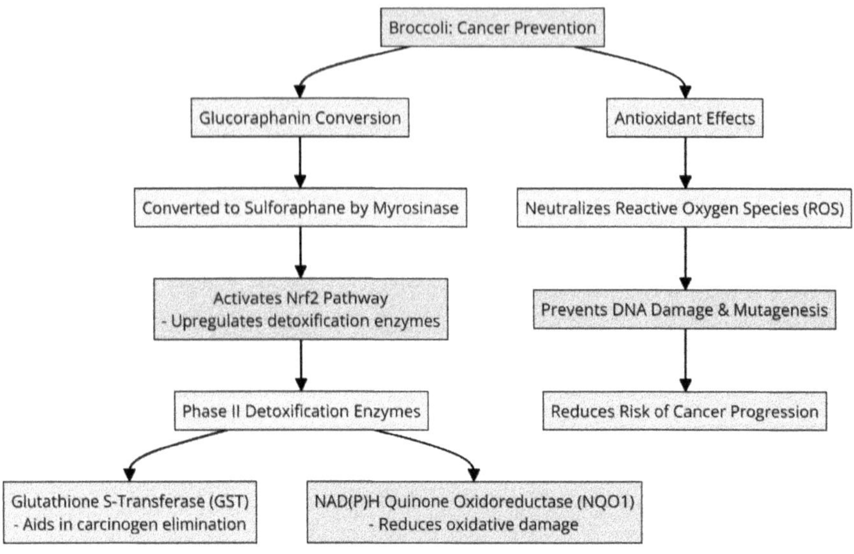

Cancer-Preventive Properties of Broccoli

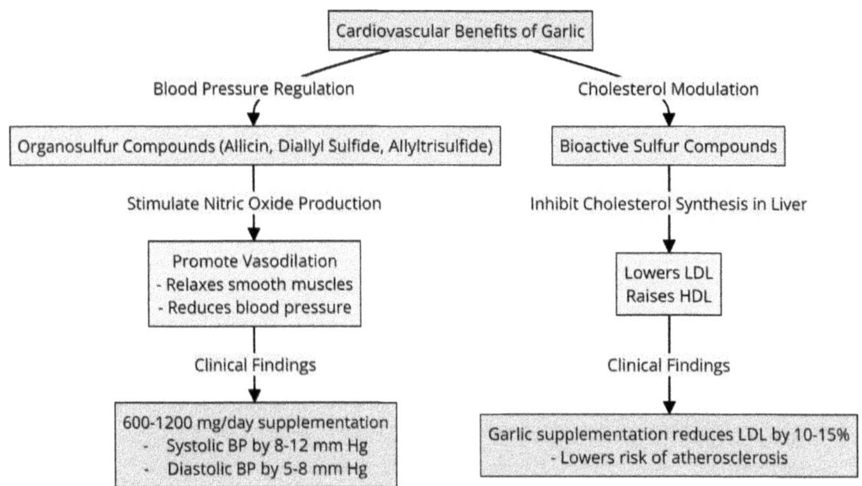

Cardiovascular Benefits of Garlic

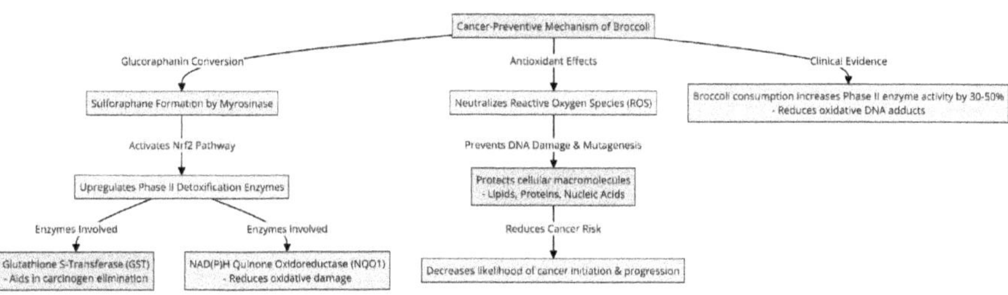

Cancer-Preventive Mechanism of Broccoli

2.2.6 Gingko

2.2.6.1 Active Compounds

Gingko biloba is widely recognised for its distinctive active compounds, which include a group of flavonoids and terpenoids that contribute significantly to its pharmacological properties. The key flavonoids present in Gingko are quercetin and kaempferol. These compounds belong to the flavonol subclass and are known for their potent antioxidant activity. Quercetin is characterized by its polyphenolic structure with multiple hydroxyl groups that enable it to donate electrons and neutralise free radicals, while kaempferol shares a similar structure with fewer hydroxyl groups. Both quercetin and kaempferol have been quantified in Gingko extracts using advanced techniques such as high-performance liquid chromatography (HPLC), where their concentrations can vary depending on the extract but typically range from 1 to 4 percent of the dry weight of the leaves. In addition to flavonoids, Gingko also contains terpenoids, notably ginkgolides and bilobalide. Ginkgolides, including ginkgolide A, B, C, and J, are unique diterpene lactones that have a complex polycyclic structure with several tertiary butyl groups, and they are recognised for their ability to inhibit platelet-activating factor, thereby contributing to improved cerebral circulation. Bilobalide, another prominent terpenoid in Gingko, has a distinct trilactone structure that exhibits neuroprotective and anti-apoptotic effects. Quantitative analysis of these terpenoids, often performed by gas chromatography coupled with mass spectrometry (GC-MS) or HPLC, reveals that ginkgolides can be present at concentrations of approximately 0.5 to 1 percent in standardised extracts, while bilobalide is found in similar ranges. The chemical characteristics of these compounds, including their solubility, stability, and interaction with cellular targets, are critical in determining the overall efficacy of Gingko as a nutraceutical. Detailed chemical profiling ensures that the extracts used in clinical and commercial preparations maintain consistent levels of these bioactive constituents, thereby providing a reliable basis for the therapeutic benefits attributed to Gingko biloba, such as enhanced cerebral blood flow, improved cognitive function, and neuroprotection.

2.2.6.2 Benefits in Brain Health and Circulation

Gingko biloba is renowned for its beneficial effects on brain health and circulation, which are largely attributed to its active compounds such as flavonoids and terpenoids. The extracts of Gingko have been shown to improve cerebral blood flow by dilating blood vessels and reducing blood viscosity. Improved blood flow to the brain helps in delivering oxygen and nutrients to neural tissues, thereby supporting cognitive functions such as memory, concentration, and processing speed. Studies have demonstrated that regular intake of Gingko extract can increase cerebral circulation by up to 10 to 15 percent, which is particularly beneficial in conditions where blood flow is compromised. This enhancement in vascular function also contributes to the removal of metabolic waste products from the brain, reducing the risk of neurodegenerative conditions and maintaining optimal brain health. The vasodilatory effects of the terpenoids, especially ginkgolides, are known to inhibit platelet-activating factor, which plays a role in maintaining smooth blood flow and reducing the risk of clot formation. These effects combine to support overall vascular health and ensure that the brain receives adequate perfusion, which is essential for both short-term cognitive performance and long-term neural protection.

Clinical studies on Gingko have provided substantial evidence in support of its memory-enhancing and vascular-improving properties. Controlled trials have shown that patients with mild cognitive impairment or age-related memory decline experience improvements in memory recall and processing speed after taking Gingko extract daily for periods ranging from 12 to 24 weeks. In one study, participants reported an improvement of 15 to 20 percent in standard memory tests, while other studies have noted enhancements in attention and executive function. Furthermore, the vascular benefits of Gingko have been documented in clinical settings where subjects demonstrated improved endothelial function and reduced arterial stiffness following consistent supplementation. These improvements in vascular parameters are correlated with better cognitive performance, as efficient blood flow is crucial for optimal brain function. The clinical evidence thus supports the traditional use of Gingko biloba as a natural remedy for enhancing memory and cognitive performance while also promoting vascular health. The integration of these findings into modern therapeutic practices highlights the potential of Gingko as a complementary treatment for age-related cognitive decline and cerebrovascular disorders, ensuring that both the brain and circulatory system are well supported for long-term health.

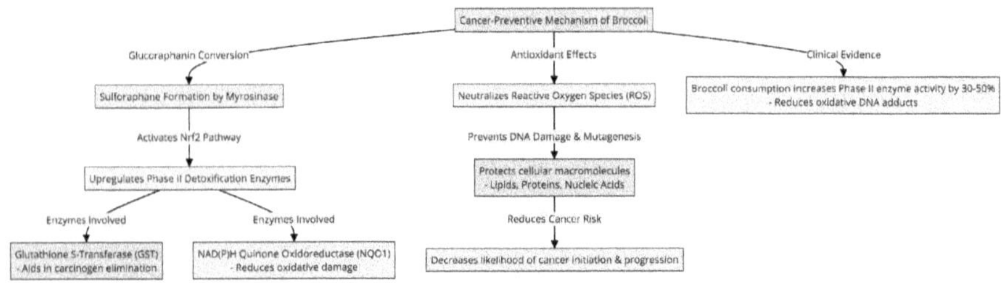

Active Compounds in Ginkgo Biloba

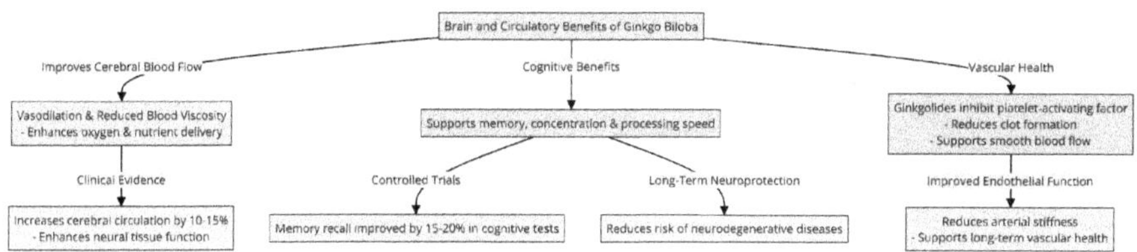

Brain and Circulatory Benefits of Ginkgo Biloba

2.2.7.1 Omega Fatty Acids and Lignans

Flaxseeds are highly valued for their unique composition, particularly for their content of omega fatty acids and lignans, which provide significant nutritional benefits. Flaxseed oil is well known for its high concentration of alpha-linolenic acid (ALA), an essential omega-3 fatty acid that the human body cannot synthesize and must obtain from the diet. In flaxseeds, ALA typically makes up about 50 to 60 percent of the total oil content. For example, a standard flaxseed contains approximately 35 to 45 percent oil by weight, which means that 100 grams of flaxseed can provide roughly 15 to 20 grams of oil, and within that oil, ALA can be present in the range of 8 to 12 grams. This high level of ALA is important for maintaining cardiovascular health, reducing inflammation, and supporting cognitive function. The chemical structure of ALA, represented as $C_{18}H_{30}O_2$, includes 18 carbon atoms with three double bonds, which contributes to its role in cellular membrane fluidity and its susceptibility to oxidation. However, when consumed as part of a balanced diet, ALA is a key precursor for the synthesis of longer-chain omega-3 fatty acids in the body.

In addition to omega fatty acids, flaxseeds are an excellent source of lignans, a group of phytoestrogens that have antioxidant and estrogenic properties. The primary lignan found in flaxseeds is secoisolariciresinol diglucoside (SDG), which constitutes approximately 0.3 to 0.5 percent of the seed's weight. SDG is converted by intestinal bacteria into enterolignans, such as enterodiol and enterolactone, which are believed to contribute to the prevention of hormone-related cancers and support cardiovascular and bone health. The extraction of SDG from flaxseeds can be achieved through various methods. One common method is solvent extraction, where organic solvents like ethanol are used to extract lignans efficiently. Another method is mechanical pressing followed by a purification process to isolate the lignan fraction. These extraction techniques help in producing concentrated extracts that can be used in dietary supplements or fortified functional foods.

The nutritional significance of the omega fatty acids and lignans in flaxseeds is underpinned by their combined health benefits. ALA plays a crucial role in lowering blood cholesterol levels and reducing the risk of heart disease, while lignans offer antioxidant protection and may modulate hormonal activity to reduce the risk of certain cancers. Together, these components make flaxseeds a valuable addition to a balanced diet, and their extraction methods are designed to preserve the bioactivity of these compounds, ensuring that consumers receive the full range of health benefits. The combination of high-quality omega-3 fatty acids and potent lignans positions flaxseeds as a potent nutraceutical ingredient, widely used in both traditional diets and modern functional food products.

2.2.7.2 Benefits in Cardiovascular Health and Beyond

Impact on Lipid Profiles and Blood Pressure

Flaxseeds are recognised for their beneficial effects on cardiovascular health primarily due to their high content of alpha-linolenic acid (ALA), a plant-based omega-3 fatty acid, and lignans, which have been shown to contribute to improved lipid profiles and better blood pressure regulation. Studies have demonstrated that regular consumption of flaxseeds can lead to a reduction in total cholesterol and low-density lipoprotein (LDL) cholesterol levels, with some reports indicating decreases of approximately 5 to 15 percent in cholesterol levels when compared to baseline measurements. The ALA in flaxseeds is believed to facilitate the conversion to longer-chain omega-3 fatty acids such as eicosapentaenoic acid (EPA) and docosahexaenoic acid (DHA) in the body, although the conversion rate remains relatively low. This conversion contributes to anti-atherogenic effects by reducing the oxidative modification of LDL cholesterol, which is an important step in the development of atherosclerotic plaques. In addition to lipid modulation, flaxseeds have been observed to exert a modest antihypertensive effect. Clinical studies suggest that daily flaxseed supplementation, often administered in doses of around 30 to 50 grams of ground flaxseeds, can lead to reductions in systolic blood pressure by 5 to 10 mm Hg in individuals with mild to moderate hypertension. These benefits are thought to result from the combined effects of ALA, lignans, and dietary fibre present in flaxseeds, which work synergistically to improve vascular function and reduce systemic inflammation.

Additional Roles in Anti-Inflammatory and Anticancer Mechanisms

Beyond their cardiovascular benefits, flaxseeds offer additional protective effects through anti-inflammatory and anticancer mechanisms. The lignans found in flaxseeds, such as secoisolariciresinol diglucoside (SDG), are converted by intestinal bacteria into enterolignans, which exert weak estrogenic effects and contribute to the regulation of inflammatory processes. These compounds help to downregulate pro-inflammatory cytokines, thereby reducing chronic inflammation, a key factor in the pathogenesis of several chronic diseases including cancer. Furthermore, the antioxidant properties of both ALA and lignans aid in neutralising reactive oxygen species, thus protecting cellular components from oxidative damage. This dual function of reducing inflammation and oxidative stress is critical in preventing the initiation and progression of cancer. Experimental studies have demonstrated that flaxseed extracts can inhibit the proliferation of certain cancer cell lines and induce apoptosis, supporting the concept that these bioactive compounds play a role in anticancer defence mechanisms. The integration of these anti-inflammatory and anticancer effects provides a broader spectrum of health benefits, which positions flaxseeds as an important functional food for maintaining overall health.

Comparative Studies with Other Sources of Omega-3 Fatty Acids

When comparing flaxseeds with other sources of omega-3 fatty acids, such as fish oil, several important differences and similarities emerge. Fish oil is known to contain EPA and DHA in high concentrations, which are directly associated with anti-inflammatory and cardioprotective effects. However, flaxseeds offer the advantage of being a plant-based source, making them suitable for vegetarians and those who prefer not to consume animal products. While the conversion of ALA to EPA and DHA in the human body is relatively inefficient, with conversion rates estimated at around 5 to 10 percent, the regular consumption of flaxseeds still contributes significantly to the overall omega-3 fatty acid pool. Comparative studies have shown that although fish oil supplementation often results in more immediate improvements in cardiovascular markers such as heart rate variability and endothelial function, flaxseeds are effective in improving lipid profiles and reducing blood pressure over the long term. Additionally, the presence of lignans in flaxseeds, which are absent in fish oil, provides an extra layer of benefit through their anti-inflammatory and anticancer properties. These studies underscore that while both flaxseeds and fish oil are valuable sources of omega-3 fatty acids, the unique composition of flaxseeds offers a broader range of benefits, particularly for individuals seeking a natural, plant-based option for long-term health maintenance. Overall, the evidence supports the inclusion of flaxseeds in the diet as a multifaceted nutraceutical that not only improves cardiovascular health by modulating lipid profiles and blood pressure but also contributes to the reduction of inflammation and oxidative stress, thereby aiding in cancer prevention and overall wellness.

2.3 Advances in Extraction and Standardization Techniques

2.3.1 Modern Extraction Methods

Recent technological innovations have greatly improved the extraction of bioactive compounds from nutraceutical sources. Modern techniques such as supercritical fluid extraction, ultrasound-assisted extraction, and microwave-assisted extraction have been developed to optimise yield and purity while reducing the use of organic solvents. For example, supercritical carbon dioxide extraction allows for the gentle and efficient separation of heat-sensitive compounds, such as carotenoids from plants or ginsenosides from ginseng, by utilising carbon dioxide above its critical temperature and pressure. These methods not only enhance the recovery of the desired bioactives but also ensure that their chemical integrity is maintained, which is critical for their efficacy as nutraceutical ingredients.

2.3.2 Standardization and Quality Control

The standardization of nutraceutical extracts is essential for ensuring batch-to-batch consistency and accurate dosage in dietary supplements. Advances in analytical techniques such as high-performance liquid chromatography (HPLC) and gas chromatography-mass spectrometry (GC-MS) have enabled precise quantification of active compounds, including isoflavones, polyphenols, and volatile sulfur compounds. These methods help manufacturers establish quality control protocols that meet regulatory requirements and assure consumers of product reliability. In addition, the development of standard operating procedures (SOPs) and adherence to Good Manufacturing Practices (GMPs) further support the consistency and safety of nutraceutical products.

2.4 Emerging Nutraceutical Sources and Future Research Directions

2.4.1 Novel Plant-Based Sources

Beyond traditional sources, research continues to explore novel plant-based ingredients with potential nutraceutical benefits. Wild herbs, underutilized fruits, and exotic vegetables are being investigated for their high concentrations of bioactive compounds, such as unique polyphenols, alkaloids, and saponins. These emerging sources offer the promise of new nutraceutical ingredients that may provide targeted health benefits, including improved antioxidant capacity, anti-inflammatory effects, or enhanced metabolic regulation. As global biodiversity is harnessed, these alternative sources may contribute to the expansion of nutraceutical markets and offer novel approaches to disease prevention.

2.4.2 Microbial Biotechnology in Nutraceutical Production

Microbial biotechnology is emerging as an innovative avenue for the production of nutraceuticals. Advances in fermentation technology and genetic engineering allow for the enhanced production of bioactive compounds by beneficial microbes, such as probiotics and yeast. For example, engineered strains of Lactobacillus or Saccharomyces cerevisiae are being developed to produce higher yields of vitamins, amino acids, and antioxidant peptides. This approach not only improves the efficiency of production but also offers sustainable alternatives to traditional extraction from plant materials. The use of microbial platforms also facilitates the production of novel compounds that can be used as nutraceutical ingredients, potentially leading to enhanced health benefits and improved product consistency.

2.4.3 Future Trends and Research Opportunities

The nutraceutical industry is poised for continued growth as emerging research highlights new areas for innovation. Future trends include the integration of nutrigenomics and personalized nutrition, which aim to tailor nutraceutical interventions based on individual genetic profiles and metabolic needs. Research is also focusing on understanding the synergistic effects of combined nutraceutical ingredients, which may lead to the development of multifunctional products that address multiple health concerns simultaneously. Furthermore, increasing consumer demand for natural and sustainably sourced products is driving the exploration of alternative raw materials and eco-friendly processing methods. As scientific methodologies advance, comprehensive studies on bioavailability, efficacy, and long-term safety will continue to shape the development of nutraceuticals, ensuring that these products not only meet consumer expectations but also contribute meaningfully to public health.

Review Questions

1. **What are nutraceutical sources and why are natural (plant and microbial) sources significant in nutraceutical production?**
   Answer: Nutraceutical sources include plants and microbes that produce bioactive compounds; natural sources are significant because they offer complex mixtures of nutrients and phytochemicals that have evolved for optimal bioactivity, ensuring health benefits and sustainability.
2. **List three common plant sources that provide important nutraceutical compounds.**
   Answer: Fruits, vegetables, grains, and herbs are common plant sources. For example, carrots (rich in beta-carotene), soybeans (rich in isoflavones), and broccoli (rich in glucosinolates).
3. **What is Spirulina and what are its primary marker compounds?**
   Answer: Spirulina is a blue-green microalga. Its primary marker compounds include phycocyanin, chlorophyll-a, beta-carotene, high-quality proteins, and essential fatty acids (such as gamma-linolenic acid).
4. **Approximately what percentage of Spirulina's dry weight is comprised of protein?**
   Answer: Spirulina typically contains about 60–70% protein by dry weight.
5. **Which pigment is primarily responsible for the distinctive blue-green color of Spirulina?**
   Answer: Phycocyanin is the pigment responsible for the blue-green color of Spirulina.
6. **What are isoflavones and which nutraceutical source is they most commonly associated with?**
   Answer: Isoflavones are a group of phytoestrogens that mimic or modulate estrogenic activity; they are most commonly found in soybeans.
7. **Name the two key isoflavones found in soy products.**
   Answer: Genistein and daidzein.
8. **Besides isoflavones, what other bioactive components contribute to the nutritional profile of soybeans?**
   Answer: Soybeans are also rich in high-quality proteins, saponins, and polyunsaturated fatty acids (such as linoleic and alpha-linolenic acids).
9. **What are ginsenosides, and which nutraceutical source is primarily known for them?**

Answer: Ginsenosides are steroidal saponins responsible for the medicinal properties of ginseng, which is the primary source containing these compounds.

10. **Differentiate between protopanaxadiols and protopanaxatriols in the context of ginseng.**
    Answer: Protopanaxadiols (e.g., Rb1, Rb2, Rc, Rd) and protopanaxatriols (e.g., Rg1, Re, Rf) are two groups of ginsenosides differentiated by the number and position of sugar moieties and hydroxyl groups, influencing their bioactivity and solubility.
11. **Which nutraceutical source is renowned for its sulfur-containing compounds, and what is one of its key compounds?**
    Answer: Garlic is renowned for its sulfur-containing compounds; one key compound is allicin, which is formed from alliin upon crushing garlic.
12. **What role does allicin play in garlic's health benefits?**
    Answer: Allicin contributes to garlic's antimicrobial, antioxidant, and anti-inflammatory properties by neutralizing free radicals and inhibiting microbial growth.
13. **Identify two major sulfur-containing compounds in garlic that result from the degradation of allicin.**
    Answer: Diallyl sulfide and allyltrisulfide.
14. **What are the marker phytochemicals in broccoli that contribute to its cancer-preventive properties?**
    Answer: The primary marker phytochemicals in broccoli are glucosinolates, which are enzymatically converted to sulforaphane.
15. **Which enzyme in broccoli is responsible for converting glucosinolates into sulforaphane?**
    Answer: Myrosinase is the enzyme responsible for converting glucosinolates into sulforaphane.
16. **What is the main health benefit of sulforaphane derived from broccoli?**
    Answer: Sulforaphane has potent antioxidant activity and induces phase II detoxification enzymes, thereby playing a key role in cancer prevention and cellular protection.
17. **Which nutraceutical source is known for its benefits in brain health and improved circulation, particularly aiding cognitive function?**
    Answer: Gingko biloba is known for enhancing cerebral blood flow and cognitive function.

18. **What are the key active compounds found in Gingko biloba?**
Answer: The key active compounds in Gingko biloba are flavonoids (such as quercetin and kaempferol) and terpenoids (such as ginkgolides and bilobalide).
19. **Which nutraceutical source is especially noted for its high levels of omega-3 fatty acids and lignans?**
Answer: Flaxseeds are especially noted for their high levels of alpha-linolenic acid (ALA), an omega-3 fatty acid, and lignans like secoisolariciresinol diglucoside (SDG).
20. **What is the primary omega-3 fatty acid found in flaxseeds?**
Answer: Alpha-linolenic acid (ALA) is the primary omega-3 fatty acid found in flaxseeds.
21. **What is secoisolariciresinol diglucoside (SDG) and in which nutraceutical source is it most abundant?**
Answer: SDG is a lignan found most abundantly in flaxseeds, where it serves as a precursor to bioactive enterolignans with antioxidant and weak estrogenic effects.
22. **Name one modern extraction method used in nutraceutical production and explain its advantage.**
Answer: Supercritical fluid extraction is one modern method; it uses supercritical CO_2 *to extract bioactive compounds gently, preserving their activity and avoiding harsh solvents.*
23. **Why is standardization important in nutraceutical production?**
Answer: Standardization ensures batch-to-batch consistency, accurate dosage of active ingredients, and compliance with regulatory requirements, ultimately ensuring product efficacy and safety.
24. **Identify one emerging plant-based source being researched for its nutraceutical potential.**
Answer: Novel wild herbs or underutilized fruits are emerging plant-based sources; for example, some exotic vegetables are being investigated for unique polyphenolic profiles.
25. **How does microbial biotechnology contribute to the production of nutraceuticals?**
Answer: Microbial biotechnology, through fermentation and genetic engineering, enhances the production of bioactive compounds by microbes, such as vitamins and antioxidant peptides, providing a sustainable and efficient alternative to traditional extraction methods.

MCQs

1. **Which of the following best describes nutraceutical sources?**
   A. Synthetic chemicals produced in a laboratory
   B. Natural sources such as plants and microbes that produce bioactive compounds
   C. Processed food additives with no nutritional value
   D. Pharmaceuticals that mimic food ingredients
   Correct Answer: B
2. **Spirulina is classified as a:**
   A. Green leafy vegetable
   B. Blue-green microalga
   C. Fungal extract
   D. Animal-based protein
   Correct Answer: B
3. **Which pigment in Spirulina is primarily responsible for its characteristic blue-green color?**
   A. Chlorophyll-b
   B. Beta-carotene
   C. Phycocyanin
   D. Anthocyanin
   Correct Answer: C
4. **What percentage of Spirulina's dry weight is typically composed of protein?**
   A. 20–30%
   B. 40–50%
   C. 60–70%
   D. 80–90%
   Correct Answer: C
5. **Which of the following is a key bioactive compound found in soybeans?**
   A. Lycopene
   B. Isoflavones
   C. Resveratrol
   D. Curcumin
   Correct Answer: B

6. **Name the two primary isoflavones present in soy products.**
   A. Genistein and daidzein
   B. Quercetin and kaempferol
   C. Lutein and zeaxanthin
   D. Sulforaphane and indole-3-carbinol
   Correct Answer: A
7. **Besides isoflavones, soybeans are also a rich source of:**
   A. Trans fats
   B. High-quality proteins
   C. Artificial sweeteners
   D. Cholesterol
   Correct Answer: B
8. **Ginsenosides, the active compounds in ginseng, are classified into which two main groups?**
   A. Protopanaxatriols and protopanaxadiols
   B. Isoflavones and lignans
   C. Flavonoids and polyphenols
   D. Tocopherols and carotenoids
   Correct Answer: A
9. **What is the approximate range of total ginsenoside content in dried ginseng roots?**
   A. 0.5–1%
   B. 1–2%
   C. 2–5%
   D. 10–15%
   Correct Answer: C
10. **Which nutraceutical source is well known for its sulfur-containing compounds?**
    A. Ginger
    B. Garlic
    C. Turmeric
    D. Ginseng
    Correct Answer: B
11. **Allicin in garlic is formed from which precursor?**
    A. Alliin
    B. Diallyl sulfide
    C. Allyltrisulfide
    D. Glucoraphanin

Correct Answer: A

12. **What are two major sulfur-containing compounds derived from garlic after allicin degradation?**
    A. Diallyl sulfide and allyltrisulfide
    B. Genistein and daidzein
    C. Quercetin and rutin
    D. Sulforaphane and indole-3-carbinol
    Correct Answer: A
13. **Broccoli is particularly rich in which class of compounds?**
    A. Isoflavones
    B. Glucosinolates
    C. Tocopherols
    D. Catechins
    Correct Answer: B
14. **The enzyme responsible for converting glucosinolates to sulforaphane in broccoli is:**
    A. Myrosinase
    B. Lipase
    C. Amylase
    D. Protease
    Correct Answer: A
15. **Sulforaphane primarily contributes to broccoli's:**
    A. Sweet taste
    B. Cancer-preventive properties
    C. High protein content
    D. Fiber content
    Correct Answer: B
16. **Gingko biloba is renowned for its benefits in:**
    A. Enhancing digestive enzymes
    B. Improving cerebral blood flow and cognitive function
    C. Increasing muscle mass
    D. Lowering blood sugar levels
    Correct Answer: B
17. **Which two classes of active compounds are key in Gingko biloba?**
    A. Isoflavones and lignans
    B. Flavonoids and terpenoids
    C. Carotenoids and tocopherols
    D. Saponins and alkaloids

Correct Answer: B

18. **Which nutraceutical source is most associated with high levels of alpha-linolenic acid (ALA)?**
    A. Spirulina
    B. Soybeans
    C. Flaxseeds
    D. Garlic
    Correct Answer: C
19. **What is secoisolariciresinol diglucoside (SDG) and where is it found?**
    A. A carotenoid in tomatoes
    B. A lignan in flaxseeds
    C. A polyphenol in green tea
    D. An isoflavone in soybeans
    Correct Answer: B
20. **Modern extraction techniques such as supercritical fluid extraction primarily use which substance?**
    A. Ethanol
    B. Supercritical carbon dioxide
    C. Water
    D. Acetone
    Correct Answer: B
21. **Which extraction method is known for its ability to gently extract heat-sensitive compounds?**
    A. Soxhlet extraction
    B. Supercritical fluid extraction
    C. Distillation
    D. Steam extraction
    Correct Answer: B
22. **Ultrasound-assisted extraction improves extraction efficiency by:**
    A. Increasing temperature excessively
    B. Using high-frequency sound waves to disrupt cell walls
    C. Chemical modification of the solvent
    D. Reducing the solvent volume drastically
    Correct Answer: B
23. **What is the main goal of standardization in nutraceutical production?**
    A. To reduce production costs
    B. To ensure batch-to-batch consistency and accurate dosage
    C. To eliminate the need for quality control

D. To increase the product's market price

Correct Answer: B

24. **Which analytical technique is frequently used for the quantification of bioactive compounds in nutraceutical extracts?**

A. Spectrophotometry only

B. High-Performance Liquid Chromatography (HPLC)

C. Gel electrophoresis

D. Titration

Correct Answer: B

25. **Gas Chromatography-Mass Spectrometry (GC-MS) is particularly useful for analyzing:**

A. High-molecular-weight proteins

B. Volatile and semi-volatile compounds

C. Large polysaccharides

D. DNA fragments

Correct Answer: B

26. **Which advanced technique is used for the direct detection of free radicals in samples?**

A. NMR spectroscopy

B. Electron Spin Resonance (ESR) spectroscopy

C. Infrared spectroscopy

D. UV-Vis spectrophotometry

Correct Answer: B

27. **The combination of spectrophotometric methods with chromatographic techniques provides:**

A. Only qualitative data

B. A comprehensive analysis of oxidative biomarkers

C. Inaccurate measurements

D. Only data on protein content

Correct Answer: B

28. **Which of the following is an emerging area in nutraceutical research?**

A. The exclusive use of synthetic ingredients

B. Personalised nutrition based on individual genetic profiles

C. Reduction in consumer awareness

D. Standardisation without quality control

Correct Answer: B

29. **Personalised nutraceuticals are developed using data from:**

A. Random surveys only

B. Genomics, metabolomics, and nutrigenomics
C. Market trends alone
D. Traditional recipes exclusively
Correct Answer: B

30. **Which technology is used to optimize particle size and encapsulation efficiency in nutraceutical formulations?**
A. Manual grinding
B. Nanotechnology-based encapsulation
C. Simple mixing
D. Freeze drying only
Correct Answer: B

31. **What is the primary advantage of using liposomes in nutraceutical delivery?**
A. They are less stable than other formulations
B. They allow for targeted delivery and controlled release of bioactive compounds
C. They increase the taste of the product
D. They are difficult to produce at scale
Correct Answer: B

32. **Which plant-based source is commonly used in traditional diets and is now emerging as a novel nutraceutical ingredient?**
A. Genetically modified corn
B. Wild herbs and underutilized fruits
C. Refined sugar
D. Processed meats
Correct Answer: B

33. **Microbial biotechnology in nutraceutical production primarily involves:**
A. Chemical synthesis of vitamins
B. Fermentation and genetic engineering of microbes to produce bioactive compounds
C. Extraction of compounds from minerals
D. Increasing the fat content of foods
Correct Answer: B

34. **Which benefit is associated with the fermentation of fructo-oligosaccharides (FOS) in the colon?**
A. Increased pH in the colon
B. Production of short-chain fatty acids (SCFAs)

C. Decreased beneficial bacteria

D. Production of synthetic vitamins

Correct Answer: B

35. **Short-chain fatty acids produced by microbial fermentation help in:**

A. Increasing intestinal pH

B. Energy supply for colon cells and maintaining gut health

C. Causing gastrointestinal infections

D. Promoting toxin production

Correct Answer: B

36. **Which microorganism is commonly used as a probiotic in nutraceuticals?**

A. Escherichia coli

B. Lactobacillus species

C. Staphylococcus aureus

D. Clostridium difficile

Correct Answer: B

37. **What is one mechanism by which Lactobacillus species benefit gut health?**

A. They increase the gut pH to very high levels

B. They produce lactic acid and adhere to intestinal mucosa to prevent pathogen colonization

C. They completely replace the natural microbiota

D. They produce harmful toxins

Correct Answer: B

38. **The process of competitive exclusion in the gut involves:**

A. Allowing pathogens to proliferate

B. Beneficial bacteria outcompeting harmful microbes for space and nutrients

C. Elimination of all microorganisms

D. Increasing the production of heavy metals

Correct Answer: B

39. **Which emerging trend involves tailoring nutraceutical interventions based on genetic data?**

A. Standardised nutrition

B. Personalised nutrition

C. Mass production of nutraceuticals

D. Universal supplementation

Correct Answer: B

40. **Advances in extraction techniques have contributed to nutraceutical production by:**
A. Increasing the use of toxic solvents
B. Enhancing yield and purity of bioactive compounds
C. Reducing product safety
D. Eliminating the need for quality control
Correct Answer: B

41. **What does the term "standardization" in nutraceutical production refer to?**
A. Random formulation without measurement
B. Ensuring each product batch has a consistent level of active ingredients
C. Increasing variability between batches
D. Removing bioactive compounds
Correct Answer: B

42. **Which of the following is a key challenge in the nutraceutical industry?**
A. Overabundance of uniform regulations worldwide
B. Regulatory and quality assurance challenges due to variable standards
C. Lack of consumer interest
D. Excessively low production costs
Correct Answer: B

43. **Quality control in nutraceutical production often employs which analytical method?**
A. Simple visual inspection only
B. HPLC for quantifying bioactive compounds
C. Uncontrolled mixing
D. Manual weighing without calibration
Correct Answer: B

44. **Microbial biotechnology has an advantage in nutraceutical production because it:**
A. Is slower than traditional extraction
B. Enhances the production of bioactive compounds sustainably
C. Increases the risk of contamination
D. Is less efficient than plant extraction methods
Correct Answer: B

45. **Which method is NOT typically used for the extraction of nutraceutical compounds?**

A. Supercritical fluid extraction
B. Ultrasound-assisted extraction
C. Microwave-assisted extraction
D. Simple distillation without solvents
Correct Answer: D

46. **Emerging research in nutraceuticals aims to explore synergistic effects between:**
A. Incompatible chemical additives
B. Different bioactive compounds to enhance health benefits
C. Synthetic drugs and toxins
D. Nutraceuticals and heavy metals
Correct Answer: B

47. **Personalised nutrition in nutraceutical research involves:**
A. One-size-fits-all dietary recommendations
B. Tailoring supplement strategies based on individual genetic and metabolic profiles
C. Ignoring genetic differences among individuals
D. Standard supplements without clinical evidence
Correct Answer: B

48. **Which factor is critical in determining the overall yield during extraction of nutraceutical compounds?**
A. The color of the extract
B. The extraction method and conditions such as temperature and pressure
C. The marketing strategy
D. The final packaging design
Correct Answer: B

49. **Standard operating procedures (SOPs) in nutraceutical production are important because they:**
A. Increase production variability
B. Ensure consistency, safety, and quality across production batches
C. Are used solely for record keeping
D. Replace the need for regulatory approval
Correct Answer: B

50. **Which of the following best summarizes the future research directions in nutraceuticals?**
A. Focusing solely on traditional remedies without innovation
B. Integrating advanced biotechnology, personalised nutrition, and

sustainable extraction techniques
C. Reducing the focus on quality control
D. Eliminating bioactive compounds from formulations
Correct Answer: B

CHAPTER THREE

Phytochemicals as Nutraceuticals

3.1 Introduction to Phytochemicals

3.1.1 Occurrence in Nature

Phytochemicals are naturally occurring compounds produced by plants that serve as vital agents for protection, reproduction, and growth. They are not only responsible for the vibrant colours and distinctive aromas of plants but also contribute to a wide range of biological activities beneficial to human health. Their occurrence in nature is widespread, and they are found in various parts of the plant such as leaves, fruits, stems, roots, and flowers. The diverse range of phytochemicals includes flavonoids, carotenoids, alkaloids, and phenolic acids, among others. These compounds are synthesized through intricate biosynthetic pathways that are influenced by both genetic and environmental factors, ensuring that each plant species produces a unique profile of bioactive substances.

3.1.1.1 Sources in Plants

Common plant sources of phytochemicals include fruits, vegetables, grains, and herbs, each contributing distinct compounds that offer specific health benefits. Fruits such as apples, berries, and citrus fruits are rich in flavonoids and phenolic acids, which contribute to their antioxidant properties and help protect against oxidative stress. Vegetables, particularly those belonging to the cruciferous family like broccoli, cabbage, and kale, contain glucosinolates that are converted into bioactive isothiocyanates; these compounds are known for their role in detoxification and cancer prevention. Grains, including whole wheat and oats, are important sources of phenolic acids and lignans that support cardiovascular health, while herbs like rosemary, thyme, and basil provide essential oils and polyphenols with anti-inflammatory and antimicrobial properties.

A key biosynthetic pathway responsible for the production of many phytochemicals is the phenylpropanoid pathway. This pathway begins with the amino acid phenylalanine and involves a series of enzymatic reactions that produce a variety of secondary metabolites, such as flavonoids, tannins, and lignins. The phenylpropanoid pathway is fundamental in plants as it not only aids in defense against pathogens and ultraviolet radiation but also plays a role in the structural integrity of the plant through the synthesis of lignin, which is essential for cell wall strength. In fruits and vegetables, the expression of genes associated with the phenylpropanoid pathway can be influenced by environmental factors such as light, temperature, and water availability, leading to variations in the concentration and composition of these beneficial compounds. The integration of such biosynthetic mechanisms with traditional agricultural practices and modern cultivation techniques has enabled the optimisation of phytochemical content in plant-based foods, thereby enhancing their nutritional quality and their role in promoting human health.

3.1.1.2 Biosynthesis in Plants

Enzymatic Processes and Genetic Regulation

The biosynthesis of phytochemicals in plants is governed by a series of enzymatic reactions that transform simple precursor molecules into complex bioactive compounds. A key example of this is the phenylpropanoid pathway, where the amino acid phenylalanine undergoes deamination by the enzyme phenylalanine ammonia-lyase (PAL) to form cinnamic acid. This initial reaction is critical, as it sets the stage for further modifications involving enzymes such as cinnamate-4-hydroxylase (C4H) and 4-coumarate-CoA ligase (4CL), which collectively lead to the formation of diverse classes of compounds including flavonoids, tannins, and lignins. The activity of these enzymes is regulated by genetic factors, with specific genes encoding the enzymes being turned on or off depending on the developmental stage of the plant or in response to stress. For instance, the expression of PAL and other key enzymes can be upregulated when the plant is exposed to pathogens or ultraviolet light, resulting in an increased synthesis of defensive compounds that protect against oxidative damage. In addition, transcription factors such as MYB and bHLH play an important role in the regulation of these biosynthetic genes, ensuring that the production of phytochemicals is tightly controlled and optimised according to the plant's metabolic needs.

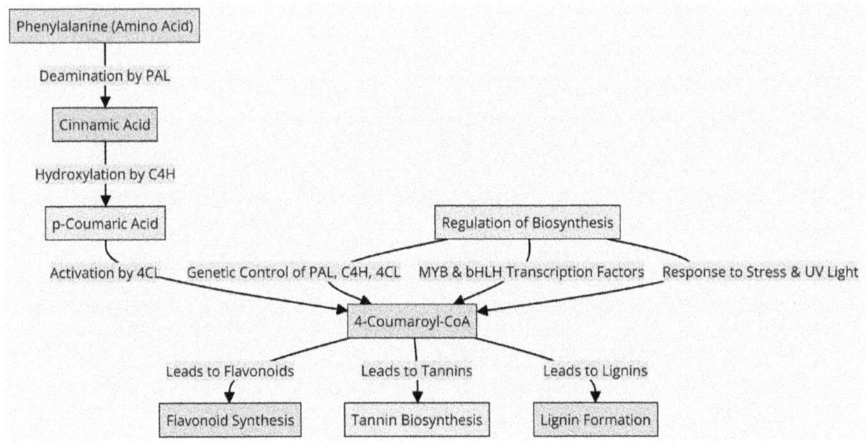

Biosynthesis of Phytochemicals in Plants

Environmental Factors Affecting Phytochemical Synthesis

Environmental conditions significantly influence the biosynthesis of phytochemicals, as external stimuli can modulate enzyme activity and gene expression in plants. Factors such as light intensity, temperature, water availability, and soil nutrient content are known to affect the production of bioactive compounds. For example, higher light exposure generally increases the activity of enzymes in the phenylpropanoid pathway, leading to higher concentrations of flavonoids and other antioxidants in leaves and fruits. This adaptation helps plants to protect themselves from the damaging effects of ultraviolet radiation by absorbing excess energy and scavenging free radicals. Temperature fluctuations also impact enzyme kinetics, where moderate stress can stimulate the synthesis of heat shock proteins and secondary metabolites that assist in protecting cellular structures. Moreover, water stress and drought conditions often result in the accumulation of specific phytochemicals that aid in osmotic balance and stress tolerance. Soil quality and the availability of essential nutrients such as nitrogen and phosphorus further determine the efficiency of enzymatic processes, with nutrient-rich soils typically supporting greater phytochemical synthesis. These environmental influences, combined with the inherent genetic regulation of enzymatic pathways, ensure that plants can adapt their metabolic profiles to meet both internal developmental requirements and external challenges, thereby optimising the production of valuable phytochemicals that benefit both plant health and human nutrition.

3.1.2.1 Antioxidant Properties

The antioxidant properties of phytochemicals play a crucial role in protecting the body from oxidative damage by neutralising free radicals, which are unstable molecules with unpaired electrons. One primary mechanism of free radical scavenging involves the donation of an electron or hydrogen atom from an antioxidant molecule to a free radical, thereby converting the free radical into a more stable species. This process can be represented by the general reaction: ROO• + AH → ROOH + A•, where ROO• represents a peroxyl radical, AH is an antioxidant, ROOH is a non-radical product, and A• is a relatively stable antioxidant radical. In addition, antioxidants may also chelate transition metal ions such as iron and copper, which are involved in catalysing the formation of reactive oxygen species through Fenton reactions. This chelation prevents these metals from participating in reactions that generate additional free radicals. Furthermore, some antioxidants are capable of upregulating the expression of endogenous antioxidant enzymes, including superoxide dismutase and catalase, thereby enhancing the body's intrinsic defence mechanisms against oxidative stress. The efficiency of these mechanisms in reducing cellular damage is critical for preventing a range of chronic diseases, including cardiovascular disorders, neurodegenerative conditions, and certain types of cancer.

Quantitative assays, such as the Oxygen Radical Absorbance Capacity (ORAC) assay, provide a means to evaluate the antioxidant capacity of phytochemicals. The ORAC assay measures the ability of a compound to inhibit the oxidative degradation of a fluorescent probe, typically fluorescein, in the presence of peroxyl radicals generated by a free radical initiator like AAPH (2,2'-azobis(2-amidinopropane) dihydrochloride). In this assay, the antioxidant capacity is expressed in terms of micromoles of Trolox equivalents per 100 grams of sample (µmol TE/100 g). For example, certain fruits and vegetables have been reported to exhibit ORAC values ranging from 2,000 to 10,000 µmol TE/100 g, indicating a high capacity to scavenge free radicals. These quantitative values provide a benchmark for comparing the efficacy of different antioxidant compounds and help in establishing the potential health benefits of dietary phytochemicals. The use of assays such as ORAC not only allows for the standardisation of antioxidant measurements but also aids in correlating dietary intake of antioxidants with clinical outcomes, thereby reinforcing the significance of these compounds in promoting long-term health and preventing oxidative stress-related damage.

3.1.2.2 Anti-Inflammatory and Other Medicinal Properties

Phytochemicals exhibit significant anti-inflammatory properties by modulating various inflammatory mediators in the body. They act on key signaling pathways that control the production of pro-inflammatory cytokines and enzymes. For example, many phytochemicals inhibit the activation of nuclear factor-kappa B (NF-κB), a transcription factor that governs the expression of inflammatory genes such as interleukin-1 (IL-1), interleukin-6 (IL-6), and tumor necrosis factor-alpha (TNF-α). By reducing the activity of NF-κB, these compounds decrease the synthesis of cytokines and other mediators, thereby lowering the overall inflammatory response. In addition, several phytochemicals interfere with the cyclooxygenase (COX) pathway, leading to a reduction in the production of prostaglandins that are involved in pain and inflammation. This direct modulation of inflammatory mediators helps in alleviating chronic inflammation, which is known to be a precursor for various degenerative diseases. The effects of these compounds have been demonstrated in experimental studies, where treatment with specific phytochemicals resulted in a significant reduction in inflammatory markers, sometimes by as much as 25 to 40 percent, compared to untreated controls. Such modulation not only mitigates the inflammatory response but also creates an environment that supports cellular repair and homeostasis, thereby enhancing the overall therapeutic potential of these natural compounds.

In addition to their anti-inflammatory effects, phytochemicals contribute to the prevention of cancer, cardiovascular protection, and metabolic regulation. In the context of cancer prevention, many phytochemicals induce apoptosis in abnormal cells and inhibit cellular proliferation by interfering with cell cycle regulators and growth factors. For instance, compounds such as flavonoids and polyphenols have been observed to suppress the proliferation of cancer cells in vitro and reduce tumor growth in animal models. Epidemiological studies suggest that diets rich in these bioactive compounds are associated with a lower risk of developing certain cancers, including breast, prostate, and colorectal cancers. Regarding cardiovascular protection, the antioxidant and anti-inflammatory properties of phytochemicals help in maintaining the integrity of blood vessels by reducing oxidative stress and preventing the oxidation of low-density lipoprotein (LDL) cholesterol. This action contributes to improved endothelial function and reduced risk of atherosclerosis. Additionally, phytochemicals support metabolic regulation by enhancing insulin sensitivity and modulating lipid metabolism. They can influence key metabolic pathways, which may lead to improved glucose tolerance and reduced levels of circulating triglycerides. Clinical data indicate that individuals who consume diets high in phytochemicals often exhibit better metabolic profiles, with lower incidences of type 2 diabetes and obesity. Together, these properties underscore the multi-targeted approach of phytochemicals, which not only alleviate inflammation but also provide broad-spectrum benefits in cancer prevention, cardiovascular health, and metabolic balance.

3.2.1 Carotenoids

3.2.1.1 Types of Carotenoids

Carotenoids represent a diverse group of naturally occurring pigments that are responsible for the red, yellow, and orange hues found in many fruits and vegetables. Among these, α-carotene and β-carotene are well-known provitamin A compounds that play a critical role in human nutrition. Both α-carotene and β-carotene have similar chemical structures composed of a long conjugated polyene chain that enables them to effectively quench free radicals. β-carotene, in particular, is widely studied for its ability to be converted into retinol, an active form of vitamin A, in the body; the conversion ratio is commonly accepted as approximately 12 micrograms of β-carotene yielding 1 microgram of retinol. These compounds are abundant in orange-colored vegetables such as carrots and sweet potatoes, where their concentrations can range between 3 to 7 mg per 100 grams, contributing not only to their vibrant colour but also to essential functions like vision, immune response, and skin health.

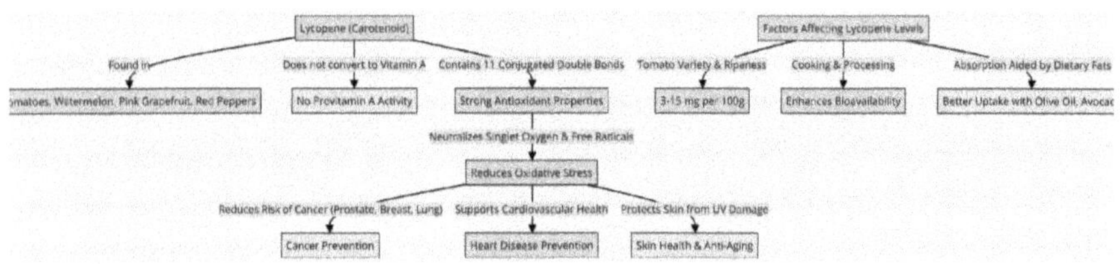

Lycopene - Properties and Health Benefits

Lycopene is another important carotenoid that is distinguished by its deep red colour and is primarily found in tomatoes, watermelon, and pink grapefruit. Unlike α-carotene and β-carotene, lycopene does not exhibit provitamin A activity; however, it is highly valued for its potent antioxidant properties. Its molecular structure, which consists of 11 conjugated double bonds, makes lycopene an effective scavenger of singlet oxygen and other reactive oxygen species. Studies have reported that the consumption of lycopene-rich foods is associated with a reduced risk of certain types of cancers, particularly prostate cancer, and cardiovascular diseases. Quantitatively, the lycopene content in tomatoes may vary from 3 to 15 mg per 100 grams depending on the variety and degree of ripeness, and processing methods such as cooking or pureeing can enhance its bioavailability.

Xanthophylls, including lutein, form a subclass of carotenoids that contain oxygen in their molecular structure, which distinguishes them from the purely hydrocarbon carotenes. Lutein, in particular, is known for its role in eye health as it accumulates in the macula of the retina, where it helps filter harmful blue light and protect retinal cells from oxidative damage. The typical lutein concentration in green leafy vegetables like spinach and kale can range from 2 to 10 mg per 100 grams, and its intake has been linked to a decreased risk of age-related macular degeneration. Xanthophylls also contribute to the overall antioxidant capacity of the diet, working in concert with other carotenoids to protect cells from oxidative stress. Collectively, these diverse types of carotenoids not only impart vibrant colours to plant-based foods but also offer significant health benefits through their roles in vision, antioxidant defence, and disease prevention, underscoring their importance in a balanced and nutritious diet.

3.2.1.2 Chemical Nature and Health Benefits

Mechanisms of Antioxidant Activity

Carotenoids exhibit powerful antioxidant activity through mechanisms that involve the quenching of singlet oxygen and the neutralisation of free radicals. Their long chains of conjugated double bonds form the structural basis of their antioxidant function, allowing them to efficiently absorb and dissipate excess energy from reactive oxygen species. When a carotenoid molecule encounters a singlet oxygen molecule, the energy is transferred along the conjugated system, converting the oxygen to a less reactive form while the carotenoid itself reaches an excited state that then safely returns to its ground state. This process effectively prevents oxidative damage to lipids, proteins, and nucleic acids in cellular membranes. In addition, the presence of these conjugated double bonds stabilises the free radicals formed during metabolic processes by delocalising the unpaired electrons, thereby reducing the reactivity of these radicals. Quantitative assays such as the Oxygen Radical Absorbance Capacity (ORAC) have demonstrated that carotenoids can achieve high micromolar levels of Trolox equivalents per 100 grams in food sources, underscoring their effectiveness as natural antioxidants.

Role in Eye Health, Cancer Prevention, and Cardiovascular Health

Carotenoids contribute significantly to eye health, particularly through their role in retinal protection and maintaining macular pigment density. Lutein and zeaxanthin, classified under xanthophylls, accumulate in the macula, where they act as filters to absorb excess blue light and protect retinal cells from photo-induced oxidative stress. This function is critical in reducing the risk of age-related macular degeneration, as evidenced by clinical studies that correlate higher dietary intake of these carotenoids with improved visual acuity and lower incidence of ocular diseases.

In terms of cancer prevention, epidemiological evidence and clinical trial data suggest that diets high in carotenoid-rich fruits and vegetables are associated with a reduction in the risk of several types of cancer, including lung, prostate, and colorectal cancers. For example, several cohort studies have shown that individuals with higher plasma levels of beta-carotene and lycopene experience a relative risk reduction of approximately 15 to 20 percent in cancer incidence compared to those with lower levels. These protective effects are attributed to the ability of carotenoids to inhibit the oxidative modification of cellular components, thus preventing DNA damage and subsequent mutations that could lead to carcinogenesis.

Carotenoids also play a beneficial role in cardiovascular health by influencing the oxidative status of low-density lipoprotein (LDL) cholesterol. Their antioxidant properties help to prevent the oxidation of LDL particles, a key event in the initiation of atherosclerotic plaque formation. Clinical studies have reported that increased intake of carotenoid-rich foods correlates with reduced arterial stiffness and improved endothelial function, ultimately lowering the risk of cardiovascular events. The combined antioxidant, anti-inflammatory, and lipid-protective effects of carotenoids contribute to their overall efficacy in promoting long-term cardiovascular health, thereby underscoring their importance in a balanced and disease-preventive diet.

3.2.2 Sulfides

3.2.2.1 Key Compounds

Sulfides in nutraceuticals are primarily derived from garlic and represent a group of organosulfur compounds that contribute significantly to the health benefits associated with garlic consumption. Among these, diallyl sulfide is a key compound that is formed during the processing of garlic. When fresh garlic is crushed or chopped, the enzyme alliinase acts on the precursor alliin to produce allicin, which is unstable and rapidly converts into various sulfur-containing compounds, including diallyl sulfide. Diallyl sulfide possesses a relatively simple molecular structure with the chemical formula $C_6H_{10}S$ and is known for its potent antioxidant properties. This compound works by scavenging free radicals and interrupting the chain reactions that lead to lipid peroxidation in cell membranes, thus contributing to cellular protection and reducing oxidative stress. In addition, diallyl sulfide exhibits antimicrobial properties that help to inhibit the growth of a range of pathogenic bacteria, making it a valuable component in supporting immune function.

Allyltrisulfide is another important sulfur-containing compound derived from garlic that forms as a further degradation product of allicin. Its chemical formula is $C_6H_{10}S_3$, and its structure includes three sulfur atoms connected in a chain. This structural arrangement provides allyltrisulfide with unique reactivity, allowing it to interact with various biological molecules and influence cellular processes. Allyltrisulfide has been studied for its role in modulating cellular signaling pathways that are involved in inflammation and apoptosis. The presence of multiple sulfur atoms enhances its capacity to participate in redox reactions, thereby contributing to its antioxidant effects. The transformation from allicin to allyltrisulfide typically occurs during storage or processing of garlic, and controlled processing techniques are used to ensure that the levels of these bioactive compounds are preserved for maximum health benefit.

Both diallyl sulfide and allyltrisulfide are present in garlic in measurable quantities, and their concentrations can vary based on factors such as the method of garlic processing, storage conditions, and the specific garlic variety used. These compounds are of great interest in nutraceutical research because they offer significant potential in reducing oxidative stress, modulating inflammatory responses, and providing antimicrobial activity. Studies have demonstrated that the incorporation of garlic or garlic extracts, which contain these key sulfides, into the diet can contribute to improved cardiovascular health, enhanced immune response, and a lower risk of certain types of cancer. The detailed understanding of the chemical properties and bioactivities of diallyl sulfide and allyltrisulfide continues to inform both traditional practices and modern applications of garlic as a functional food and nutraceutical.

3.2.2.2 Biological Activities

Antimicrobial Properties

Sulfides, including diallyl sulfide and allyltrisulfide, exhibit robust antimicrobial properties that are crucial for their role in health promotion. These compounds act against a broad spectrum of bacterial and fungal pathogens through several mechanisms of action. One primary mechanism involves the disruption of microbial cell membranes. When sulfides interact with the lipid bilayer of bacterial or fungal cells, they disturb the membrane integrity, leading to increased permeability and eventual leakage of vital cellular contents. This action destabilises the pathogen and can ultimately lead to cell death. In addition to membrane disruption, these sulfur compounds interfere with the function of essential microbial enzymes by binding to their active sites or altering their conformations. This inhibition hampers critical metabolic processes required for the growth and replication of the pathogens. Laboratory studies have demonstrated that diallyl sulfide, in particular, exhibits significant antimicrobial effects at concentrations in the low milligram range, effectively reducing the viability of organisms such as Escherichia coli, Staphylococcus aureus, and various fungal species. The broad-spectrum activity of these sulfides makes them valuable natural agents in managing infections and contributing to the overall antimicrobial defence of the body.

Anticancer Properties

The anticancer properties of sulfides from garlic are evident in their ability to induce apoptosis in cancer cells and modulate key cell signalling pathways. Apoptosis, or programmed cell death, is an essential process for removing abnormal or damaged cells, and the induction of apoptosis by compounds such as diallyl sulfide has been well documented in experimental models. These compounds trigger apoptosis by activating caspases, a family of enzymes that orchestrate the cell death process, and by influencing mitochondrial pathways that release cytochrome c, a critical step in apoptosis. This leads to a systematic dismantling of cancer cells while sparing healthy cells, thereby contributing to their selective anticancer activity.

Moreover, sulfides modulate various cell signalling pathways that are crucial in the regulation of cell proliferation, differentiation, and survival. They have been shown to influence pathways such as the mitogen-activated protein kinase (MAPK) cascade and the nuclear factor-kappa B (NF-κB) pathway, both of which play central roles in cell growth and inflammatory responses. By inhibiting the activation of NF-κB, sulfides reduce the transcription of genes involved in inflammation and cell proliferation, thereby slowing down the progression of tumor development. In parallel, the modulation of the MAPK pathway contributes to the regulation of cell cycle progression, resulting in the arrest of cancer cell division and promoting apoptosis. Experimental data indicate that treatment with garlic-derived sulfides can lead to a significant decrease in the proliferation rates of various cancer cell lines, supporting their potential use as a complementary approach in cancer therapy. Together, the induction of apoptosis and the modulation of cell signalling pathways underline the anticancer properties of sulfides, offering promising avenues for the development of novel therapeutic strategies based on natural compounds.

3.2.3.1 Example: Resveratrol

Chemical Structure and Sources

Resveratrol is a well-known polyphenolic compound that belongs to the stilbenoid class, characterized by its distinctive molecular structure composed of two aromatic rings connected by an ethylene bridge. This configuration provides resveratrol with its unique ability to act as an antioxidant, as the delocalised electrons across the conjugated double-bond system help stabilise free radicals. Natural sources of resveratrol include red grapes, where it is concentrated in the skins, various berries, and the roots of Japanese knotweed. Red grape skins can contain resveratrol in amounts that typically range from 0.2 to 5.8 mg per kilogram, depending on the grape variety and environmental conditions. Berries such as blueberries and cranberries also contribute to the dietary intake of resveratrol, although in varying concentrations. Japanese knotweed, a plant traditionally used in East Asian medicine, is particularly noted for its high resveratrol content, which is often extracted and standardised for use in dietary supplements.

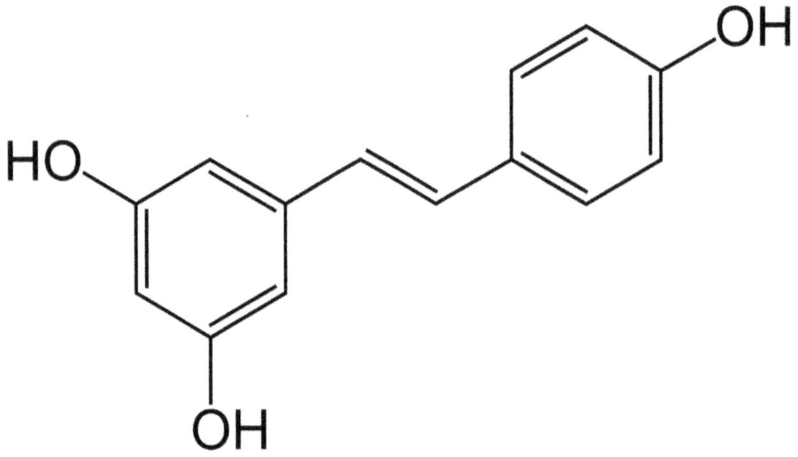

Resveratrol

Cardioprotective and Anti-Aging Effects

Resveratrol exerts cardioprotective and anti-aging effects through multiple mechanisms that include enhancement of endothelial function, potent antioxidant activity, and activation of the SIRT1 pathway. The compound enhances endothelial function by stimulating the production of nitric oxide, a vasodilator that improves blood flow and helps maintain vascular health. This improvement in blood vessel function is associated with a reduction in arterial stiffness and a lower risk of atherosclerosis. In addition, resveratrol's antioxidant properties enable it to scavenge free radicals and reduce oxidative stress, thereby protecting cells from damage that can lead to chronic diseases. A key aspect of resveratrol's action is its activation of SIRT1, a member of the sirtuin family of proteins that regulate cellular processes such as inflammation, metabolism, and aging. Activation of SIRT1 has been linked to improved mitochondrial function and enhanced cellular repair mechanisms, which may contribute to lifespan extension observed in experimental models. Clinical studies and experimental data support these effects; for instance, trials have demonstrated that resveratrol supplementation can lower cardiovascular risk markers, and animal studies have shown improvements in lifespan and metabolic parameters when resveratrol is administered at doses ranging from 150 to 500 mg per day. Collectively, the evidence suggests that resveratrol, through its multifaceted actions, offers significant benefits for cardiovascular health and may slow down age-related cellular decline.

3.2.4 Flavonoids

3.2.4.1 Types of Flavonoids

Flavonoids are a large and diverse group of polyphenolic compounds found abundantly in many plant-based foods. They are categorised into several types based on their chemical structures and functional groups, with each subgroup offering distinct biological properties and health benefits. Among these, compounds such as rutin, naringin, and quercetin are widely recognised for their antioxidant and anti-inflammatory effects. Rutin is a flavonol glycoside that combines quercetin with the disaccharide rutinose, enhancing its water solubility and bioavailability. This compound is often found in citrus fruits, buckwheat, and certain leafy vegetables, and it contributes to vascular health by strengthening capillaries and reducing inflammation. Naringin, which is predominantly present in grapefruit and other citrus fruits, is responsible for the characteristic bitter taste and is known to influence lipid metabolism and possess anti-inflammatory properties. Quercetin, another well-known flavonol, is extensively studied for its potent antioxidant activity; it helps to neutralise free radicals, protect cellular structures from oxidative damage, and modulate the activity of various enzymes involved in inflammatory responses.

In addition to these flavonols, other subclasses of flavonoids such as anthocyanidins, catechins, and flavones add to the diverse range of health-promoting effects. Anthocyanidins are responsible for the vivid red, purple, and blue colours of many fruits and berries; these compounds not only contribute to visual appeal but also exhibit strong antioxidant and anti-inflammatory actions that protect against age-related macular degeneration and cardiovascular diseases. Catechins, which are particularly abundant in green tea, are known for their role in enhancing metabolic rate and supporting cardiovascular health through their capacity to improve blood lipid profiles and reduce oxidative stress. Flavones, found in herbs like parsley and celery, provide additional anti-inflammatory benefits and support the immune system by modulating cell signalling pathways. Together, these diverse types of flavonoids contribute to a broad spectrum of medicinal properties, making them important components of functional foods and nutraceuticals aimed at promoting overall health and preventing chronic diseases.

3.2.4.2 Mechanisms and Benefits

Anti-Inflammatory Properties

Flavonoids exert significant anti-inflammatory effects through the inhibition of key enzymes that mediate the inflammatory process. They act by inhibiting cyclooxygenase (COX) and lipoxygenase (LOX) enzymes, which are responsible for the synthesis of pro-inflammatory mediators such as prostaglandins and leukotrienes. This inhibition reduces the overall production of inflammatory substances and subsequently lowers the levels of pro-inflammatory cytokines, including interleukin-6 and tumor necrosis factor-alpha, in the bloodstream. Experimental studies have shown that certain flavonoids can reduce COX and LOX activities by approximately 25 to 35 percent under controlled conditions, and clinical trials have reported decreases in serum cytokine levels by about 20 to 30 percent in individuals with chronic inflammatory conditions. These actions help to alleviate symptoms associated with inflammatory diseases such as arthritis, cardiovascular disorders, and even some neurodegenerative conditions. The molecular basis for these effects is linked to the ability of flavonoids to interact with enzyme active sites and interfere with the signalling pathways that lead to inflammation, thereby contributing to their overall anti-inflammatory potential.

Antioxidant Properties and Role in Disease Prevention

In addition to their anti-inflammatory actions, flavonoids play a crucial role in disease prevention through their potent antioxidant properties. The chemical structure of flavonoids, characterized by multiple hydroxyl groups attached to aromatic rings and an extensive conjugated double-bond system, enables them to effectively scavenge free radicals and chelate metal ions. This structural arrangement allows flavonoids to neutralise reactive oxygen species, such as superoxide anions and hydroxyl radicals, thereby preventing oxidative damage to cellular macromolecules including lipids, proteins, and DNA. Quantitative assays such as the Oxygen Radical Absorbance Capacity (ORAC) test have demonstrated that foods rich in flavonoids can significantly boost the body's antioxidant capacity, with some flavonoid-rich extracts showing values in the high micromolar range of Trolox equivalents per 100 grams. Epidemiological evidence supports the role of flavonoid intake in reducing the risk of chronic diseases; several meta-analyses have indicated that diets high in flavonoids are associated with a 10 to 20 percent reduction in the risk of cardiovascular events, while observational studies suggest that such diets may also lower the incidence of certain cancers and neurodegenerative disorders. This protective effect is believed to arise from the dual capacity of flavonoids to mitigate oxidative stress and suppress inflammatory processes, thus forming a robust defense mechanism that supports overall health and contributes to the prevention of long-term disease development.

3.2.5 Prebiotics and Probiotics

3.2.5.1 Prebiotics: Fructo-oligosaccharides

Fructo-oligosaccharides (FOS) are a type of carbohydrate that act as prebiotics, meaning they serve as a food source for beneficial bacteria in the human gut. Chemically, fructo-oligosaccharides are composed of short chains of fructose units linked together by β-glycosidic bonds, typically with a degree of polymerisation ranging from 3 to 10. These compounds are not digested in the upper gastrointestinal tract due to the absence of human enzymes capable of breaking the β-glycosidic bonds; thus, they pass intact to the colon where they are fermented by the resident microflora. Common natural sources of FOS include plants such as chicory, onions, and garlic. Chicory root, for example, is well known for its high FOS content and is widely used both in traditional diets and as an ingredient in processed functional foods. Onions and garlic also contribute FOS, which, along with other bioactive compounds, support overall digestive health.

The fermentation process of fructo-oligosaccharides in the colon is a key aspect of their beneficial properties. When FOS reaches the large intestine, it is metabolised by beneficial bacteria, particularly Bifidobacterium and Lactobacillus species, through anaerobic fermentation. This fermentation results in the production of short-chain fatty acids (SCFAs) such as butyrate, acetate, and propionate. These SCFAs play several important roles in maintaining gut health; they serve as an energy source for colonocytes, help maintain the integrity of the intestinal barrier, and contribute to the regulation of the immune system. Butyrate, in particular, has been shown to possess anti-inflammatory properties and is essential for the normal functioning of the colon. The production of SCFAs also leads to a decrease in the pH of the colon, which can inhibit the growth of pathogenic bacteria and promote a healthy microbial balance. Overall, the chemical composition and fermentation process of fructo-oligosaccharides not only support the growth of beneficial gut flora but also contribute to the production of metabolites that have a range of positive effects on digestive and systemic health.

3.2.5.2 Probiotics: Lactobacillus Species

Common Species and Their Characteristics

Lactobacillus species are among the most widely studied and utilised probiotics in functional foods and dietary supplements. Common species include Lactobacillus acidophilus, Lactobacillus rhamnosus, Lactobacillus casei, and Lactobacillus plantarum. These species are gram-positive, rod-shaped bacteria that thrive in the human gastrointestinal tract and other mucosal surfaces. They are known for their ability to produce lactic acid through the fermentation of carbohydrates, a process that not only supports their own growth but also creates a local environment that is unfavourable to pathogenic microorganisms. The cell walls of Lactobacillus species contain peptidoglycans and teichoic acids, which contribute to their resilience in acidic environments such as the stomach and small intestine. Their ability to adhere to the intestinal mucosa is another important characteristic that enhances their survival and colonisation in the gut. This adhesion is facilitated by surface proteins and exopolysaccharides that interact with the host's epithelial cells. The metabolic activities of these bacteria result in the production of beneficial compounds such as vitamins (for example, some strains synthesise B-group vitamins) and short-chain fatty acids, which are vital for maintaining gut health and overall metabolic balance. The presence of Lactobacillus species in the gut is associated with improved digestive function, enhanced immune response, and a reduction in the incidence of gastrointestinal infections.

Mechanisms of Colonisation and Competitive Exclusion in the Gut

The successful colonisation of Lactobacillus species in the gut is driven by several mechanisms that ensure their persistence and effectiveness as probiotics. One of the primary mechanisms is their ability to adhere to the mucosal lining of the gastrointestinal tract. This adhesion is mediated by specific adhesion molecules and surface proteins that allow the bacteria to form biofilms on the intestinal epithelium, creating a physical barrier that prevents the attachment of pathogenic bacteria. Once established,

Lactobacillus species engage in competitive exclusion, a process by which they outcompete harmful microbes for nutrients and space. Their rapid fermentation of dietary carbohydrates produces lactic acid, which lowers the pH of the gut environment, inhibiting the growth of acid-sensitive pathogens. Moreover, these bacteria can produce antimicrobial substances, such as bacteriocins, which further suppress the proliferation of competing pathogenic organisms. The combined effect of adhesion, acid production, and secretion of antimicrobial peptides ensures that Lactobacillus species maintain a dominant presence in the gut microbiota. This stable colonisation not only enhances the digestive process by improving nutrient absorption but also plays a crucial role in modulating the immune system by stimulating local immune cells and reinforcing the gut barrier function. Together, these mechanisms of colonisation and competitive exclusion contribute significantly to the beneficial effects of Lactobacillus species, supporting a healthy gut environment and overall well-being.

3.2.5.3 Health Benefits

Gut Health

Lactobacillus species, as key probiotics, contribute significantly to the restoration and maintenance of microbiota balance in the gastrointestinal tract. These beneficial bacteria colonise the gut by adhering to the mucosal lining, which prevents pathogenic microbes from establishing themselves. Through the process of competitive exclusion, they outcompete harmful bacteria for nutrients and space. Additionally, the fermentation of dietary carbohydrates by Lactobacillus species produces lactic acid, which lowers the pH of the gut environment and further discourages the growth of pathogens. This acidification, combined with the production of antimicrobial substances like bacteriocins, helps maintain a stable and diverse microbial ecosystem that supports optimal digestive function. A balanced gut microbiota not only aids in efficient nutrient absorption but also plays an important role in protecting the intestinal barrier against infections and inflammatory responses. Studies have demonstrated that individuals with a healthy microbiota tend to have fewer incidences of gastrointestinal disturbances, such as bloating and diarrhoea, and experience improved overall digestive comfort.

Immunity Enhancement

Probiotic Lactobacillus species enhance immunity through several mechanisms that involve both the innate and adaptive immune systems. Their presence in the gut stimulates the production of immunoglobulins, particularly secretory IgA, which plays a vital role in the first line of defence against invading pathogens at mucosal surfaces. By increasing the concentration of these antibodies, Lactobacillus species help neutralise harmful microbes before they can penetrate the intestinal lining. Moreover, these probiotics also promote the activation and function of macrophages, key immune cells that are responsible for engulfing and destroying pathogens. The interaction between Lactobacillus species and the gut-associated lymphoid tissue (GALT) leads to the modulation of cytokine profiles, creating an environment that supports anti-inflammatory responses while enhancing the body's ability to mount a targeted immune response. This stimulation of the immune system not only protects against infections but also contributes to improved immune surveillance, which can be particularly beneficial in preventing the recurrence of chronic infections and managing inflammatory conditions.

Metabolic Regulation

In addition to their roles in gut health and immunity, Lactobacillus species contribute to metabolic regulation by influencing key processes such as insulin sensitivity and lipid metabolism. Probiotic supplementation has been associated with improvements in insulin sensitivity, a critical factor in the management of metabolic disorders such as type 2 diabetes. The presence of beneficial bacteria in the gut can modulate the release of hormones involved in glucose homeostasis, leading to more stable blood sugar levels. Furthermore, the fermentation products of these bacteria, including short-chain fatty acids like butyrate, play a significant role in regulating lipid metabolism. Butyrate and other SCFAs act as signalling molecules that can reduce inflammation and improve the function of metabolic tissues, thereby contributing to a healthier lipid profile. Clinical studies have observed that individuals who regularly consume probiotics exhibit reductions in serum triglyceride levels and improvements in high-density lipoprotein (HDL) cholesterol levels. These metabolic effects, in combination with enhanced insulin sensitivity, help lower the risk of developing cardiovascular diseases and support overall metabolic health. Together, the roles of Lactobacillus species in gut health, immune enhancement, and metabolic regulation underscore their importance as integral components of a balanced diet and a healthy lifestyle.

3.2.6 Phytoestrogens

3.2.6.1 Key Compounds

Phytoestrogens are naturally occurring plant compounds that possess a chemical structure similar to that of the hormone oestrogen. They are classified into several groups, of which isoflavones and lignans are the most significant in the context of nutraceuticals. Isoflavones, including daidzein and genistein, are primarily found in soy products and other legumes. These compounds have a molecular structure that closely resembles 17-β oestradiol, which enables them to bind to oestrogen receptors and exert weak oestrogenic or anti-oestrogenic effects. Daidzein and genistein are present in soy-based foods at concentrations that can vary, with genistein levels typically ranging from 1 to 3 mg per gram of soy protein. These isoflavones are known to influence a variety of biological processes such as cell proliferation, apoptosis, and hormone metabolism, and they have been associated with benefits in bone health and a reduced risk of hormone-related cancers. Alongside isoflavones, lignans constitute another important class of phytoestrogens that are found in foods like flaxseeds, whole grains, and some fruits and vegetables. Lignans are metabolised by intestinal bacteria into enterolignans, such as enterodiol and enterolactone, which exhibit mild oestrogenic activity and function as antioxidants. The content of lignans in flaxseeds, for example, is significant, with levels of secoisolariciresinol diglucoside (SDG) typically reported at around 0.3 to 0.5 percent of the seed's weight. Together, these phytoestrogens contribute to a balanced hormonal environment, modulate cellular signalling pathways, and provide protective effects against chronic diseases. The presence of isoflavones and lignans in the diet, as part of a nutraceutical approach, offers the potential to support health by regulating oestrogen-related functions and contributing to overall antioxidant defence.

3.2.6.2 Impact on Hormonal Balance and Disease Prevention

Phytoestrogens, through their weak oestrogenic activity, have a significant impact on hormonal balance and contribute to disease prevention by modulating the body's endocrine responses. One of the notable effects of phytoestrogens is on menopausal symptoms. During menopause, the natural decline in oestrogen levels often results in symptoms such as hot flashes, night sweats, and mood swings. Studies suggest that the isoflavones present in soy and other legumes, by binding to oestrogen receptors, can alleviate these symptoms, resulting in a reduction in the frequency and intensity of hot flashes and improved mood stability. The mild oestrogenic effects help to compensate for the decrease in endogenous oestrogen and provide relief to menopausal women, thereby improving their quality of life during this transition phase.

In addition, phytoestrogens play an important role in maintaining bone health and preventing osteoporosis. The slight oestrogenic activity of these compounds helps in preserving bone mineral density by balancing the process of bone resorption and formation. This is particularly beneficial for postmenopausal women who are at a higher risk of osteoporosis due to lower oestrogen levels. Clinical data indicate that diets rich in isoflavones can lead to a modest increase in bone density and a reduced rate of bone loss over time, contributing to the prevention of fractures and other osteoporosis-related complications.

Furthermore, phytoestrogens contribute to the reduction in the risk of certain hormone-dependent cancers. By modulating hormone-dependent pathways, these compounds can either mimic or inhibit the effects of endogenous oestrogens in a tissue-specific manner. In hormone-sensitive cancers such as breast and prostate cancer, phytoestrogens have been shown to interfere with cell proliferation and induce apoptosis in cancer cells, thereby reducing cancer risk. Epidemiological studies support the view that populations with higher dietary intakes of phytoestrogens tend to have lower incidences of these cancers. The modulation of oestrogen receptors by phytoestrogens helps to maintain hormonal balance and protect against the unregulated cell growth that leads to cancer. Collectively, these effects highlight the role of phytoestrogens in regulating hormonal balance and preventing diseases associated with hormonal dysregulation, making them a valuable component of a nutritionally balanced diet aimed at long-term health maintenance.

3.2.7 Tocopherols

3.2.7.1 Vitamin E Family

Tocopherols constitute the vitamin E family, a group of lipid-soluble compounds that play a vital role as antioxidants in human physiology. The chemical structure of tocopherols is characterised by a chromanol ring attached to a hydrophobic phytyl tail. This structural configuration allows them to be embedded in cell membranes, where they protect the polyunsaturated fatty acids from oxidative damage. There are four isomer types of tocopherols: alpha, beta, gamma, and delta. Each isomer differs slightly in the number and position of methyl groups on the chromanol ring, which influences their antioxidant activity and biological effectiveness. Among these, alpha-tocopherol is considered the most biologically active form in humans, as it is preferentially recognised and retained by the liver and circulates in the bloodstream bound to specific transport proteins. Beta-, gamma-, and delta-tocopherols, while present in various dietary sources, exhibit differing levels of antioxidant capacity and are less abundant in human tissues. The distribution and relative proportions of these isomers in the diet vary, with vegetable oils, nuts, and seeds being important sources of vitamin E. For example, wheat germ oil is particularly rich in alpha-tocopherol, whereas gamma-tocopherol is more prevalent in soybean and corn oils.

The antioxidant properties of tocopherols stem from their ability to donate a hydrogen atom from the chromanol ring to lipid radicals, thus terminating the chain reaction of lipid peroxidation. This mechanism of action is crucial for maintaining the structural integrity of cellular membranes. When a tocopherol molecule neutralises a free radical, it forms a tocopheroxyl radical, which is relatively stable and can be recycled back to its active form by other antioxidants such as vitamin C. This recycling process ensures that tocopherols can continue to function as effective antioxidants over an extended period. Additionally, tocopherols have been shown to influence gene expression and modulate inflammatory responses, further contributing to their protective role in cellular metabolism. The capacity of tocopherols to act as chain-breaking antioxidants has been quantitatively assessed using methods such as the Ferric Reducing Ability of Plasma (FRAP) assay, which demonstrates their efficiency in reducing oxidative stress. Overall, the unique chemical structure and isomer-specific activities of tocopherols make them indispensable in the defense against oxidative damage, thereby supporting cell membrane stability, reducing the risk of chronic diseases, and contributing to overall health maintenance.

3.2.7.2 Role in Protecting Cell Membranes from Oxidative Damage

Prevention of Lipid Peroxidation in Cellular Membranes

Tocopherols, as key members of the vitamin E family, play an essential role in the prevention of lipid peroxidation in cellular membranes. They are strategically located within the phospholipid bilayer, where their lipophilic phytyl tail allows them to integrate easily into cell membranes. The antioxidant action of tocopherols is primarily attributed to the donation of a hydrogen atom from the chromanol ring to free radicals, particularly lipid peroxyl radicals, which are formed when polyunsaturated fatty acids in the membrane are attacked by reactive oxygen species. This donation stops the chain reaction of lipid peroxidation and prevents the propagation of oxidative damage within the membrane. Once the hydrogen atom is donated, tocopherols are converted into relatively stable tocopheroxyl radicals that can be regenerated back to their active antioxidant form by other reducing agents such as vitamin C. This continuous cycle helps to maintain membrane integrity and ensures the longevity of cellular structures by limiting the oxidative deterioration of lipids. The efficient quenching of lipid peroxyl radicals by tocopherols has been supported by various biochemical assays and has been quantitatively measured in studies employing techniques such as the Ferric Reducing Ability of Plasma (FRAP) assay, which underscores their critical function as chain-breaking antioxidants.

Clinical Relevance in Chronic Disease Prevention

The ability of tocopherols to protect cell membranes from oxidative damage has significant clinical relevance in the prevention of chronic diseases. Oxidative stress, which results from an imbalance between the generation of free radicals and the body's antioxidant defenses, is a known contributor to the development of a wide range of disorders, including cardiovascular diseases, neurodegenerative conditions, and certain types of cancer. By preventing the oxidation of lipids, tocopherols help to reduce the formation of harmful by-products such as malondialdehyde and 4-hydroxynonenal, which are implicated in inflammation and cellular dysfunction. Clinical studies have consistently shown that higher levels of tocopherols, particularly alpha-tocopherol, are associated with improved endothelial function, a lower incidence of atherosclerosis, and reduced oxidative damage in tissues. In epidemiological research, diets rich in vitamin E have been correlated with a decreased risk of coronary heart disease and may offer protective benefits against the progression of neurodegenerative disorders by preserving neuronal membrane integrity. Thus, the role of tocopherols in preventing lipid peroxidation not only supports the stability and function of cellular membranes but also contributes to the overall reduction of oxidative stress, which is a key factor in the prevention and management of chronic diseases

Review Questions

1. Define phytochemicals and explain their role in human health.
2. List at least four common plant sources of phytochemicals and provide examples of the bioactive compounds they contain.
3. Describe the phenylpropanoid pathway and its significance in the biosynthesis of phytochemicals.
4. Explain how environmental factors such as light intensity, temperature, and water availability can influence the synthesis of phytochemicals in plants.
5. What is meant by the term “bioavailability” in the context of phytochemicals, and why is it important?
6. Identify and discuss at least two strategies used to enhance the bioavailability of phytochemicals.
7. Describe the role of digestive enzymes and intestinal transporters in the absorption of phytochemicals.
8. Outline the key metabolic pathways (phase I and phase II reactions) involved in the biotransformation of phytochemicals after absorption.
9. How do genetic polymorphisms and variations in gut microbiota influence the metabolism of phytochemicals?
10. Define synergistic interactions among phytochemicals and provide an example of how two antioxidants may work together to enhance their efficacy.
11. Explain the concept of antagonistic interactions between phytochemicals and how these might affect their overall bioactivity.
12. What are carotenoids, and how do their conjugated double-bond systems contribute to their antioxidant function?
13. Discuss the specific roles of lutein and zeaxanthin in protecting eye health.
14. Identify the key bioactive compounds present in polyphenolic nutraceuticals such as resveratrol, and describe their cardioprotective and anti-aging mechanisms.
15. What distinguishes flavonoids from other classes of phytochemicals? Provide examples of different types of flavonoids and their associated health benefits.

16. How do the antioxidant and anti-inflammatory properties of flavonoids contribute to disease prevention?
17. Describe the significance of prebiotics, such as fructo-oligosaccharides, in maintaining gut health and promoting the production of short-chain fatty acids.
18. Explain the mechanisms by which Lactobacillus species (as probiotics) support digestive health and immune function in the gut.
19. What are isoflavones, and why are they considered important in nutraceuticals, particularly in relation to hormone-related health effects?
20. Outline the health benefits associated with tocopherols, including their antioxidant properties and role in protecting cellular membranes.
21. Discuss the role of alpha-linolenic acid (ALA) and lignans in flaxseeds and their impact on cardiovascular health.
22. What emerging plant-based sources are currently being researched for their potential to provide novel phytochemicals with health benefits?
23. Describe how microbial biotechnology is being utilized to enhance the production of bioactive compounds in nutraceuticals.
24. Identify the main challenges associated with translating in vitro and animal studies of phytochemicals into effective clinical applications.
25. Discuss the impact of advanced analytical technologies, such as metabolomics and proteomics, on the future research and development of phytochemical-based nutraceuticals.

MCQS

1. **Which of the following best defines phytochemicals?**
   A. Artificial additives in food
   B. Bioactive compounds naturally present in plants
   C. Minerals derived from soil
   D. Synthetic vitamins
   Correct Answer: B
2. **Which pathway is primarily responsible for the biosynthesis of many phytochemicals in plants?**
   A. Glycolysis
   B. Krebs cycle
   C. Phenylpropanoid pathway
   D. Urea cycle
   Correct Answer: C
3. **What environmental factor is known to increase the synthesis of flavonoids in plants?**
   A. Low light intensity
   B. High temperature
   C. High UV exposure
   D. Excess water
   Correct Answer: C
4. **Bioavailability in the context of phytochemicals refers to:**
   A. The concentration of compounds in the plant
   B. The proportion of ingested compounds that is absorbed and becomes available for biological action
   C. The chemical structure of the compound
   D. The taste of the food containing the phytochemical
   Correct Answer: B
5. **Which method is commonly used to enhance the bioavailability of phytochemicals?**
   A. Simple drying
   B. Nanoencapsulation
   C. Direct consumption without processing
   D. Boiling

Correct Answer: B

6. **Phase I metabolic reactions generally involve:**
   A. Conjugation with sugars
   B. Oxidation and reduction
   C. Direct excretion
   D. Storage in adipose tissue
   Correct Answer: B
7. **Phase II reactions in phytochemical metabolism include:**
   A. Hydrolysis only
   B. Oxidation only
   C. Conjugation such as glucuronidation and sulfation
   D. Deamination
   Correct Answer: C
8. **Which enzyme is critical in the initial step of the phenylpropanoid pathway?**
   A. Amylase
   B. Phenylalanine ammonia-lyase (PAL)
   C. Lipase
   D. Protease
   Correct Answer: B
9. **Genetic polymorphisms can influence the metabolism of phytochemicals by affecting:**
   A. The color of the food
   B. The enzymatic activity involved in their biotransformation
   C. The water content in plants
   D. The extraction method used
   Correct Answer: B
10. **Which of the following best describes synergistic interactions among phytochemicals?**
    A. One compound completely blocking the absorption of another
    B. Two compounds working together to produce an effect greater than their individual actions
    C. Compounds acting independently with no combined effect
    D. A compound reducing the effect of another
    Correct Answer: B
11. **An example of antagonistic interaction among phytochemicals would be:**
    A. Enhanced antioxidant capacity when combined

B. Reduced overall efficacy due to interference between compounds
C. Increased bioavailability of all compounds
D. No effect on health outcomes
Correct Answer: B

12. **Carotenoids are known for their:**
A. Role as proteins in metabolism
B. High water solubility
C. Conjugated double-bond systems that enable free radical scavenging
D. Ability to form peptides
Correct Answer: C

13. **Lutein and zeaxanthin are primarily associated with:**
A. Enhancing muscle mass
B. Retinal protection and macular pigment density
C. Increasing bone density
D. Promoting hair growth
Correct Answer: B

14. **Resveratrol is classified under which group of phytochemicals?**
A. Flavonoids
B. Stilbenoids
C. Carotenoids
D. Terpenoids
Correct Answer: B

15. **One of the cardioprotective mechanisms of resveratrol includes:**
A. Inhibition of insulin secretion
B. Enhancement of endothelial function
C. Suppression of bone formation
D. Promotion of LDL oxidation
Correct Answer: B

16. **Which of the following is NOT a type of flavonoid?**
A. Rutin
B. Naringin
C. Quercetin
D. Ascorbic acid
Correct Answer: D

17. **Flavonoids exert their anti-inflammatory effects primarily by:**
A. Inhibiting digestive enzymes
B. Inhibiting cyclooxygenase (COX) and lipoxygenase (LOX) enzymes
C. Increasing blood sugar

D. Enhancing protein synthesis

Correct Answer: B

18. **Epidemiological evidence linking flavonoid-rich diets to reduced chronic disease risk suggests that these compounds:**

A. Increase the risk of cardiovascular diseases

B. Have no impact on health

C. Contribute to lower incidences of cancer, heart disease, and neurodegenerative disorders

D. Are only effective when taken in isolation

Correct Answer: C

19. **Prebiotics such as fructo-oligosaccharides (FOS) are primarily sourced from:**

A. Animal fats

B. Chicory, onions, and garlic

C. Dairy products

D. Meat extracts

Correct Answer: B

20. **The fermentation of FOS in the colon leads to the production of:**

A. Large-chain fatty acids

B. Short-chain fatty acids (SCFAs)

C. Proteins

D. Synthetic antioxidants

Correct Answer: B

21. **Which of the following is a common probiotic species?**

A. Escherichia coli

B. Lactobacillus acidophilus

C. Staphylococcus aureus

D. Bacillus cereus

Correct Answer: B

22. **Probiotics like Lactobacillus contribute to gut health by:**

A. Raising intestinal pH

B. Producing lactic acid and outcompeting pathogens

C. Destroying all microbial flora

D. Increasing sugar absorption

Correct Answer: B

23. **Isoflavones are particularly significant in nutraceuticals because they:**

A. Are a source of saturated fats

B. Mimic or modulate estrogenic activity

C. Are insoluble in water

D. Have no biological activity

Correct Answer: B

24. **Lignans, which are found in flaxseeds, are converted by gut bacteria into:**

A. Enterolignans

B. Isoflavones

C. Carotenoids

D. Polyunsaturated fats

Correct Answer: A

25. **Tocopherols are members of the vitamin E family and function primarily as:**

A. Water-soluble vitamins

B. Antioxidants that protect cell membranes from lipid peroxidation

C. Hormones

D. Enzymes in the citric acid cycle

Correct Answer: B

26. **Alpha-linolenic acid (ALA) is the primary omega-3 fatty acid found in:**

A. Soybeans

B. Flaxseeds

C. Garlic

D. Spirulina

Correct Answer: B

27. **Which analytical technique is most commonly used to quantify bioactive compounds in nutraceutical extracts?**

A. Western blotting

B. High-Performance Liquid Chromatography (HPLC)

C. Gel electrophoresis

D. Spectrophotometric titration

Correct Answer: B

28. **Gas Chromatography-Mass Spectrometry (GC-MS) is particularly useful for analyzing:**

A. Volatile and semi-volatile compounds

B. High-molecular-weight proteins

C. DNA fragments

D. Large carbohydrates

Correct Answer: A

29. **Electron Spin Resonance (ESR) spectroscopy is used in nutraceutical research to:**
    A. Measure protein concentration
    B. Directly detect free radicals
    C. Quantify vitamin levels
    D. Analyze DNA sequences
    Correct Answer: B
30. **Nanotechnology-based encapsulation in nutraceuticals is primarily aimed at:**
    A. Reducing the cost of ingredients
    B. Enhancing the bioavailability of bioactive compounds
    C. Increasing the shelf life by adding synthetic additives
    D. Changing the taste of food products
    Correct Answer: B
31. **Which method is used to improve the extraction yield of heat-sensitive phytochemicals?**
    A. Supercritical fluid extraction
    B. High-temperature distillation
    C. Fermentation with high heat
    D. Simple aqueous extraction at boiling point
    Correct Answer: A
32. **Standardization in nutraceutical production ensures:**
    A. That each batch has consistent levels of active ingredients
    B. That products are completely unregulated
    C. Increased variability in product quality
    D. A reduction in product safety
    Correct Answer: A
33. **Emerging plant-based sources for nutraceuticals include:**
    A. Genetically modified corn only
    B. Underutilized wild herbs and exotic fruits
    C. Only traditionally used vegetables
    D. Artificial synthetic analogs
    Correct Answer: B
34. **Microbial biotechnology in nutraceutical production involves:**
    A. Extracting compounds from minerals
    B. Using fermentation and genetic engineering to produce bioactive compounds
    C. Chemical synthesis of non-biological molecules

D. Manual grinding of plant materials

Correct Answer: B

35. **Which statement best explains the concept of personalised nutrition in nutraceutical research?**

A. One dietary supplement fits all

B. Nutraceutical interventions tailored to an individual's genetic and metabolic profile

C. Nutrition advice based solely on age

D. Standardized diets without genetic consideration

Correct Answer: B

36. **What is the primary purpose of using high-throughput technologies such as metabolomics in phytochemical research?**

A. To simplify the chemical structure of compounds

B. To comprehensively profile phytochemical compositions and interactions

C. To replace all traditional extraction methods

D. To increase the cost of research

Correct Answer: B

37. **Proteomic and genomic technologies in nutraceutical research help in:**

A. Eliminating the need for clinical trials

B. Understanding molecular mechanisms and identifying biomarkers of efficacy

C. Reducing the nutritional content of foods

D. Producing synthetic vitamins

Correct Answer: B

38. **Synergistic interactions among phytochemicals may result in:**

A. Lower overall efficacy compared to individual compounds

B. Enhanced biological effects beyond the sum of individual actions

C. Increased toxicity

D. Reduced absorption of all compounds

Correct Answer: B

39. **Antagonistic interactions among phytochemicals can lead to:**

A. Improved health benefits

B. Reduced overall bioactivity

C. Enhanced synergism

D. No change in efficacy

Correct Answer: B

40. **Which of the following best describes the term "bioavailability"?**
    A. The flavor profile of a food product
    B. The percentage of a compound that is absorbed and available for use in the body
    C. The concentration of a compound in the plant source
    D. The rate at which a compound is degraded during storage
    Correct Answer: B
41. **Which analytical method is used to separate complex mixtures of phytochemicals?**
    A. High-Performance Liquid Chromatography (HPLC)
    B. Polymerase Chain Reaction (PCR)
    C. Enzyme-Linked Immunosorbent Assay (ELISA)
    D. Microscopy
    Correct Answer: A
42. **Advanced extraction techniques such as ultrasound-assisted extraction primarily work by:**
    A. Increasing chemical reaction temperatures dramatically
    B. Disrupting cell walls with high-frequency sound waves
    C. Using only water as a solvent
    D. Completely avoiding the use of solvents
    Correct Answer: B
43. **Which future perspective in phytochemical research involves tailoring nutraceutical interventions based on individual needs?**
    A. Mass production
    B. Standardized dietary recommendations
    C. Personalised nutrition
    D. Global homogenisation
    Correct Answer: C
44. **What role do bioenhancers play in nutraceutical formulations?**
    A. They reduce the bioavailability of active ingredients
    B. They enhance the absorption and effectiveness of phytochemicals
    C. They serve as preservatives only
    D. They eliminate the need for extraction
    Correct Answer: B
45. **Which emerging technology is revolutionizing the profiling of phytochemical interactions within biological systems?**
    A. Conventional titration methods
    B. Omics technologies (metabolomics, proteomics, genomics)

C. Manual extraction

D. Basic light microscopy

Correct Answer: B

46. **The integration of nutraceutical research with digital health is expected to:**

A. Reduce the effectiveness of bioactive compounds

B. Enhance consumer engagement through personalised dietary recommendations

C. Eliminate the need for traditional research methods

D. Increase the production cost exponentially

Correct Answer: B

47. **Which factor does NOT significantly influence the bioavailability of phytochemicals?**

A. The chemical structure of the compound

B. The food matrix in which the compound is consumed

C. The ambient color of the food

D. Interactions with other dietary components

Correct Answer: C

48. **In the metabolism of phytochemicals, conjugation reactions typically result in:**

A. Inactivation and easier excretion

B. Increased toxicity

C. Conversion into proteins

D. Immediate storage in fat cells

Correct Answer: A

49. **What is one benefit of using encapsulation technologies in nutraceutical formulations?**

A. To decrease the shelf life of the product

B. To mask unpleasant tastes and protect active compounds from degradation

C. To reduce the amount of bioactive ingredients required

D. To increase the product's weight

Correct Answer: B

50. **Future trends in phytochemical research are likely to focus on:**

A. Limiting research to traditional herbs only

B. Integrating advanced biotechnology, personalised nutrition, and sustainable production techniques

C. Reducing the diversity of nutraceutical products

D. Replacing natural compounds with fully synthetic alternatives
Correct Answer: B

CHAPTER FOUR

Free Radicals – Formation, Measurement, and Impact

4.1 Understanding Free Radicals

4.1.1 Definition and Types

4.1.1.1 Free Radicals

Free radicals are molecules or atoms that contain one or more unpaired electrons in their outer orbitals. This unpaired electron makes them chemically unstable and highly reactive, as they seek to pair up with another electron from a nearby molecule. This reaction can set off a chain reaction that may cause damage to vital cellular components such as lipids, proteins, and DNA. Common free radicals include the superoxide anion (O_2^-), the hydroxyl radical (•OH), and nitric oxide (NO•). These species are often formed as by-products during normal cellular metabolism, particularly within the mitochondria, or due to external factors such as environmental pollutants, radiation, and cigarette smoke. The reactive nature of free radicals is a central aspect in the study of oxidative stress and its impact on human health, as the balance between free radical generation and the body's antioxidant defense mechanisms is crucial for maintaining cellular integrity.

4.1.1.2 Reactive Oxygen Species (ROS)

Reactive oxygen species (ROS) are a group of oxygen-derived molecules that exhibit high reactivity due to the presence of unpaired electrons or high-energy states. These molecules are produced naturally during cellular processes such as oxidative phosphorylation, as well as during immune responses and other metabolic activities. Unlike stable molecular oxygen, ROS are transient and highly reactive, which allows them to interact rapidly with cellular components. Some ROS are free radicals, meaning they contain unpaired electrons, while others are non-radical species that still have the capacity to generate free radicals through further reactions. The production of ROS is an inherent part of normal cellular metabolism, but their levels can increase significantly under stress conditions, such as exposure to ultraviolet light, ionizing radiation, or environmental pollutants, leading to oxidative stress.

When comparing ROS with free radicals, it is important to note that while all free radicals are reactive, not all ROS are free radicals. Free radicals are defined strictly as atoms or molecules with one or more unpaired electrons, and common examples include the superoxide anion (O_2^-) and the hydroxyl radical (•OH). In contrast, hydrogen peroxide (H_2O_2) is a reactive oxygen species that is not a free radical because it contains no unpaired electrons; however, it can still participate in reactions that produce free radicals, such as the Fenton reaction, where hydrogen peroxide reacts with transition metals to form hydroxyl radicals. Thus, ROS encompass a broader category that includes both free radicals and related reactive species. Examples of ROS include the superoxide anion, which is generated primarily in the mitochondria during electron transport; the hydroxyl radical, which is one of the most reactive and damaging ROS known; and hydrogen peroxide, which, despite its relative stability, plays a central role in signaling processes and can lead to further radical formation under certain conditions. These characteristics of ROS highlight their dual nature as both essential signaling molecules at low concentrations and as potential inducers of cellular damage when present in excess.

4.1.2 Cellular Production of Free Radicals

4.1.2.1 Mitochondrial Metabolism

Mitochondrial metabolism is a major source of free radicals within cells, predominantly through the process of oxidative phosphorylation. During this process, electrons are transferred through a series of protein complexes in the electron transport chain (ETC) embedded in the inner mitochondrial membrane, ultimately reducing molecular oxygen to water while generating adenosine triphosphate (ATP). However, this electron transport is not perfectly efficient; a small percentage of electrons can leak from the ETC, particularly from complexes I and III. These leaked electrons prematurely react with oxygen to form superoxide anions, one of the primary free radicals generated in cells. This process is exacerbated under conditions of metabolic stress or when mitochondrial function is compromised, leading to an increase in the production of reactive oxygen species (ROS). The superoxide anions generated can be converted to other reactive species, such as hydrogen peroxide, through the action of superoxide dismutase. Although hydrogen peroxide is not a free radical itself, it can undergo further reactions, such as the Fenton reaction, in the presence of transition metals, to form the highly reactive hydroxyl radical. Therefore, the inherent process of oxidative phosphorylation, while essential for energy production, also contributes to the formation of free radicals due to electron leakage, highlighting the delicate balance between energy generation and oxidative stress in cellular physiology.

4.1.2.2 Enzymatic Reactions

In addition to mitochondrial processes, various enzymatic reactions significantly contribute to the production of free radicals within cells. Key enzymes such as xanthine oxidase, cytochrome P450 oxidases, and NADPH oxidase play pivotal roles in this context. Xanthine oxidase, for example, is involved in the catabolism of purines, where it catalyses the oxidation of hypoxanthine to xanthine and subsequently to uric acid. During these reactions, xanthine oxidase reduces molecular oxygen to superoxide anions and hydrogen peroxide, particularly under conditions of tissue hypoxia or ischemia. Similarly, cytochrome P450 oxidases, which are critical for the metabolism of various endogenous and exogenous compounds, can inadvertently generate free radicals as by-products of their catalytic cycle. These enzymes may leak electrons during the metabolism of substrates, leading to the partial reduction of oxygen and formation of ROS. NADPH oxidase is another key enzyme complex that deliberately produces free radicals as part of the immune response; it transfers electrons from NADPH to oxygen, forming superoxide anions that are utilized by phagocytes to kill invading pathogens. During inflammatory responses, the upregulation of NADPH oxidase activity contributes significantly to the overall burden of ROS in tissues, which, while beneficial for pathogen clearance, can also result in collateral oxidative damage. Collectively, the activity of these enzymes during normal metabolic processes, inflammation, and detoxification reactions underscores their contribution to free radical generation, highlighting the importance of tightly regulated antioxidant systems to mitigate potential cellular damage.

4.2.1.1 Lipids

Free radicals target lipids in cellular membranes primarily through a process known as lipid peroxidation. This process is initiated when a free radical, such as the hydroxyl radical (•OH), abstracts a hydrogen atom from a polyunsaturated fatty acid present in the phospholipid bilayer. This initial step, termed initiation, creates a lipid radical that is unstable and highly reactive. During the propagation phase, the lipid radical reacts with molecular oxygen to form a lipid peroxyl radical. This newly formed radical then abstracts a hydrogen atom from a neighboring lipid molecule, generating another lipid radical and a lipid hydroperoxide (LOOH). This chain reaction can continue for several cycles, causing extensive damage to the cell membrane by creating many lipid radicals and hydroperoxides. The termination phase occurs when two free radicals combine to form a stable non-radical product, effectively ending the chain reaction. However, even after termination, the lipid hydroperoxides that have formed can decompose into secondary products such as malondialdehyde (MDA) and 4-hydroxynonenal (4-HNE). These secondary products are highly reactive and can form adducts with proteins, DNA, and other cellular components, further contributing to cellular dysfunction and damage. Quantitative assays often measure the levels of MDA as an index of lipid peroxidation, with higher concentrations indicating greater oxidative stress. This detailed cascade of initiation, propagation, and termination underscores the vulnerability of cellular membranes to free radical attack and the importance of antioxidants in protecting lipid structures from oxidative damage.

4.2.1.2 Proteins

Free radicals can attack proteins and induce various structural modifications that compromise their function. The process often begins with the oxidation of amino acid side chains, particularly those containing sulfur such as cysteine and methionine, as well as aromatic residues like tryptophan and tyrosine. This oxidation results in the formation of protein carbonyls, which are stable products used as markers of oxidative protein damage. The introduction of carbonyl groups into proteins not only alters their molecular structure but also predisposes them to further aggregation and degradation. The formation of these oxidised groups is a clear indicator that the protein has undergone significant chemical modification, and such alterations can be measured using spectrophotometric assays that quantify carbonyl content. This biochemical modification disrupts the protein's native conformation and can impair its functional domains, making the protein more susceptible to proteolytic degradation.

The functional consequences of these structural modifications are profound. Oxidative modifications can lead to the inactivation of enzymes by affecting the active sites, thereby hindering catalytic activity. When key amino acid residues that are essential for substrate binding or catalysis are oxidised, the enzyme loses its ability to perform its biological function effectively. Additionally, the altered conformation may disrupt protein–protein interactions that are critical for forming multi-protein complexes or for signal transduction pathways. Such disruptions can interfere with cellular communication and compromise the integrity of various metabolic and regulatory processes. In some cases, the accumulation of oxidised proteins can lead to cellular dysfunction, contributing to the pathogenesis of chronic diseases such as neurodegenerative disorders, cardiovascular diseases, and diabetes. Thus, the oxidation of proteins by free radicals not only affects their structural stability but also has significant implications for overall cellular function and health, underscoring the need for efficient antioxidant defenses to preserve protein integrity.

4.2.1.3 Carbohydrates and Nucleic Acids

Free radicals can also cause significant oxidative damage to carbohydrates and nucleic acids, compromising the integrity and functionality of these essential biomolecules. In the case of carbohydrates, oxidative stress leads to the modification of sugars and glycoproteins through the formation of reactive carbonyl groups. This process, known as glycoxidation, alters the structure of polysaccharides and glycoproteins, which can disrupt their normal roles in cell signaling and structural support. The oxidation of carbohydrates often results in the cross-linking of proteins and the generation of advanced glycation end-products (AGEs). These AGEs accumulate in tissues and have been implicated in the development of various chronic conditions, including diabetes and age-related diseases, by interfering with normal cellular functions and promoting inflammatory responses.

Nucleic acids, particularly DNA, are highly susceptible to oxidative damage caused by free radicals. One of the most common types of DNA damage is the formation of strand breaks, which can occur when reactive species attack the sugar-phosphate backbone of the DNA molecule. In addition, free radicals can modify the nitrogenous bases in DNA, leading to base alterations that disrupt the normal base-pairing mechanisms essential for accurate replication and transcription. A well-recognised marker of oxidative DNA damage is the formation of 8-hydroxy-2'-deoxyguanosine (8-OHdG), which results from the oxidation of the guanine base. The accumulation of 8-OHdG and other oxidised bases can lead to mutagenesis, as these modifications increase the likelihood of errors during DNA replication. Over time, the persistence of such mutations may contribute to the onset of various diseases, including cancer and neurodegenerative disorders, by initiating abnormal cellular proliferation and impairing the function of critical genes. The damage to carbohydrates and nucleic acids underscores the importance of effective antioxidant systems in preventing oxidative stress and maintaining cellular health.

4.3.1.1 Lipid Peroxidation Products

Lipid peroxidation products serve as important biomarkers of oxidative damage in cell membranes. During the initial stage of lipid peroxidation, free radicals attack polyunsaturated fatty acids to form lipid radicals. These radicals quickly react with molecular oxygen to produce lipid peroxyl radicals, which in turn abstract hydrogen from neighbouring lipid molecules to generate lipid hydroperoxides. Lipid hydroperoxides are regarded as primary products in this oxidative chain reaction. When these primary products further decompose, they form a range of secondary products. Notable secondary products include malondialdehyde (MDA) and 4-hydroxynonenal (4-HNE). Malondialdehyde, often measured as an index of oxidative stress, is generated by the breakdown of polyunsaturated fatty acids and is chemically characterized by its reactivity with thiobarbituric acid. Similarly, 4-hydroxynonenal is formed from the oxidation of omega-6 fatty acids and is known to react with proteins and DNA, further contributing to cellular damage.

Quantification of lipid hydroperoxides and secondary products requires specific analytical methods that provide accurate and reproducible results. One commonly used method is the thiobarbituric acid reactive substances (TBARS) assay, which measures the concentration of MDA by reacting it with thiobarbituric acid to produce a colored complex. This complex is then quantified spectrophotometrically at a wavelength of around 532 nm. Although the TBARS assay is widely used due to its simplicity, it may suffer from interferences and lack specificity. To improve accuracy, high-performance liquid chromatography (HPLC) is employed, as it separates the individual lipid peroxidation products before detection. HPLC coupled with UV-visible or fluorescence detectors offers enhanced sensitivity and specificity for measuring lipid hydroperoxides. Gas chromatography-mass spectrometry (GC-MS) is another advanced technique that provides detailed molecular identification and quantification of both primary and secondary lipid peroxidation products. In several studies, lipid hydroperoxide levels have been reported in micromoles per liter or as nanomoles per milligram of protein, providing a quantitative measure of oxidative stress in biological samples. These methods, when applied under controlled conditions, allow researchers to assess the extent of lipid peroxidation and correlate the data with cellular damage and disease progression, thereby underscoring the clinical relevance of these biomarkers.

4.3.1.2 Malondialdehyde (MDA)

Malondialdehyde (MDA) is widely recognised as a key biomarker for assessing oxidative stress and lipid peroxidation in biological systems. As a secondary product of lipid peroxidation, MDA is formed when reactive oxygen species attack polyunsaturated fatty acids present in cell membranes. The breakdown of these peroxidised lipids leads to the generation of MDA, which is chemically stable enough to be measured in various biological samples. Due to its formation through the oxidation of lipids, MDA levels provide a direct indication of the extent of oxidative damage within cells. This correlation has been exploited in numerous studies to monitor the oxidative status in tissues, blood, and other fluids, serving as an essential tool for understanding the role of oxidative stress in the development of chronic diseases. The utility of MDA as a biomarker lies in its ability to reflect cumulative lipid peroxidation, thereby offering insight into both acute and long-term oxidative damage. Its measurement is typically carried out using spectrophotometric methods such as the thiobarbituric acid reactive substances (TBARS) assay, which quantifies the coloured complex formed between MDA and thiobarbituric acid at a specific wavelength, or through more precise techniques like high-performance liquid chromatography (HPLC) that separate MDA from interfering substances. These analytical approaches allow researchers to correlate MDA levels with the intensity of oxidative stress, as higher concentrations of MDA often signal an imbalance between free radical production and antioxidant defenses. Numerous clinical and experimental studies have demonstrated that elevated MDA levels are associated with conditions such as cardiovascular diseases, diabetes, and neurodegenerative disorders, further emphasizing its importance as a diagnostic and prognostic biomarker in both research and clinical settings.

4.3.2 Analytical Techniques

4.3.2.1 Spectrophotometric Methods

Spectrophotometric methods are among the most commonly employed techniques for measuring biomarkers of oxidative stress, particularly malondialdehyde (MDA). One widely used approach is the thiobarbituric acid reactive substances (TBARS) assay. In this assay, MDA reacts with thiobarbituric acid (TBA) under high temperature and acidic conditions to form a coloured complex, which is typically pink in appearance. The chemical reaction can be summarised by the equation:

$MDA + 2\ TBA \rightarrow MDA\text{–}(TBA)_2$ complex.

The intensity of the colour produced is directly proportional to the concentration of MDA in the sample and is measured spectrophotometrically at a wavelength of approximately 532 nm. This method is popular because it is relatively simple, cost-effective, and does not require highly sophisticated equipment.

One of the advantages of the TBARS assay is its ease of use, making it accessible in many laboratory settings, especially where resources are limited. It allows for rapid processing of multiple samples simultaneously, which is beneficial in both clinical and research environments. Moreover, the assay is sensitive enough to detect changes in MDA levels that correlate with varying degrees of oxidative stress. The straightforward protocol and relatively low cost of reagents further contribute to its widespread application in studies investigating lipid peroxidation and oxidative damage.

However, the TBARS assay also has certain limitations. One major drawback is its lack of specificity; other aldehydic compounds formed during lipid peroxidation may also react with TBA, potentially leading to overestimation of MDA levels. Interferences from sugars, amino acids, and other cellular components can further complicate the interpretation of results. In addition, the assay conditions, such as high temperature and acidic environment, may induce artificial formation of MDA during sample processing. These limitations necessitate careful standardisation and the use of appropriate controls to ensure accuracy. Despite these challenges, the TBARS assay remains a valuable tool for assessing oxidative stress, particularly when combined with other analytical techniques such as high-performance liquid chromatography (HPLC) for more precise quantification of MDA.

3.2.2 Chromatographic Techniques

High-Performance Liquid Chromatography (HPLC)

High-Performance Liquid Chromatography (HPLC) is a powerful analytical technique used to separate, identify, and quantify components in complex mixtures. In the context of free radical damage, HPLC is employed to measure biomarkers such as malondialdehyde and other lipid peroxidation products. The technique utilises a high-pressure pump to force a liquid mobile phase through a column packed with a stationary phase. As the sample passes through the column, its components interact with the stationary phase to different extents, leading to their separation based on differences in polarity, molecular weight, or other chemical properties. The separated compounds are then detected using various detectors, such as ultraviolet-visible (UV-Vis) or fluorescence detectors, which provide sensitive and specific quantification. HPLC is particularly advantageous because it offers high resolution, repeatability, and the capacity to handle complex biological matrices with minimal interference. The use of calibration standards and internal controls further enhances the accuracy of the measurements. Additionally, HPLC methods can be coupled with derivatisation techniques that improve the detectability of compounds like malondialdehyde by converting them into more stable, chromophore-containing derivatives. Overall, HPLC provides robust quantitative data that are essential for assessing the extent of oxidative damage in tissues and fluids, contributing to a deeper understanding of the role of free radicals in various pathological conditions.

Gas Chromatography-Mass Spectrometry (GC-MS)

Gas Chromatography-Mass Spectrometry (GC-MS) is another advanced analytical method that combines the separation capabilities of gas chromatography with the identification power of mass spectrometry. This technique is particularly useful for analysing volatile and semi-volatile compounds. In studies of free radical damage, GC-MS is used to detect and quantify lipid peroxidation products such as malondialdehyde, 4-hydroxynonenal, and other aldehydes that result from the oxidation of polyunsaturated fatty acids. During the GC phase, the sample is vaporised and carried by an inert gas through a capillary column, where components are separated based on their volatility and interactions with the column's stationary phase. The separated analytes then enter the mass spectrometer, where they are ionised, fragmented, and detected based on their mass-to-charge ratios. The resulting mass spectra provide detailed structural information, which facilitates the identification of each compound with high specificity. GC-MS offers the advantage of high sensitivity, making it possible to detect even trace levels of oxidative biomarkers. Moreover, the technique allows for the simultaneous analysis of multiple compounds, enabling comprehensive profiling of oxidative damage in a single run. Despite the requirement for derivatisation of non-volatile compounds to render them suitable for GC analysis, GC-MS remains a gold standard for the precise quantification and structural elucidation of lipid peroxidation products. Together, HPLC and GC-MS form a complementary toolkit that enables researchers to obtain both quantitative and qualitative insights into free radical-induced damage, ultimately enhancing our understanding of oxidative stress and its implications in health and disease.

4.3.2.3 Advanced Methods

Electron Spin Resonance (ESR) Spectroscopy for Direct Free Radical Detection

Electron Spin Resonance (ESR) spectroscopy is a highly specialized technique that directly detects free radicals based on their unpaired electrons. In ESR spectroscopy, samples are exposed to a constant magnetic field and microwave radiation, which causes the unpaired electrons to transition between spin states. This transition produces a characteristic signal that provides detailed information about the type and environment of the free radical. The strength and pattern of the ESR signal allow researchers to identify the free radical species present in a sample without the need for indirect chemical reactions or derivatisation. ESR is particularly valuable because it can measure the concentration and dynamics of free radicals in real time, offering insights into the kinetics of radical formation and decay. This technique is widely used in studies of oxidative stress, as it enables the direct observation of free radicals generated during metabolic processes, under environmental stress, or as a result of pathological conditions. Despite its high sensitivity and specificity, ESR requires specialised equipment and expertise, which can limit its accessibility. Nevertheless, its ability to provide direct evidence of free radical presence makes it an essential tool in advanced oxidative stress research.

Integration of Multiple Techniques for Comprehensive Analysis

While each analytical method offers unique advantages, integrating multiple techniques can provide a more comprehensive analysis of free radical damage. For instance, the combination of spectrophotometric methods such as the TBARS assay with chromatographic techniques like HPLC and GC-MS can yield both quantitative and qualitative data on lipid peroxidation products. The TBARS assay offers rapid screening, while HPLC and GC-MS allow for precise identification and quantification of individual biomarkers such as malondialdehyde and 4-hydroxynonenal. ESR spectroscopy further complements these methods by directly detecting free radicals and offering real-time insights into their dynamics. The integration of these advanced techniques enables researchers to cross-validate results, improve measurement accuracy, and obtain a more detailed understanding of the oxidative processes occurring in biological systems. This comprehensive analytical approach is particularly useful in clinical and experimental settings where understanding the full spectrum of oxidative damage is critical. By employing a combination of methods, scientists can better correlate oxidative stress with disease progression, ultimately contributing to the development of targeted therapeutic strategies and improved antioxidant interventions.

REVIEW Questions

1. Define free radicals and describe their chemical characteristics. How does the presence of an unpaired electron affect their reactivity?
2. Explain what reactive oxygen species (ROS) are and discuss how they differ from other free radicals. Provide examples of both radical and non-radical ROS.
3. Describe the process of oxidative phosphorylation in mitochondria. How does this process contribute to the formation of free radicals?
4. Discuss the mechanism of electron leakage from the electron transport chain in mitochondria. Why does this leakage lead to the production of superoxide anions?
5. Identify key enzymatic reactions that contribute to free radical production. What role do enzymes such as xanthine oxidase, cytochrome P450 oxidases, and NADPH oxidase play in this process?
6. Explain how xanthine oxidase catalyzes the oxidation of purines and how this reaction results in the generation of free radicals.
7. Describe the function of cytochrome P450 oxidases in the metabolism of xenobiotics and how these enzymes inadvertently produce reactive oxygen species.
8. Discuss the role of NADPH oxidase in the immune response. How does its activity during inflammation lead to increased free radical production?
9. Outline the three main phases of lipid peroxidation: initiation, propagation, and termination. What key events characterize each phase?
10. What are lipid hydroperoxides, and why are they important as primary products of lipid peroxidation?
11. Describe how malondialdehyde (MDA) is formed during lipid peroxidation and discuss its significance as a biomarker for oxidative stress.
12. Explain the process by which free radicals oxidize proteins. What structural modifications occur, and how are protein carbonyls formed?
13. Discuss the functional consequences of protein oxidation. How does the formation of protein carbonyls lead to enzyme inactivation and the disruption of protein–protein interactions?

14. Explain how free radicals can cause oxidative damage to carbohydrates and glycoproteins. What impact does this have on cellular function?
15. Describe the types of damage that free radicals can inflict on nucleic acids, particularly DNA. What are some of the specific modifications observed?
16. What is 8-hydroxy-2'-deoxyguanosine (8-OHdG), and how is it used to assess oxidative damage to DNA?
17. Outline the principle behind the TBARS assay for measuring lipid peroxidation. How does this assay work to detect malondialdehyde (MDA)?
18. Discuss the advantages and limitations of using spectrophotometric methods, such as the TBARS assay, in assessing oxidative damage.
19. Explain how High-Performance Liquid Chromatography (HPLC) is used to separate, identify, and quantify lipid peroxidation products. What makes HPLC suitable for this purpose?
20. Describe the application of Gas Chromatography-Mass Spectrometry (GC-MS) in the analysis of free radical-induced oxidative damage. What types of compounds does GC-MS best detect?
21. What is Electron Spin Resonance (ESR) spectroscopy and how does it directly detect free radicals? Explain the underlying principle that enables this technique.
22. Discuss the benefits of integrating multiple analytical techniques (e.g., spectrophotometry, HPLC, GC-MS, ESR) when assessing oxidative stress in biological systems.
23. How does oxidative stress contribute to cellular ageing and the progression of age-related diseases? Provide a mechanistic explanation based on the accumulation of damage over time.
24. Describe the overall impact of free radical damage on the structural and functional integrity of cellular components such as lipids, proteins, carbohydrates, and nucleic acids.
25. Summarize how the measurement and analysis of oxidative stress biomarkers help in understanding the role of free radicals in disease development and overall cellular health.

MCQS

1. **Which of the following best defines a free radical?**
   A. A molecule with paired electrons
   B. A molecule or atom with one or more unpaired electrons
   C. A stable molecule that does not react
   D. A type of antioxidant
   Correct Answer: B
2. **Reactive oxygen species (ROS) include:**
   A. Only free radicals
   B. Only non-radical molecules
   C. Both free radicals and non-radical oxygen derivatives
   D. Only molecules with paired electrons
   Correct Answer: C
3. **Which of the following is an example of a free radical?**
   A. Hydrogen peroxide (H_2O_2)
   B. Superoxide anion (O_2^-)
   C. Water (H_2O)
   D. Ozone (O_3)
   Correct Answer: B
4. **Hydrogen peroxide (H_2O_2) is classified as:**
   A. A free radical
   B. A non-radical reactive oxygen species
   C. A stable antioxidant
   D. A metal ion
   Correct Answer: B
5. **What is the primary site of free radical generation during cellular respiration?**
   A. Cytoplasm
   B. Mitochondria
   C. Nucleus
   D. Endoplasmic reticulum
   Correct Answer: B
6. **During oxidative phosphorylation, electron leakage primarily occurs at which mitochondrial complexes?**

A. Complexes I and II
B. Complexes I and III
C. Complexes III and IV
D. Complex IV only
Correct Answer: B

7. **Which enzyme converts superoxide anions to hydrogen peroxide?**
A. Catalase
B. Glutathione peroxidase
C. Superoxide dismutase (SOD)
D. Xanthine oxidase
Correct Answer: C

8. **Xanthine oxidase contributes to free radical production by oxidizing:**
A. Lipids
B. Purines
C. Carbohydrates
D. Proteins
Correct Answer: B

9. **NADPH oxidase is primarily active in:**
A. Muscle contraction
B. Mitochondrial energy production
C. Immune cells during the respiratory burst
D. DNA replication
Correct Answer: C

10. **Which phase of lipid peroxidation involves the initial attack by free radicals?**
A. Propagation
B. Initiation
C. Termination
D. Stabilization
Correct Answer: B

11. **During the propagation phase of lipid peroxidation, a lipid radical reacts with:**
A. Water
B. Oxygen
C. Nitrogen
D. Glucose
Correct Answer: B

12. **The termination phase of lipid peroxidation occurs when:**
    A. Free radicals are generated continuously
    B. Two radicals combine to form a stable product
    C. Antioxidants are depleted
    D. Lipid hydroperoxides form
    Correct Answer: B
13. **Malondialdehyde (MDA) is considered a biomarker of:**
    A. Protein synthesis
    B. DNA replication
    C. Lipid peroxidation
    D. Carbohydrate metabolism
    Correct Answer: C
14. **Which assay is commonly used to measure MDA levels?**
    A. Bradford assay
    B. TBARS assay
    C. BCA assay
    D. ELISA
    Correct Answer: B
15. **At what wavelength is the MDA-TBA complex typically measured in the TBARS assay?**
    A. 280 nm
    B. 450 nm
    C. 532 nm
    D. 600 nm
    Correct Answer: C
16. **Which technique is best for separating and quantifying lipid peroxidation products in complex mixtures?**
    A. Gel electrophoresis
    B. High-Performance Liquid Chromatography (HPLC)
    C. UV-Visible spectrophotometry only
    D. Atomic absorption spectroscopy
    Correct Answer: B
17. **Gas Chromatography-Mass Spectrometry (GC-MS) is especially useful for analyzing:**
    A. Volatile and semi-volatile oxidation products
    B. High molecular weight proteins
    C. Large polysaccharides
    D. Nucleic acids

Correct Answer: A

18. **Electron Spin Resonance (ESR) spectroscopy detects free radicals by measuring:**
    A. Fluorescence intensity
    B. Absorption of ultraviolet light
    C. Magnetic properties of unpaired electrons
    D. Thermal conductivity
    Correct Answer: C
19. **The formation of 8-hydroxy-2'-deoxyguanosine (8-OHdG) is an indicator of oxidative damage to:**
    A. Lipids
    B. Proteins
    C. DNA
    D. Carbohydrates
    Correct Answer: C
20. **Which of the following best describes the impact of oxidative stress on proteins?**
    A. Enhances enzymatic activity
    B. Causes oxidation of amino acid residues and formation of protein carbonyls
    C. Increases protein solubility
    D. Promotes protein synthesis
    Correct Answer: B
21. **What is a common consequence of protein oxidation in cells?**
    A. Improved cell signaling
    B. Enzyme inactivation and disruption of protein–protein interactions
    C. Increased cell proliferation
    D. Enhanced nutrient absorption
    Correct Answer: B
22. **Oxidative damage to carbohydrates may lead to the formation of:**
    A. Advanced glycation end-products (AGEs)
    B. Proteoglycans
    C. Amino acids
    D. Free fatty acids
    Correct Answer: A
23. **Which process describes the formation of advanced glycation end-products?**
    A. Lipid peroxidation

B. Glycoxidation
C. Protein synthesis
D. Nucleic acid replication
Correct Answer: B

24. **In the context of free radical damage, what does the term "propagation" refer to?**
A. The initiation of free radical formation
B. The continuous chain reaction where radicals react with neighboring molecules
C. The termination of the reaction
D. The recycling of antioxidants
Correct Answer: B

25. **Which of the following is a secondary product of lipid peroxidation?**
A. Hydrogen peroxide
B. Malondialdehyde (MDA)
C. Glutathione
D. Catalase
Correct Answer: B

26. **What role do antioxidants play in counteracting free radical damage?**
A. They increase free radical production
B. They donate electrons to stabilize free radicals
C. They bind to DNA to prevent replication
D. They enhance protein oxidation
Correct Answer: B

27. **Which of the following enzymes converts hydrogen peroxide into water and oxygen?**
A. Superoxide dismutase
B. Xanthine oxidase
C. Catalase
D. Glutathione peroxidase
Correct Answer: C

28. **Glutathione peroxidase reduces hydrogen peroxide using which substrate?**
A. NADH
B. Glutathione (GSH)
C. Ascorbic acid
D. Vitamin E
Correct Answer: B

29. **The term "oxidative stress" is defined as:**
    A. A state of complete absence of free radicals
    B. An imbalance between free radical production and antioxidant defenses
    C. Excessive protein synthesis
    D. Overproduction of ATP in mitochondria
    Correct Answer: B
30. **What is one effect of free radical-induced DNA damage?**
    A. Increased cell division
    B. DNA strand breaks and base modifications
    C. Enhanced replication fidelity
    D. Immediate repair without mutation
    Correct Answer: B
31. **Which analytical method provides a direct measurement of free radicals in a sample?**
    A. HPLC
    B. GC-MS
    C. ESR spectroscopy
    D. TBARS assay
    Correct Answer: C
32. **What is the primary advantage of combining multiple analytical techniques (e.g., TBARS, HPLC, GC-MS, ESR) when assessing oxidative stress?**
    A. It increases the cost of analysis
    B. It provides comprehensive qualitative and quantitative data
    C. It reduces the need for regulatory approval
    D. It limits the detection to only one type of biomarker
    Correct Answer: B
33. **The Fenton reaction is associated with the conversion of hydrogen peroxide into which highly reactive species?**
    A. Superoxide anion
    B. Hydroxyl radical
    C. Singlet oxygen
    D. Nitric oxide
    Correct Answer: B
34. **What is a major consequence of lipid peroxidation in cell membranes?**
    A. Increased membrane fluidity and enhanced function

B. Loss of membrane integrity and cell dysfunction
C. Immediate repair without any damage
D. Conversion of lipids into proteins
Correct Answer: B

35. **Which of the following biomarkers is most commonly used to assess protein oxidation?**
A. Malondialdehyde (MDA)
B. Protein carbonyl content
C. 8-OHdG
D. Glutathione levels
Correct Answer: B

36. **The accumulation of advanced glycation end-products (AGEs) is associated with damage to which macromolecule?**
A. DNA
B. Lipids
C. Carbohydrates and glycoproteins
D. Minerals
Correct Answer: C

37. **What is the significance of measuring 8-OHdG levels in biological samples?**
A. It indicates lipid peroxidation only
B. It serves as a marker of oxidative DNA damage
C. It measures protein synthesis rates
D. It determines mitochondrial efficiency
Correct Answer: B

38. **Which of the following best describes the function of superoxide dismutase (SOD) in oxidative stress?**
A. It generates free radicals
B. It converts superoxide radicals into hydrogen peroxide
C. It degrades hydrogen peroxide
D. It synthesizes antioxidants
Correct Answer: B

39. **Catalase primarily protects cells by decomposing:**
A. Superoxide anions
B. Hydrogen peroxide
C. Lipid hydroperoxides
D. Protein carbonyls
Correct Answer: B

40. **Lipid peroxidation can lead to the formation of which of the following secondary products?**
    A. Glutathione
    B. 4-Hydroxynonenal (4-HNE)
    C. Ascorbic acid
    D. Catalase
    Correct Answer: B
41. **In the context of free radical damage, what does the term "chain reaction" refer to?**
    A. The sequential repair of damaged DNA
    B. The process by which one radical generates another, propagating oxidative damage
    C. The formation of a protein complex
    D. The assembly of antioxidant molecules
    Correct Answer: B
42. **Which factor does NOT directly contribute to the generation of free radicals in the body?**
    A. Mitochondrial respiration
    B. Enzymatic reactions such as those catalyzed by NADPH oxidase
    C. Exposure to UV radiation
    D. High concentration of dietary fiber
    Correct Answer: D
43. **Oxidative stress is implicated in the pathogenesis of many chronic diseases because:**
    A. It always increases energy production
    B. It damages essential biomolecules like DNA, proteins, and lipids
    C. It enhances cellular repair mechanisms
    D. It reduces the need for antioxidants
    Correct Answer: B
44. **The term "antioxidant" refers to a substance that:**
    A. Enhances free radical production
    B. Neutralizes free radicals by donating electrons or hydrogen atoms
    C. Breaks down cellular membranes
    D. Increases the rate of DNA replication
    Correct Answer: B
45. **Which of the following best describes the role of electron leakage in mitochondrial ROS production?**
    A. It is a sign of efficient energy production

B. It leads to the formation of superoxide anions that contribute to oxidative stress

C. It results in the synthesis of ATP exclusively

D. It prevents any oxidative damage in the cell

Correct Answer: B

46. **In a healthy cell, the balance between free radical production and antioxidant defenses is known as:**

A. Redox equilibrium

B. Enzymatic imbalance

C. Metabolic overdrive

D. Oxidative hyperactivity

Correct Answer: A

47. **Which assay is used to assess the antioxidant capacity of a sample by measuring its ability to quench free radicals?**

A. ORAC (Oxygen Radical Absorbance Capacity) assay

B. BCA protein assay

C. PCR

D. ELISA

Correct Answer: A

48. **The measurement of lipid hydroperoxides in a sample is important because:**

A. They are primary markers of protein oxidation

B. They indicate the initial stages of lipid peroxidation

C. They are used to measure DNA damage

D. They reflect the overall water content of the cell

Correct Answer: B

49. **What does GC-MS stand for in analytical chemistry?**

A. Gas Chromatography-Mass Spectrometry

B. Gel Chromatography-Microwave Spectroscopy

C. General Chromatography-Mass Screening

D. Gas Cyclotron-Magnetic Spectroscopy

Correct Answer: A

50. **Which of the following best summarizes the overall impact of free radicals on cellular health?**

A. Free radicals only serve beneficial signaling functions

B. Excessive free radical production leads to oxidative stress, damaging lipids, proteins, carbohydrates, and nucleic acids

C. Free radicals improve the efficiency of all metabolic processes

D. The body produces no free radicals under normal conditions
Correct Answer: B

CHAPTER FIVE

Free Radicals in Disease and the Role of Antioxidants

5.1.1.1 Diabetes Mellitus

Diabetes Mellitus is a chronic metabolic disorder characterised by persistent hyperglycaemia resulting from defects in insulin secretion, insulin action, or both, and oxidative stress plays a crucial role in its pathogenesis. Oxidative stress arises when the production of free radicals, particularly reactive oxygen species, exceeds the capacity of the body's antioxidant defenses. In the context of diabetes, chronic high blood glucose levels lead to the overproduction of free radicals through several mechanisms, including the auto-oxidation of glucose and the enhanced flux through the polyol pathway. These free radicals then initiate a cascade of damaging reactions that impair cellular functions and contribute to insulin resistance. One key mechanism linking oxidative stress to insulin resistance involves the activation of stress-sensitive signaling pathways, such as the c-Jun N-terminal kinase (JNK) and p38 mitogen-activated protein kinase (MAPK) pathways. The activation of these kinases results in the serine phosphorylation of insulin receptor substrate (IRS) proteins, which interferes with their ability to transduce the insulin signal, ultimately reducing glucose uptake in peripheral tissues like muscle and adipose tissue. Additionally, oxidative stress can lead to the formation of advanced glycation end products (AGEs), which further impair insulin action by binding to specific receptors on cell surfaces and activating inflammatory cascades. This interaction not only exacerbates the inflammatory state but also perpetuates a cycle of oxidative damage and insulin resistance. Pancreatic β-cells, which are responsible for insulin production, are particularly vulnerable to oxidative stress due to their relatively low levels of endogenous antioxidants. As a result, prolonged exposure to high oxidative stress can lead to β-cell dysfunction and apoptosis, reducing insulin secretion and worsening hyperglycaemia. Clinical and experimental studies have consistently demonstrated that markers of oxidative stress, such as malondialdehyde (MDA) and 8-hydroxy-2'-deoxyguanosine (8-OHdG), are elevated in individuals with diabetes and are strongly correlated with impaired insulin sensitivity. Overall, the interplay between oxidative stress and insulin resistance forms a critical component of diabetes pathophysiology, highlighting the importance of antioxidants in potentially mitigating these deleterious effects and improving glycaemic control.

5.1.1.2 Inflammation

Free radicals, particularly reactive oxygen species (ROS), play a central role in chronic inflammatory processes by acting as signalling molecules that modulate the activity of various pro-inflammatory pathways. Under normal physiological conditions, ROS are generated in controlled amounts during cellular metabolism, serving functions in cell signalling and homeostasis. However, when their production exceeds the capacity of the antioxidant defence system, a state of oxidative stress is established. This state is characterised by an imbalance that can lead to the activation of transcription factors such as nuclear factor-kappa B (NF-κB), which in turn upregulates the expression of pro-inflammatory cytokines including tumor necrosis factor-alpha (TNF-α), interleukin-1 beta (IL-1β), and interleukin-6 (IL-6). Elevated levels of these cytokines can perpetuate the inflammatory response by recruiting additional immune cells to the site of injury or infection, thus creating a self-sustaining cycle of inflammation.

The continuous presence of free radicals can also lead to the oxidation of cellular components, which further exacerbates the inflammatory response. For example, oxidative modifications of lipids result in the formation of oxidised low-density lipoprotein (LDL) particles, which are known to contribute to the development of atherosclerotic plaques. These oxidised particles are recognised by specific receptors on macrophages, leading to foam cell formation and the propagation of vascular inflammation. Additionally, the oxidative damage to proteins and nucleic acids not only impairs cellular function but also generates molecular patterns that can be recognised by the innate immune system, triggering further inflammatory signalling. In chronic inflammatory conditions such as rheumatoid arthritis, inflammatory bowel disease, and even neurodegenerative disorders, elevated levels of oxidative markers such as malondialdehyde (MDA) and

8-hydroxy-2'-deoxyguanosine (8-OHdG) have been consistently observed. These biomarkers correlate with the severity of inflammation and tissue damage.

Overall, the role of free radicals in chronic inflammation is multifaceted, involving the activation of key signalling pathways, the promotion of oxidative modifications in biomolecules, and the amplification of cytokine production. This creates an environment where inflammation is not only sustained but also contributes to the progression of various chronic diseases. Understanding these mechanisms is crucial for developing antioxidant strategies aimed at mitigating the deleterious effects of chronic inflammation.

5.1.1.3 Ischemic Reperfusion Injury

Ischemic reperfusion injury occurs when blood supply returns to tissue after a period of ischemia, or lack of oxygen. The restoration of oxygen triggers a burst of free radical production that leads to severe tissue damage. During the ischemic phase, cells adapt to a low oxygen environment by shifting their metabolism to anaerobic pathways, which results in the accumulation of metabolic by-products such as lactate and a decrease in cellular pH. When oxygen is suddenly reintroduced during reperfusion, the mitochondria, which had been compromised during the ischemic phase, generate a large number of reactive oxygen species (ROS) due to the rapid reactivation of the electron transport chain. This surge in ROS overwhelms the endogenous antioxidant defence mechanisms, resulting in oxidative damage to cellular lipids, proteins, and nucleic acids. The lipid peroxidation of cell membranes leads to loss of membrane integrity and cellular leakage, while protein oxidation alters the structure and function of enzymes and structural proteins, further compromising cellular function.

In addition to oxidative stress, the reperfusion phase also involves a robust inflammatory response. The sudden influx of oxygen and nutrients triggers the activation of resident immune cells and the recruitment of neutrophils to the affected area. These immune cells release additional ROS, proteases, and pro-inflammatory cytokines, which amplify the tissue injury. The combination of oxidative stress and inflammation leads to endothelial dysfunction, increased vascular permeability, and edema. Furthermore, the activation of apoptotic pathways during reperfusion contributes to the programmed cell death of damaged cells, exacerbating tissue loss and impairing the overall recovery process. Together, these mechanisms—massive ROS production, lipid peroxidation, protein oxidation, and the ensuing inflammatory response—underscore the complex and damaging nature of ischemic reperfusion injury, highlighting the need for therapeutic strategies that can mitigate these processes and protect tissues from further damage.

5.1.1.4 Cancer

Free radicals play a critical role in the process of oncogenesis by causing DNA damage and inducing mutagenesis. When free radicals, especially reactive oxygen species (ROS), are generated in excess, they interact with the DNA molecules in cells and can induce a variety of structural changes. These interactions may result in single-strand breaks, double-strand breaks, or modifications to the nitrogenous bases, such as the formation of 8-hydroxy-2'-deoxyguanosine (8-OHdG). The formation of 8-OHdG is a well-documented marker of oxidative DNA damage, as it results from the oxidation of the guanine base, and its increased levels have been correlated with a higher incidence of mutations. Additionally, the oxidative damage can lead to base mispairing during DNA replication, which may result in point mutations or small insertions and deletions. When these mutations occur in genes that regulate cell cycle control, apoptosis, or DNA repair, they can disrupt normal cellular functions. This disruption may in turn lead to uncontrolled cell proliferation, a hallmark of cancer development. Studies have shown that increased levels of oxidative DNA damage markers, such as 8-OHdG, are often observed in cancerous tissues compared to normal tissues, highlighting the link between free radical-induced DNA damage and mutagenesis.

Furthermore, the accumulation of genetic mutations over time due to persistent oxidative stress contributes significantly to oncogenesis. As DNA repair mechanisms work to correct damage, they may become overwhelmed or may themselves be impaired by the oxidative environment, leading to errors in the repair process. This failure to correctly repair DNA damage allows mutations to accumulate, and if these mutations affect critical regulatory genes like tumor suppressor genes or oncogenes, they can initiate the transformation of normal cells into cancerous cells. The mutagenic effects of free radicals are also compounded by chronic inflammatory states, where continuous production of ROS not only damages DNA directly but also promotes a pro-tumorigenic environment. In such environments, inflammatory cytokines and growth factors further stimulate cell division and reduce the effectiveness of normal apoptosis, thereby increasing the likelihood of malignant transformation. Overall, the process by which free radicals induce DNA damage and mutagenesis is a fundamental aspect of cancer development, emphasizing the importance of antioxidant systems in protecting genomic integrity and reducing the risk of oncogenesis.

5.1.1.5 Atherosclerosis

Atherosclerosis is a chronic condition in which the oxidative modification of low-density lipoprotein (LDL) plays a pivotal role in the formation of arterial plaques. During normal metabolic processes, LDL circulates in the bloodstream carrying cholesterol to various tissues. However, under conditions of oxidative stress, free radicals such as reactive oxygen species interact with LDL, leading to the oxidation of its lipid and protein components. This oxidative modification results in the formation of oxidised LDL, a form of LDL that is more readily taken up by macrophages in the arterial wall. When macrophages engulf oxidised LDL, they transform into foam cells, which are lipid-laden cells that accumulate within the intima of the blood vessels. The aggregation of these foam cells forms fatty streaks, which are the earliest visible lesions of atherosclerosis. Over time, these fatty streaks progress into more complex plaques that consist of a necrotic core, fibrous cap, and calcified regions. The continued accumulation of oxidised LDL and the subsequent inflammatory response contribute to the enlargement of plaques, narrowing of the arterial lumen, and reduced elasticity of the blood vessel walls. This process not only hinders blood flow but also increases the risk of plaque rupture, which can lead to thrombosis and potentially result in acute cardiovascular events such as heart attacks or strokes. Studies have shown that a higher concentration of oxidised LDL correlates with an increased risk of cardiovascular disease, and clinical evidence suggests that interventions aimed at reducing oxidative stress can lower the progression of atherosclerosis. The complex interplay between lipid oxidation, foam cell formation, and chronic inflammation underscores the central role of oxidative modification of LDL in the pathogenesis of atherosclerosis.

5.1.1.6 Neurological Disorders

Free radicals play a significant role in impacting brain metabolism and contributing to various pathological conditions in the central nervous system. The brain, being rich in polyunsaturated fatty acids and having a high oxygen consumption rate, is particularly vulnerable to oxidative stress. When free radicals are produced in excess, they can damage neuronal cell membranes, proteins, and nucleic acids. This oxidative damage disrupts the normal function of neurons and interferes with energy metabolism in the brain. In particular, the mitochondria in neurons are sensitive to oxidative injury, which affects the production of adenosine triphosphate (ATP) and leads to impaired cellular energy homeostasis. The reduction in mitochondrial efficiency not only hampers the overall brain function but also promotes an environment where inflammation and apoptosis are more likely to occur.

This oxidative stress is closely linked to the development of neurodegenerative disorders such as Alzheimer's and Parkinson's diseases. In Alzheimer's disease, the accumulation of oxidative damage in brain tissues contributes to the formation of amyloid plaques and neurofibrillary tangles, which are hallmarks of the disease. Similarly, in Parkinson's disease, oxidative damage to dopaminergic neurons in the substantia nigra leads to a reduction in dopamine levels, resulting in the characteristic motor symptoms of the disorder. Clinical studies have observed elevated levels of oxidative biomarkers in patients suffering from these conditions, which further supports the association between free radical damage and the progression of neurodegenerative diseases. Overall, the impact of free radicals on brain metabolism and neuronal integrity highlights the need for effective antioxidant strategies to protect against the oxidative stress that underlies these debilitating neurological disorders.

5.1.1.7 Other Disorders

Free radicals are not limited to affecting a single organ system; their excessive production and the resultant oxidative stress can contribute to damage in various tissues, including the kidneys, muscles, and other organs. In the kidneys, oxidative stress plays a crucial role in the development of nephropathies by damaging the delicate structures within the renal glomeruli and tubules. The generation of reactive oxygen species (ROS) leads to lipid peroxidation of cell membranes and oxidation of proteins, which in turn impairs the filtering capacity of the kidneys and promotes inflammation. Over time, these changes can result in chronic kidney damage and a gradual decline in renal function. Elevated levels of oxidative biomarkers have been observed in patients with kidney diseases, supporting the link between free radical-induced damage and renal dysfunction.

Muscle tissues are also vulnerable to the detrimental effects of free radicals, especially during periods of intense physical exertion or in conditions of metabolic imbalance. The production of ROS in muscle cells can lead to the oxidation of proteins and lipids, resulting in structural damage and impaired muscle function. This oxidative damage can contribute to muscle fatigue, reduced strength, and slower recovery after exercise. In addition, chronic oxidative stress in muscle tissues has been associated with the development of myopathies, where ongoing damage can impair muscle regeneration and promote inflammation.

Other tissue injuries, including those in the liver, lungs, and skin, can also be attributed to the actions of free radicals. In the liver, for instance, oxidative stress can contribute to the progression of conditions such as non-alcoholic fatty liver disease (NAFLD) and cirrhosis by triggering inflammatory responses and fibrotic changes. Similarly, the lungs are susceptible to oxidative damage from environmental pollutants and cigarette smoke, which can exacerbate conditions such as chronic obstructive pulmonary disease (COPD) and asthma. The cumulative impact of free radical damage across various tissues underscores the importance of robust antioxidant defence mechanisms in protecting the body from a wide range of disorders. Overall, the evidence suggests that maintaining a balance between free radical production and antioxidant capacity is essential for preserving the health of multiple organ systems and reducing the risk of chronic tissue injuries.

5.1.2.1 Concept and Historical Development

The free radical theory of ageing proposes that the accumulation of damage caused by free radicals over time is a major contributor to the ageing process and the development of age-related diseases. According to this theory, free radicals, which are highly reactive molecules with unpaired electrons, are continuously generated during normal metabolic processes and by external factors such as radiation and pollution. These reactive species can damage vital cellular components, including DNA, proteins, and lipids, leading to impaired cellular function and increased vulnerability to degenerative diseases. The concept was first introduced in the mid-20th century when scientists observed that oxidative damage increased with age, and further research provided evidence linking higher levels of oxidative stress with reduced longevity. Early studies demonstrated that organisms with enhanced antioxidant defenses often experienced slower rates of ageing, while those with compromised antioxidant systems tended to show accelerated signs of ageing and a higher incidence of chronic diseases. Over the years, the theory has been refined and expanded through experimental research and clinical observations, leading to the understanding that a balance between the production of free radicals and the effectiveness of the body's antioxidant defenses is critical in determining the rate of ageing. This historical development has established the free radical theory as a fundamental explanation for how cumulative oxidative damage contributes to the physiological decline seen in ageing, and it has guided further investigations into antioxidant therapies as potential strategies to delay ageing and improve overall health.

5.1.2.2 Evidence Linking Oxidative Stress to Ageing

Experimental and clinical data provide strong support for the concept that oxidative stress plays a key role in the ageing process. Laboratory studies using model organisms such as mice, fruit flies, and worms have consistently shown that the accumulation of free radical-induced damage correlates with a reduction in lifespan and the onset of age-related deterioration. For example, experiments with genetically modified animals that overexpress antioxidant enzymes like superoxide dismutase (SOD) and catalase have demonstrated a delay in the development of age-related phenotypes, along with improved mitochondrial function and decreased levels of oxidative biomarkers. These findings suggest that enhanced antioxidant capacity can slow the ageing process by reducing the damage caused by reactive oxygen species (ROS).

In addition to experimental research, clinical studies involving human subjects have provided corroborative evidence linking oxidative stress to ageing. Measurements of oxidative biomarkers such as malondialdehyde (MDA) and 8-hydroxy-2'-deoxyguanosine (8-OHdG) have shown that older individuals generally exhibit higher levels of these markers compared to younger subjects, indicating a greater burden of oxidative damage. Epidemiological studies have also highlighted that diets rich in natural antioxidants, such as fruits, vegetables, and whole grains, are associated with a lower incidence of age-related diseases including cardiovascular disorders, neurodegenerative conditions, and certain cancers. Moreover, clinical trials investigating the effects of antioxidant supplementation have demonstrated improvements in biomarkers of oxidative stress and modest enhancements in health outcomes among elderly populations. Although the translation of these findings into significant extensions of human lifespan remains complex and is still under investigation, the overall body of evidence supports the idea that oxidative stress contributes to the molecular and cellular processes that underlie ageing. This evidence continues to drive research into antioxidant therapies as potential strategies to delay ageing and reduce the risk of chronic, age-associated diseases.

5.2.1.1 Superoxide Dismutase (SOD)

Superoxide dismutase (SOD) is a critical enzymatic antioxidant that serves as the first line of defense against oxidative stress by catalysing the dismutation of the superoxide anion into oxygen and hydrogen peroxide. This process is vital because the superoxide anion is a highly reactive free radical generated during normal metabolic processes, particularly within the mitochondria during oxidative phosphorylation. The mechanism of action of SOD involves the binding of the superoxide anion to the active site of the enzyme, where a metal ion—commonly copper, zinc, or manganese—facilitates the conversion of two superoxide molecules into molecular oxygen and hydrogen peroxide. This reaction can be expressed by the following chemical equation: $2\,O_2^- + 2\,H^+ \rightarrow O_2 + H_2O_2$. By rapidly converting the superoxide anion into less reactive species, SOD prevents the propagation of free radical damage and protects cellular components from oxidative injury.

SOD exists in multiple isoforms, each of which is strategically distributed within different cellular compartments to provide comprehensive protection against oxidative stress. The primary isoforms include cytosolic Cu/Zn-SOD, mitochondrial Mn-SOD, and extracellular SOD. Cu/Zn-SOD is predominantly found in the cytosol and the nucleus, where it acts to neutralise superoxide radicals generated by various metabolic activities. Mn-SOD, on the other hand, is located in the mitochondrial matrix, a region where the production of superoxide is particularly high due to the electron transport chain's activity; its presence is essential for maintaining mitochondrial integrity and function. The extracellular form of SOD, though less abundant, is important for scavenging free radicals in the extracellular space, thereby protecting the cell membrane and interstitial tissues from oxidative damage. The distribution and functionality of these isoforms are regulated by genetic factors and can be influenced by environmental stresses and nutritional status. Together, these isoforms form a robust and dynamic antioxidant system that mitigates the harmful effects of reactive oxygen species, thereby playing a pivotal role in cellular homeostasis and the prevention of oxidative damage-related diseases.

5.2.1.2 Catalase

Catalase is an essential enzymatic antioxidant that plays a critical role in decomposing hydrogen peroxide (H_2O_2), a reactive oxygen species generated during normal cellular metabolism and by various environmental stressors. Hydrogen peroxide, although not a free radical, can be harmful because it has the potential to generate the highly reactive hydroxyl radical via Fenton reactions when transition metals such as iron or copper are present. Catalase protects cells by rapidly converting hydrogen peroxide into water and oxygen, following the chemical equation: $2 H_2O_2 \rightarrow 2 H_2O + O_2$. This reaction prevents the accumulation of hydrogen peroxide to toxic levels and minimizes the risk of oxidative damage to lipids, proteins, and nucleic acids.

The enzyme catalase is found in nearly all aerobic organisms and is particularly abundant in organs with high metabolic activity such as the liver and kidneys. Its active site typically contains a heme group that is vital for the enzyme's catalytic function. Catalase exhibits an exceptionally high turnover rate; a single molecule of catalase can convert millions of hydrogen peroxide molecules per second under optimal conditions. This high catalytic efficiency ensures that even small amounts of hydrogen peroxide are quickly decomposed, maintaining cellular redox balance.

Catalase operates by binding hydrogen peroxide at its active site, where the heme iron facilitates the transfer of electrons. The reaction occurs in two main steps: first, hydrogen peroxide oxidises the heme group to form an intermediate known as compound I, and second, a second molecule of hydrogen peroxide reduces compound I back to its resting state while releasing water and molecular oxygen. This cyclic process is crucial for protecting cells against oxidative stress and preserving cellular function.

The importance of catalase in maintaining cellular health is underscored by clinical observations where deficiencies in catalase activity are linked to increased susceptibility to oxidative damage and various disorders. Overall, catalase is a vital component of the body's defense system, efficiently decomposing hydrogen peroxide and thereby reducing the potential for harmful oxidative reactions within the cell.

5.2.1.3 Glutathione Peroxidase

Function in Reducing Lipid Hydroperoxides and H_2O_2

Glutathione peroxidase is an important enzyme in the cellular antioxidant defense system that functions primarily to reduce both hydrogen peroxide (H_2O_2) and lipid hydroperoxides to less harmful compounds. The enzyme utilises reduced glutathione (GSH) as a substrate in order to carry out its catalytic reaction, in which one molecule of hydrogen peroxide is converted into water while oxidising two molecules of GSH to form glutathione disulfide (GSSG). This reaction can be summarised by the equation: $2 GSH + H_2O_2 \rightarrow GSSG + 2 H_2O$. In addition to detoxifying H_2O_2, glutathione peroxidase is also capable of reducing lipid hydroperoxides (LOOH) that are formed in the membranes during the process of lipid peroxidation. By converting these lipid hydroperoxides into their corresponding alcohols, the enzyme prevents the propagation of free radical-induced damage in the cell membranes and maintains the integrity of cellular structures.

Glutathione peroxidase is a selenium-dependent enzyme, meaning that its active site contains selenium in the form of the amino acid selenocysteine, which is crucial for its catalytic efficiency. This enzyme is present in various cellular compartments, including the cytosol and mitochondria, thereby providing widespread protection against oxidative stress throughout the cell. The ability of glutathione peroxidase to act on both H_2O_2 and lipid hydroperoxides underscores its dual role in preventing oxidative damage; while H_2O_2 is relatively stable, its accumulation can lead to the generation of more reactive species through metal-catalyzed reactions, and lipid hydroperoxides, if left unchecked, can cause severe damage to the phospholipid bilayer.

Experimental studies have demonstrated that the activity of glutathione peroxidase is critical for cellular survival under conditions of high oxidative stress. In many clinical and biochemical assays, the enzyme's activity is measured in units per milligram of protein, and reductions in its activity have been correlated with increased susceptibility to oxidative damage and various diseases. Supplementation with selenium, for instance, has been shown to increase the activity of glutathione peroxidase, thereby enhancing the cell's ability to neutralise both H_2O_2 and lipid hydroperoxides. This enzymatic action not only protects cellular membranes and organelles but also contributes to the overall maintenance of redox balance within the cell, preventing the cascade of events that lead to cell dysfunction and death. In summary, the role of glutathione peroxidase in reducing both hydrogen peroxide and lipid hydroperoxides is central to the body's defense against oxidative stress, thereby playing a vital role in maintaining cellular health and preventing the onset of various chronic diseases.

5.2.2.1 Glutathione

Glutathione is a tripeptide composed of three amino acids: glutamate, cysteine, and glycine. Its structure is unique in that the glutamate residue is linked to cysteine through a gamma-glutamyl bond rather than the usual alpha-carboxyl linkage, which provides glutathione with a high degree of stability and reactivity. This structure is critical for its function as a powerful antioxidant, as it allows glutathione to donate electrons readily to neutralise free radicals and reactive oxygen species.

Glutathione is synthesised in a two-step ATP-dependent process within the cytosol. The first step involves the enzyme glutamate-cysteine ligase, which catalyses the formation of gamma-glutamylcysteine from glutamate and cysteine. This reaction is the rate-limiting step in glutathione synthesis. The second step is catalysed by glutathione synthetase, which adds glycine to gamma-glutamylcysteine to form the complete tripeptide glutathione. The availability of cysteine is often the critical factor that determines the overall rate of glutathione synthesis, and its levels can be influenced by dietary intake and cellular stress.

Once oxidised during the detoxification of free radicals, glutathione is converted into glutathione disulfide (GSSG). To maintain its antioxidant capacity, cells employ a recycling mechanism where the enzyme glutathione reductase uses NADPH as a reducing agent to convert GSSG back into its reduced form, GSH. This recycling process is essential for sustaining intracellular levels of active glutathione, ensuring that cells remain equipped to combat oxidative stress continuously. The efficiency of glutathione recycling directly impacts the overall redox state of the cell, and any disruption in this cycle can lead to increased vulnerability to oxidative damage and related diseases.

5.2.2.2 α-Lipoic Acid

α-Lipoic acid, also known as thioctic acid, is a naturally occurring compound that functions as a universal antioxidant due to its unique chemical properties and its ability to operate in both aqueous and lipid environments. Its structure consists of an eight-carbon chain with two sulfur atoms in a cyclic disulfide ring that can be reduced to dihydrolipoic acid. This reversible redox property is central to its antioxidant activity, allowing it to neutralise a broad spectrum of reactive oxygen species and regenerate other antioxidants, such as vitamins C and E, back to their active forms. α-Lipoic acid is endogenously synthesised in the mitochondria and is essential for aerobic metabolism, where it acts as a cofactor for critical enzyme complexes involved in energy production. Its capacity to function in both hydrophilic and lipophilic compartments of the cell makes it particularly versatile, as it is able to protect a wide range of cellular components from oxidative damage. Experimental studies have shown that α-lipoic acid can reduce oxidative stress markers and improve mitochondrial function, with potential benefits observed in conditions characterized by high levels of oxidative stress such as diabetes, neurodegenerative diseases, and cardiovascular disorders. Additionally, clinical research suggests that supplementation with α-lipoic acid, typically in doses ranging from 300 to 600 mg per day, may improve insulin sensitivity and lower inflammation, thus supporting overall metabolic health. Its role as a universal antioxidant is further reinforced by its ability to chelate metal ions, which prevents these ions from catalysing the formation of additional free radicals through Fenton reactions. The dual action of α-lipoic acid in scavenging reactive species and regenerating other antioxidants underscores its critical role in maintaining cellular redox balance, making it a valuable component of the body's antioxidant defense system.

5.2.2.3 Melatonin

Melatonin is a hormone primarily produced by the pineal gland in the brain, well known for its key role in regulating circadian rhythms and sleep-wake cycles. It is synthesised from the amino acid tryptophan and is released in response to darkness, signalling the body to prepare for sleep. The regulation of circadian rhythms by melatonin is essential for synchronising various physiological processes with the environmental light-dark cycle, ensuring that many bodily functions such as metabolism, hormone release, and immune responses occur at appropriate times of the day. By maintaining a regular sleep pattern and overall circadian rhythm, melatonin indirectly supports numerous aspects of health, including cognitive function, mood regulation, and overall metabolic balance. Clinical studies have shown that disruptions in melatonin production and secretion are often associated with sleep disorders, mood disturbances, and an increased risk of chronic conditions, highlighting its vital role in preserving human health.

In addition to its function in circadian regulation, melatonin also exhibits potent free radical scavenging activity, making it an important non-enzymatic antioxidant. It can directly neutralise a variety of reactive oxygen and nitrogen species, thus protecting cellular components from oxidative damage. The molecular structure of melatonin allows it to easily cross cellular membranes, enabling it to exert its antioxidant effects in both aqueous and lipid environments. This dual characteristic is particularly beneficial as it ensures that melatonin can safeguard various cellular compartments, including mitochondria and the cell nucleus, from oxidative stress. Furthermore, melatonin has been observed to stimulate the activity of other antioxidant enzymes, thereby reinforcing the body's overall antioxidant defence system. Its ability to regulate the balance between free radical production and antioxidant protection is thought to contribute to the slowing of the ageing process and the prevention of neurodegenerative diseases. Research in both animal models and human subjects has provided evidence that melatonin supplementation can reduce markers of oxidative stress, support immune function, and improve mitochondrial efficiency. Thus, melatonin serves a dual role by not only regulating circadian rhythms but also protecting cells from oxidative injury, which underscores its importance as a critical component of the body's defense system against both environmental and metabolic stress.

5.3.1.1 Butylated Hydroxy Toluene (BHT)

Butylated Hydroxy Toluene, commonly abbreviated as BHT, is a synthetic phenolic antioxidant that has been extensively employed in the food industry as well as in other sectors such as cosmetics and pharmaceuticals. Chemically, BHT is known as 2,6-di-tert-butyl-4-methylphenol, which reflects its structure based on a toluene ring substituted with two tert-butyl groups at the 2 and 6 positions and a hydroxyl group at the 4 position. This configuration provides BHT with a high lipophilicity and excellent stability against thermal and oxidative degradation. The phenolic hydroxyl group in BHT is responsible for its antioxidant activity; it functions by donating a hydrogen atom to free radicals, thereby converting them into more stable, non-reactive species. This hydrogen donation results in the formation of a relatively stable BHT radical, which does not propagate further radical reactions. The presence of the bulky tert-butyl groups not only stabilises the radical form but also enhances the overall antioxidant capacity by sterically hindering the access of free radicals to the reactive center.

BHT is widely applied in food preservation to prevent the oxidation of fats and oils, which can lead to rancidity and the loss of nutritional quality as well as flavour. In many food products, such as snack foods, baked goods, and cereals, BHT is added in concentrations typically ranging from 100 to 200 parts per million (ppm), ensuring effective protection against lipid peroxidation without adversely affecting the sensory properties of the food. Its use extends to stabilising vegetable oils and shortening during storage, where BHT effectively inhibits the chain reactions of lipid oxidation that produce harmful aldehydes and other secondary oxidation products. Due to its lipophilic nature, BHT is particularly suitable for use in lipid-rich food matrices, where its distribution within the fat phase maximises its capacity to neutralise free radicals at their site of formation.

The application of BHT in food preservation is supported by its proven efficacy in extending shelf life and maintaining food quality, and its usage is regulated by food safety authorities around the world. For example, in many countries, the maximum allowable concentration of BHT in food products is strictly monitored to ensure consumer safety, based on toxicological evaluations that assess its safety profile over long-term exposure. While BHT is generally recognised as safe when used within regulated limits, ongoing research continues to assess its metabolic fate and potential health effects. Nonetheless, the chemical stability, ease of incorporation into food systems, and robust antioxidant properties make BHT a valuable synthetic antioxidant that plays a significant role in preserving the quality and safety of food products by inhibiting the oxidative degradation of fats and oils.

5.3.1.2 Butylated Hydroxy Anisole (BHA)

Butylated Hydroxy Anisole, commonly known as BHA, is a synthetic antioxidant widely used in the food industry to prevent the oxidation of fats and oils, similar to BHT. Chemically, BHA is a mixture of two isomeric compounds that consist of a phenolic structure with tert-butyl groups attached to the aromatic ring. The presence of the hydroxyl group allows BHA to donate a hydrogen atom to free radicals, thereby terminating the chain reactions of lipid peroxidation. In comparative terms with BHT, BHA exhibits a slightly different molecular configuration which can influence its solubility and reactivity. While both BHA and BHT act as effective antioxidants, BHA is generally considered to be more versatile in certain applications because it can function in both lipid and aqueous phases, albeit with some limitations in terms of thermal stability when compared to BHT. This versatility makes BHA particularly useful in a wider range of food products where the distribution of the antioxidant across different phases of the product is required to prevent rancidity.

In typical uses, BHA is incorporated into foods such as baked goods, snack items, and cereals, as well as in cosmetic and pharmaceutical products. The concentrations used in food applications are usually in the range of 50 to 200 parts per million, depending on the product formulation and regulatory guidelines. The efficacy of BHA in preventing oxidative spoilage is well-documented, and its application is often chosen based on factors such as the type of fat present in the food matrix and the desired shelf life. In comparative studies, both BHA and BHT have been shown to effectively inhibit the oxidation of fats, although BHA is sometimes preferred for products that require better performance in polar systems due to its relative solubility in both aqueous and lipid environments. Overall, the differences in chemical structure and functional properties between BHA and BHT allow manufacturers to select the most appropriate antioxidant for a given application, ensuring the stability and quality of food products while maintaining compliance with safety standards.

5.3.2 Comparative Effectiveness and Safety

5.3.2.1 Advantages of Synthetic Antioxidants

Synthetic antioxidants offer several distinct advantages in comparison to their natural counterparts, which makes them widely used in various industries such as food, cosmetics, and pharmaceuticals. One of the primary advantages is their stability. Synthetic antioxidants like BHT and BHA are designed to withstand harsh processing conditions, including high temperatures and prolonged storage, without significant degradation. This chemical stability ensures that the antioxidant properties are maintained throughout the shelf life of the product, preventing the oxidation of fats and oils even under conditions that would normally lead to rapid spoilage. The robust stability of these compounds not only helps to preserve the quality and safety of food products but also reduces the frequency of product replacement due to oxidative deterioration.

In addition to their stability, synthetic antioxidants are also noted for their cost-effectiveness. The production processes for these compounds have been optimised over many years, allowing for large-scale manufacture at relatively low cost. This makes them an economically viable option for food manufacturers who require effective antioxidants in substantial quantities. The lower cost of synthetic antioxidants translates to reduced overall production costs for a wide range of products, which is particularly beneficial in large-scale industrial applications where cost margins are critical.

Furthermore, the ease of formulation is another significant advantage of synthetic antioxidants. Their well-defined chemical structures and consistent quality allow manufacturers to incorporate them into products with predictable outcomes. This ease of formulation means that synthetic antioxidants can be easily mixed into diverse matrices, ranging from oil-based systems to aqueous formulations, without causing undesirable changes in taste, colour, or texture. The predictable behavior of synthetic antioxidants in various formulations enables product developers to design and standardise products more efficiently, ensuring that the antioxidant protection is both effective and reliable across different batches. These combined advantages of high stability, cost-effectiveness, and ease of formulation have established synthetic antioxidants as an integral component in the preservation of food quality and the enhancement of product longevity in a variety of consumer goods.

5.3.2.2 Limitations and Safety Concerns

While synthetic antioxidants such as BHT and BHA offer significant advantages in terms of stability and cost-effectiveness, they also have certain limitations and safety concerns that distinguish them from natural antioxidants. One of the primary concerns is the potential toxicity associated with prolonged exposure to synthetic antioxidants. Some studies have raised questions regarding the carcinogenic and mutagenic potential of these compounds when consumed in high doses or over long periods, although regulatory agencies generally consider them safe when used within established limits. Regulatory bodies such as the U.S. Food and Drug Administration (FDA) and the European Food Safety Authority (EFSA) have evaluated the safety profiles of these substances and set maximum allowable concentrations in food products. These limits are intended to minimize any health risks while ensuring that the antioxidants effectively prevent oxidative degradation.

In contrast, natural antioxidants, which are derived from plant sources, are often perceived as being safer due to their occurrence in whole foods and the complex mixture of bioactive compounds they provide. However, it is important to note that natural antioxidants can also exhibit toxicity at very high doses, and their effects can vary based on the method of extraction and processing. The regulatory status of synthetic antioxidants is generally well defined, with extensive toxicological data supporting their use at levels deemed safe for human consumption. Nonetheless, concerns remain regarding the potential for adverse effects in sensitive populations and the long-term impact of chronic exposure. As a result, there is ongoing research into improving the safety profiles of synthetic antioxidants and exploring alternative strategies, such as combining lower doses of synthetic antioxidants with natural compounds, to achieve effective antioxidant protection while minimising potential health risks.

Review Questions

1. Describe how oxidative stress contributes to the development of diabetes mellitus, particularly in relation to insulin resistance and β-cell dysfunction.
2. Explain the mechanisms by which free radicals trigger and sustain chronic inflammation, including the role of key signaling pathways such as NF-κB.
3. Outline the process of ischemic reperfusion injury, emphasizing how the sudden reintroduction of oxygen leads to tissue damage through free radical production.
4. Discuss how free radicals can induce DNA damage, including the formation of strand breaks and base modifications (such as 8-OHdG), and explain how these changes contribute to oncogenesis.
5. Explain the process of oxidative modification of LDL cholesterol and describe how this leads to foam cell formation and the progression of atherosclerosis.
6. Describe the impact of oxidative stress on the brain, and discuss how free radical-induced damage contributes to neurological disorders such as Alzheimer's and Parkinson's diseases.
7. Identify other disorders that have been linked to oxidative stress (such as kidney and muscle damage) and explain the mechanisms by which free radicals contribute to these conditions.
8. Summarize the free radical theory of ageing, including its historical development and the main ideas that underpin the theory.
9. Discuss experimental evidence that supports the role of oxidative stress in ageing. What types of studies have been used to demonstrate this relationship?
10. Explain how clinical studies have used biomarkers of oxidative stress to correlate increased free radical damage with age-related diseases.
11. Describe the mechanism of action of superoxide dismutase (SOD) in neutralizing free radicals, and explain the significance of its different isoforms (cytosolic, mitochondrial, extracellular).
12. Outline the role of catalase in cellular defense, particularly how it decomposes hydrogen peroxide, and discuss why this reaction is important for maintaining redox balance.

13. Explain how glutathione peroxidase functions to reduce both hydrogen peroxide and lipid hydroperoxides, and discuss its role in preventing cellular damage.
14. Describe the structure of glutathione, its synthesis within the cell, and the importance of its recycling mechanism in maintaining antioxidant defenses.
15. Discuss the chemical structure of α-lipoic acid and explain why its ability to function in both aqueous and lipid environments makes it a "universal" antioxidant.
16. Explain the dual role of melatonin in regulating circadian rhythms and scavenging free radicals, and discuss how these functions might contribute to neuroprotection.
17. Compare the roles and mechanisms of enzymatic antioxidants (such as SOD, catalase, and glutathione peroxidase) with those of non-enzymatic antioxidants (like glutathione, α-lipoic acid, and melatonin).
18. Describe the chemical properties of synthetic antioxidants such as BHT and BHA, and explain how these properties contribute to their use in food preservation.
19. Discuss the potential toxicity and safety concerns associated with synthetic antioxidants compared to natural antioxidants, and explain how regulatory agencies address these concerns.
20. Outline the major components of the endogenous antioxidant defense system and discuss how they interact to maintain cellular redox balance.
21. Explain how free radicals activate inflammatory signaling pathways and how this activation contributes to tissue damage and disease progression.
22. Discuss the role of oxidative stress in the pathogenesis of insulin resistance, and explain the cellular mechanisms involved in this process.
23. Describe how free radicals can induce apoptosis in cancer cells and discuss potential therapeutic strategies that might target these mechanisms.
24. Examine the potential benefits of antioxidant therapies in cardiovascular diseases. How might such therapies mitigate oxidative stress and improve clinical outcomes?
25. Provide an overview of how the combined actions of enzymatic and non-enzymatic antioxidants protect cells from age-related damage and contribute to the prevention of chronic diseases.

MCQS

1. **Which of the following best describes oxidative stress?**
   A. A state where antioxidant levels exceed free radical production
   B. A balanced state between free radical production and antioxidant defenses
   C. A condition where free radical production overwhelms the body's antioxidant defenses
   D. A process that exclusively occurs during exercise
   Correct Answer: C
2. **How does oxidative stress contribute to the pathogenesis of diabetes mellitus?**
   A. By enhancing insulin secretion
   B. By triggering the oxidation of insulin molecules
   C. By promoting insulin resistance and β-cell dysfunction
   D. By increasing glucose absorption in muscles
   Correct Answer: C
3. **Which signaling pathway is activated by oxidative stress and plays a role in inflammation?**
   A. Wnt signaling
   B. NF-κB pathway
   C. mTOR pathway
   D. Hedgehog pathway
   Correct Answer: B
4. **During ischemic reperfusion injury, the sudden reintroduction of oxygen leads to a burst of free radical production primarily due to:**
   A. Increased glycolysis
   B. Enhanced DNA replication
   C. Rapid reactivation of the mitochondrial electron transport chain
   D. Decreased enzyme activity
   Correct Answer: C
5. **Which of the following best describes the role of free radicals in cancer development?**
   A. They enhance immune surveillance
   B. They cause oxidative DNA damage and mutagenesis
   C. They reduce cellular proliferation

D. They improve DNA repair mechanisms

Correct Answer: B

6. **The oxidative modification of low-density lipoprotein (LDL) is critical in the development of atherosclerosis because:**

   A. It increases the LDL concentration in the blood

   B. Oxidized LDL is taken up by macrophages, leading to foam cell formation

   C. It promotes the synthesis of HDL cholesterol

   D. It directly triggers platelet aggregation

   Correct Answer: B

7. **In neurological disorders such as Alzheimer's disease, oxidative stress contributes to pathology by:**

   A. Enhancing synaptic plasticity

   B. Promoting the accumulation of amyloid plaques and tau tangles

   C. Increasing dopamine production

   D. Reducing the need for mitochondrial ATP

   Correct Answer: B

8. **Which biomarker is commonly used to indicate oxidative damage to DNA?**

   A. Malondialdehyde (MDA)

   B. 8-hydroxy-2'-deoxyguanosine (8-OHdG)

   C. Glutathione

   D. Protein carbonyl content

   Correct Answer: B

9. **Free radicals can cause protein oxidation leading to enzyme inactivation primarily by:**

   A. Enhancing the formation of disulfide bonds

   B. Forming protein carbonyls on amino acid side chains

   C. Increasing the solubility of proteins

   D. Stimulating protein synthesis

   Correct Answer: B

10. **In the context of free radical damage, what does the term "propagation" refer to?**

    A. The initiation of free radical formation

    B. The termination of free radical reactions

    C. The chain reaction where free radicals continuously generate more radicals

    D. The recycling of antioxidants

Correct Answer: C

11. **Malondialdehyde (MDA) is formed during lipid peroxidation and is used as a biomarker for:**
    A. DNA synthesis
    B. Oxidative stress
    C. Protein degradation
    D. Carbohydrate metabolism
    Correct Answer: B
12. **Which analytical method is commonly used to detect MDA levels?**
    A. BCA protein assay
    B. TBARS assay
    C. PCR
    D. SDS-PAGE
    Correct Answer: B
13. **At approximately what wavelength is the MDA-TBA complex measured in the TBARS assay?**
    A. 280 nm
    B. 450 nm
    C. 532 nm
    D. 600 nm
    Correct Answer: C
14. **Superoxide dismutase (SOD) catalyzes the dismutation of superoxide anions into:**
    A. Hydrogen peroxide and water
    B. Hydrogen peroxide and oxygen
    C. Oxygen and water
    D. Carbon dioxide and water
    Correct Answer: B
    (Reaction: $2\,O_2^{-} + 2\,H^{+} \rightarrow H_2O_2 + O_2$ *)*
15. **Catalase protects cells by decomposing hydrogen peroxide into:**
    A. Water and carbon dioxide
    B. Water and oxygen
    C. Oxygen and superoxide
    D. Water and hydroxyl radicals
    Correct Answer: B
    (Reaction: $2\,H_2O_2 \rightarrow 2\,H_2O + O_2$ *)*
16. **Glutathione peroxidase reduces hydrogen peroxide by using which substrate?**

A. NADPH
B. Glutathione (GSH)
C. Ascorbic acid
D. Vitamin E
Correct Answer: B

17. **Glutathione is a tripeptide composed of which three amino acids?**
A. Alanine, cysteine, and glycine
B. Glutamate, cysteine, and glycine
C. Glutamine, serine, and glycine
D. Tyrosine, cysteine, and alanine
Correct Answer: B

18. **α-Lipoic acid is termed a "universal" antioxidant because it can function in which types of environments?**
A. Only aqueous environments
B. Only lipid environments
C. Both aqueous and lipid environments
D. Only gaseous environments
Correct Answer: C

19. **Melatonin plays a dual role in the body by regulating circadian rhythms and:**
A. Enhancing ATP production
B. Scavenging free radicals
C. Increasing free radical production
D. Promoting protein oxidation
Correct Answer: B

20. **Which synthetic antioxidant is known by the abbreviation BHT?**
A. Butylated Hydroxy Toluene
B. Butylated Hydroxy Anisole
C. Benzoyl Hydroxyl Toluene
D. Butoxy Hydroxyl Toluene
Correct Answer: A

21. **Butylated Hydroxy Anisole (BHA) is primarily used for:**
A. Enhancing flavor
B. Preventing lipid oxidation in food products
C. Increasing vitamin content
D. Acting as a preservative by killing bacteria
Correct Answer: B

22. **One advantage of synthetic antioxidants like BHT and BHA is that they:**
    A. Are completely natural and unregulated
    B. Provide high stability and are cost-effective
    C. Have no limitations or safety concerns
    D. Can cure diseases
    Correct Answer: B
23. **A limitation of synthetic antioxidants compared to natural ones is:**
    A. Their inability to prevent oxidation
    B. Potential toxicity and safety concerns at high doses
    C. Their unstable chemical structure
    D. Their excessive water solubility
    Correct Answer: B
24. **The free radical theory of ageing suggests that ageing is primarily caused by:**
    A. A decrease in metabolism over time
    B. Accumulated oxidative damage from free radicals
    C. Genetic mutations unrelated to oxidative stress
    D. Increased antioxidant production
    Correct Answer: B
25. **Which of the following is an experimental method used to measure free radicals directly?**
    A. UV-Vis spectroscopy
    B. Electron Spin Resonance (ESR) spectroscopy
    C. High-Performance Liquid Chromatography (HPLC)
    D. Enzyme-linked immunosorbent assay (ELISA)
    Correct Answer: B
26. **In diabetes mellitus, oxidative stress contributes to insulin resistance by:**
    A. Enhancing insulin receptor sensitivity
    B. Promoting serine phosphorylation of insulin receptor substrates
    C. Increasing insulin secretion from β-cells
    D. Reducing blood glucose levels
    Correct Answer: B
27. **Chronic inflammation is exacerbated by free radicals through the upregulation of:**
    A. Anti-inflammatory cytokines
    B. Pro-inflammatory cytokines such as TNF-α and IL-6

C. Antioxidant enzymes exclusively

D. Insulin production

Correct Answer: B

28. **Ischemic reperfusion injury is characterized by tissue damage resulting from:**

A. Prolonged oxygen deprivation without reperfusion

B. Sudden reoxygenation leading to a burst of ROS generation

C. Continuous oxygen supply without any interruption

D. Inadequate nutrient absorption

Correct Answer: B

29. **Which of the following diseases is directly linked to oxidative modification of LDL cholesterol?**

A. Diabetes mellitus

B. Atherosclerosis

C. Alzheimer's disease

D. Parkinson's disease

Correct Answer: B

30. **Oxidative stress in the brain contributes to neurological disorders by:**

A. Enhancing neuronal regeneration

B. Causing mitochondrial dysfunction and neuronal damage

C. Reducing amyloid plaque formation

D. Increasing neurotransmitter synthesis

Correct Answer: B

31. **Kidney damage from oxidative stress is primarily due to:**

A. Increased filtration rate

B. Damage to renal glomeruli and tubules by ROS

C. Excessive water absorption

D. Overproduction of urea

Correct Answer: B

32. **Muscle damage due to free radicals often results in:**

A. Increased muscle strength

B. Protein oxidation leading to impaired muscle function

C. Enhanced regeneration of muscle fibers

D. Increased blood flow

Correct Answer: B

33. **The accumulation of advanced glycation end-products (AGEs) is a result of oxidative damage to:**

A. Lipids only

B. Nucleic acids only

C. Carbohydrates and glycoproteins

D. Proteins exclusively

Correct Answer: C

34. **Which of the following is a common consequence of oxidative DNA damage?**

A. Increased accuracy of DNA replication

B. Mutagenesis and potential oncogenesis

C. Enhanced repair mechanisms without mutation

D. Complete resistance to further oxidative damage

Correct Answer: B

35. **In the context of free radicals, what does the term "chain reaction" imply?**

A. A process where antioxidants repair DNA

B. A sequential reaction where one free radical generates another, perpetuating damage

C. The complete inhibition of free radical formation

D. The recycling of metabolic substrates

Correct Answer: B

36. **What is the primary function of endogenous antioxidants in cells?**

A. To increase free radical production

B. To neutralize free radicals and protect cellular components from oxidative damage

C. To synthesize new proteins

D. To enhance the formation of lipid peroxides

Correct Answer: B

37. **Which enzyme is responsible for reducing lipid hydroperoxides into non-reactive alcohols?**

A. Catalase

B. Glutathione peroxidase

C. Superoxide dismutase

D. Xanthine oxidase

Correct Answer: B

38. **What role does melatonin play in protecting against oxidative stress in the brain?**

A. It enhances the production of free radicals

B. It directly scavenges reactive oxygen and nitrogen species

C. It inhibits mitochondrial function

D. It increases blood sugar levels

Correct Answer: B

39. **Which synthetic antioxidant is known for its high thermal stability and is widely used in food preservation?**

A. BHA

B. BHT

C. Ascorbic acid

D. α-Tocopherol

Correct Answer: B

40. **A key safety concern regarding synthetic antioxidants compared to natural ones is:**

A. Their inability to prevent oxidation

B. Their potential toxicity at high doses

C. Their extremely high water solubility

D. Their lack of regulatory oversight

Correct Answer: B

41. **The free radical theory of ageing suggests that:**

A. Ageing is solely determined by genetic factors

B. Cumulative oxidative damage from free radicals contributes significantly to ageing

C. Free radicals are beneficial for prolonging lifespan

D. Antioxidants accelerate the ageing process

Correct Answer: B

42. **Which type of evidence supports the role of oxidative stress in ageing?**

A. Only in vitro studies

B. Experimental studies in model organisms and clinical biomarker analyses

C. Anecdotal evidence from consumer testimonials

D. Studies showing no change in antioxidant levels with age

Correct Answer: B

43. **In the context of free radical damage, what is the significance of protein carbonyls?**

A. They are markers of protein oxidation and damage

B. They indicate increased protein synthesis

C. They promote cellular regeneration

D. They are solely produced during healthy metabolism

Correct Answer: A

44. **Which of the following best explains the role of antioxidants in mitigating ischemic reperfusion injury?**
    A. They increase free radical production during reperfusion
    B. They neutralize the burst of ROS generated upon reoxygenation
    C. They block oxygen delivery to tissues
    D. They accelerate cell apoptosis
    Correct Answer: B
45. **How do free radicals contribute to the progression of atherosclerosis?**
    A. By lowering LDL cholesterol levels
    B. By oxidizing LDL cholesterol, leading to foam cell formation and plaque development
    C. By enhancing the elasticity of arterial walls
    D. By increasing HDL cholesterol levels
    Correct Answer: B
46. **Which of the following is an outcome of oxidative stress-induced damage to nucleic acids?**
    A. Enhanced DNA repair without mutation
    B. DNA strand breaks and potential mutagenesis
    C. Increased protein synthesis
    D. Immediate cell division
    Correct Answer: B
47. **What is the main purpose of measuring biomarkers like MDA and 8-OHdG in clinical studies?**
    A. To determine cell viability exclusively
    B. To assess the level of oxidative stress and damage in tissues
    C. To measure enzyme activity
    D. To quantify dietary intake
    Correct Answer: B
48. **Which of the following best explains the relationship between chronic inflammation and free radical production?**
    A. Free radicals reduce the production of inflammatory cytokines
    B. Chronic inflammation can increase free radical production, which in turn sustains the inflammatory response
    C. Inflammation completely stops free radical formation
    D. Free radicals and inflammation are unrelated processes
    Correct Answer: B
49. **Why is it important to maintain a balance between free radical production and antioxidant defenses?**

A. To maximize free radical generation

B. To prevent oxidative damage to cellular components and maintain cellular homeostasis

C. To increase metabolic rates indefinitely

D. To promote enzyme inactivation

Correct Answer: B

50. **Overall, what is the significance of studying free radicals and oxidative stress in the context of disease prevention?**

A. It only provides information on metabolic rates

B. It helps in understanding the molecular mechanisms underlying various diseases and guides the development of antioxidant therapies

C. It is solely a theoretical concept with no practical applications

D. It indicates that free radicals are always beneficial

Correct Answer: B

CHAPTER SIX

Food Laws, Regulations, and Safety

6.1.1.1 Food and Drug Administration (FDA)

The Food and Drug Administration (FDA) is a principal regulatory agency tasked with overseeing the safety, efficacy, and quality of a wide range of products including food, drugs, dietary supplements, cosmetics, and medical devices. Established under the U.S. Department of Health and Human Services, the FDA's jurisdiction covers all aspects of product development from manufacturing through to marketing and post-market surveillance. The agency plays a crucial role in setting and enforcing standards to ensure that food products, including those containing nutraceuticals, meet strict safety criteria before reaching consumers. One of the primary responsibilities of the FDA is to evaluate and approve new drugs and dietary supplements, which involves rigorous preclinical and clinical testing to ensure that these products do not pose significant health risks. In addition, the FDA is responsible for reviewing and approving health claims on product labels, ensuring that any statements regarding the benefits of a food or supplement are supported by sound scientific evidence. The agency also monitors compliance with Good Manufacturing Practices (GMPs) to maintain product consistency and safety, and it carries out inspections of manufacturing facilities both in the United States and abroad. The FDA has the authority to issue warnings, recall products, or impose sanctions on companies that do not comply with regulatory requirements, thereby safeguarding public health. With a commitment to scientific integrity, the agency employs experts in various fields such as toxicology, microbiology, and nutrition to assess risk and establish guidelines, and it frequently updates its regulations in response to emerging scientific research. The comprehensive oversight provided by the FDA ensures that products in the marketplace are not only safe for consumption but also accurately labelled, thereby fostering consumer trust and maintaining the integrity of the food and pharmaceutical industries.

6.1.1.2 Food Products Order (FPO)

The Food Products Order (FPO) is a regulatory framework established to ensure that food products meet quality, safety, and labeling standards before they reach consumers. It is a significant tool in quality assurance that sets clear criteria for the composition, packaging, and presentation of food items. The FPO mandates the use of proper ingredients and prohibits the use of adulterants, thereby protecting public health and maintaining consumer trust. It specifies standards for various food categories, including dairy products, oils, cereals, and nutraceuticals, ensuring that these products conform to prescribed quality parameters. Through the FPO, manufacturers must adhere to strict quality control measures during production and processing. These measures include proper handling of raw materials, adherence to Good Manufacturing Practices (GMPs), and regular testing of finished products for compliance with the set standards. The significance of the FPO lies in its ability to provide a consistent framework that supports fair trade practices and protects consumers from substandard or unsafe food products. By enforcing quality assurance protocols, the FPO plays a crucial role in preventing food adulteration and contamination, thus contributing to the overall integrity of the food supply chain.

6.1.1.3 Meat Products Order (MPO)

Regulations Specific to Meat Products

The Meat Products Order (MPO) is a regulatory framework designed specifically to ensure the quality, safety, and proper labelling of meat and meat products. It sets forth detailed standards and procedures that meat processing units and manufacturers must follow to guarantee that the products meet stringent hygienic and quality requirements. The MPO outlines clear guidelines for the handling, processing, storage, and transportation of meat, thereby ensuring that the entire supply chain maintains high standards of safety and sanitation. Under these regulations, meat products must be produced in facilities that adhere to strict sanitary practices, including proper cleaning, disinfection, and temperature control to prevent microbial contamination. The order also stipulates limits on the use of additives, preservatives, and other chemicals, ensuring that any substances used are within safe and acceptable ranges as determined by scientific studies and regulatory benchmarks.

Additionally, the MPO requires that meat products are accurately labelled with information regarding ingredients, nutritional content, production dates, and expiry dates, which helps consumers make informed choices and prevents misleading claims. Regular inspections and quality control checks are mandated under the MPO to monitor compliance with these regulations. These measures are critical in preventing adulteration and ensuring that the meat available in the market is of high quality and safe for consumption. The Meat Products Order thus plays a vital role in maintaining public health, promoting fair trade practices, and ensuring that meat products meet the expectations of both consumers and regulatory authorities.

6.1.1.4 AGMARK

AGMARK is a certification system and a set of standards established by the Government of India to assure the quality and purity of agricultural produce. Administered by the Directorate of Marketing and Inspection, this scheme is designed to standardise and certify a wide range of agricultural products, ensuring that they meet rigorous quality benchmarks before they reach consumers. The AGMARK certification covers numerous aspects such as product purity, quality parameters, packaging, and labelling, thereby providing a comprehensive framework that facilitates the reliable identification of genuine produce in the market. This system plays a crucial role in safeguarding the interests of both consumers and producers by promoting transparency, enhancing market access, and boosting consumer confidence in agricultural products.

The significance of AGMARK lies in its ability to ensure that agricultural products such as fruits, vegetables, grains, and processed food items are produced, handled, and marketed in adherence to nationally recognised standards. By providing certification, AGMARK helps prevent adulteration and substandard quality, which in turn protects public health and supports fair trade practices. Products that meet the AGMARK standards are awarded a quality mark, which serves as a guarantee of their authenticity and compliance with established norms. This certification is not only a mark of quality but also acts as a tool for market differentiation, enabling consumers to make informed choices based on the assurance of quality. In addition, AGMARK standards facilitate international trade by aligning Indian agricultural produce with global quality benchmarks, thus enhancing the competitiveness of Indian products in the global market. Overall, the AGMARK scheme represents an essential element of the agricultural quality assurance system in India, contributing significantly to the promotion of high standards in agricultural production, processing, and marketing.

6.2.1.1 Principles of HACCP

Hazard Analysis Critical Control Point (HACCP) is a systematic and preventive approach designed to ensure food safety through the identification and control of hazards from production to consumption. One of the key principles of HACCP is the identification of Critical Control Points (CCPs), which are steps in the production process where potential hazards—such as microbial contamination, chemical residues, or physical contaminants—can be prevented, eliminated, or reduced to acceptable levels. During this process, food manufacturers assess every stage of production, from raw material handling to processing, packaging, and storage, to determine points where the control of hazards is critical for ensuring the safety of the final product. Once these critical points are identified, each is assigned specific critical limits, which are measurable parameters such as temperature, pH, or time limits that must be maintained to prevent food safety risks.

In addition to identifying CCPs, HACCP incorporates risk assessment and management strategies to monitor and control hazards effectively. Risk assessment involves a thorough evaluation of potential hazards by analysing their likelihood of occurrence and the severity of their impact on food safety. This step allows manufacturers to prioritise control measures and allocate resources efficiently. Based on the risk assessment, management strategies are then developed to monitor these critical points continuously. These strategies include the implementation of regular monitoring procedures, where data is collected and compared against established critical limits, and the establishment of corrective actions that are triggered whenever a critical limit is breached. Furthermore, HACCP requires that all control measures, monitoring procedures, and corrective actions are documented and verified regularly to ensure that the entire system functions effectively. By combining the identification of CCPs with rigorous risk assessment and management strategies, HACCP provides a robust framework for preventing food safety hazards and ensuring that only safe, high-quality food products reach consumers.

6.2.1.2 Application in Food Processing

The application of HACCP in food processing is demonstrated through numerous case studies and practical examples that underscore its effectiveness in ensuring food safety. In the dairy industry, for instance,

HACCP has been implemented to monitor the critical control point of pasteurization, where maintaining precise temperature and time parameters is essential to inactivate pathogenic microorganisms such as Listeria monocytogenes and Escherichia coli. A case study from a major dairy plant revealed that strict adherence to HACCP protocols resulted in a significant reduction in microbial counts in the final product, thereby extending shelf life and ensuring consumer safety. Similarly, in meat processing, the identification and management of critical control points during slaughter, chilling, and packaging stages have proven to be instrumental in reducing the risk of contamination. In one practical example, a meat processing facility introduced HACCP measures that focused on controlling temperature during storage and transport, which led to a measurable decrease in the incidence of spoilage and foodborne illnesses among consumers.

Another illustrative case is found in the processing of fresh produce, where HACCP principles are applied to washing, cutting, and packaging operations. Here, the risk of microbial contamination is mitigated by setting critical limits for water quality and sanitisation procedures. A notable example is a fruit processing plant that integrated real-time monitoring systems to check water pH and chlorine levels during the washing process, ensuring that the risk of contamination from waterborne pathogens was minimized. These practical implementations of HACCP not only demonstrate the system's ability to identify and control critical points throughout the production process but also highlight its role in standardizing quality assurance practices across diverse food processing sectors. The successful integration of HACCP in these real-world scenarios provides compelling evidence of its utility in enhancing food safety, reducing product recalls, and ultimately protecting public health.

6.2.2.1 Ensuring Quality in Production

Good Manufacturing Practices (GMPs) are a set of guidelines and regulations that are critical in ensuring the quality, safety, and consistency of food, pharmaceuticals, and nutraceutical products throughout the production process. These guidelines are developed and enforced by regulatory agencies to establish standardized procedures that cover every aspect of production, including raw material handling, processing, packaging, storage, and distribution. The primary objective of GMPs is to ensure that products are manufactured in a controlled environment that minimizes the risk of contamination, error, and variability. This is achieved by implementing rigorous documentation protocols, maintaining hygienic conditions, and enforcing strict quality control measures at each stage of production. For example, GMPs require that manufacturing facilities be designed to prevent cross-contamination between products, with designated areas for specific processing activities and proper separation of raw and finished products. Additionally, GMPs mandate regular equipment maintenance, calibration, and validation of processes to ensure that production conditions remain within predefined critical limits.

The regulatory frameworks surrounding GMPs are provided by national and international bodies such as the World Health Organization (WHO), the U.S. Food and Drug Administration (FDA), and the European Medicines Agency (EMA). These agencies issue detailed guidelines that outline the minimum requirements for facilities, personnel, equipment, and processes. They also conduct periodic inspections and audits to verify compliance with GMP standards. In India, the Food Safety and Standards Authority of India (FSSAI) along with other relevant bodies establishes specific GMP guidelines for food and nutraceutical manufacturing. These guidelines specify criteria such as the need for proper documentation of standard operating procedures (SOPs), batch production records, and quality control test results. Training of personnel is a key component, as staff are required to be well-versed in GMP principles and to follow procedures meticulously to maintain product quality. Furthermore, GMP guidelines emphasize the importance of environmental monitoring, including control of temperature, humidity, and cleanliness, which are essential for preventing microbial contamination and ensuring the stability of sensitive bioactive compounds. By adhering to these regulatory frameworks, manufacturers can produce products that are not only safe for consumption but also meet the high standards required for market approval, thereby protecting public health and building consumer confidence.

6.2.2.2 Implementation in the Food Industry

Best Practices and Compliance Measures

Implementing Good Manufacturing Practices (GMPs) in the food industry involves a systematic approach that combines best practices with rigorous compliance measures to ensure that products meet safety and quality standards consistently. One of the key best practices is the establishment of detailed Standard Operating Procedures (SOPs) for every step of the manufacturing process. These SOPs provide clear instructions for handling raw materials, operating equipment, and performing quality control tests. For example, food processing plants are required to document procedures for washing, sanitising, and storing raw produce to prevent cross-contamination and microbial growth. Maintaining comprehensive records of batch production and process controls is also essential, as it allows manufacturers to trace any issues back to their source and implement corrective actions swiftly.

In addition, implementing a robust environmental monitoring program is critical. This includes regular testing of air quality, water quality, and surfaces for microbial contamination, as well as continuous monitoring of temperature, humidity, and ventilation in processing areas. Many food companies employ automated systems to monitor these parameters in real time, ensuring that any deviations from critical limits are immediately detected and corrected. For instance, cold storage facilities are often equipped with digital sensors that track temperature variations to within ±1°C, thereby ensuring that perishable items remain within safe limits and reducing the risk of spoilage.

Training and education of personnel form another cornerstone of GMP implementation. Employees must receive regular training on hygiene practices, proper equipment use, and emergency procedures. Periodic refresher courses help maintain high standards and ensure that all staff understand the importance of compliance with GMP guidelines. Additionally, companies frequently perform internal audits and inspections to assess compliance with established procedures. These internal checks are often complemented by external audits from regulatory bodies such as the FDA or FSSAI, which verify that the facility meets the required standards.

Compliance measures also include the adoption of quality control measures such as in-process testing and final product verification. This may involve testing for microbial contamination, chemical residues, and physical contaminants using methods like high-performance liquid chromatography (HPLC) or gas chromatography-mass spectrometry (GC-MS) for accurate quantification. Manufacturers may also employ hazard analysis techniques to identify potential risks at critical control points, followed by the implementation of corrective actions when deviations are observed. For example, if an unexpected rise in microbial counts is detected in a particular batch, the affected production run may be halted and investigated to prevent distribution of compromised products.

6.3.1.1 Common Practices

Adulteration of foods refers to the deliberate addition or substitution of inferior or harmful substances in food products, which compromises their quality, safety, and nutritional value. Common practices of food adulteration involve the use of chemical, physical, and microbial adulterants that can occur at various stages of food processing and distribution.

Chemical adulterants include substances that are intentionally added to mimic or enhance the appearance, texture, or shelf life of food products. These can include synthetic dyes to improve colour, preservatives to extend shelf life, and even chemicals that mimic the nutritional content of the food. In some cases, cheaper substances such as water, starch, or non-food-grade additives are used to dilute or substitute high-value ingredients. The use of these chemicals not only reduces the nutritional quality of the food but may also pose significant health risks to consumers if they are toxic or produce harmful metabolites upon ingestion.

Physical adulterants refer to the inclusion of non-food materials that do not belong in the product. This type of adulteration might involve the addition of extraneous matter such as sand, sawdust, or other foreign objects that are used to increase the bulk of the product or lower production costs. Physical adulterants can also include the misrepresentation of food portions by substituting one type of ingredient with another that is inferior in quality. Such practices are not only deceptive but can also lead to contamination and injury, especially if the foreign objects are sharp or abrasive.

Microbial adulterants involve the unintentional or deliberate introduction of harmful microorganisms into food products. In some instances, poor handling practices and inadequate hygiene during processing lead to microbial contamination, while in other cases, the deliberate addition of microbes might be used to ferment or alter the characteristics of a food product in an unsafe manner. These microbial contaminants can include pathogenic bacteria, viruses, and fungi, which have the potential to cause foodborne illnesses. The presence of microbial adulterants is particularly concerning as it poses a direct risk to public health by causing infections and outbreaks of disease.

6.3.1.2 Impact on Health

Adulteration of foods poses a significant threat to public health by introducing substances that can lead to a wide range of adverse effects. Chemical adulterants such as synthetic dyes and unauthorized preservatives have been associated with acute poisoning, allergic reactions, and long-term risks such as carcinogenicity and endocrine disruption. For instance, the use of Sudan dyes, which are industrial chemicals, in spices and oils is linked to liver damage and an increased risk of cancer. Similarly, the addition of non-permitted preservatives may lead to toxic metabolite formation and cumulative health hazards over time.

Physical adulterants, including inert materials like sawdust, stone powder, or plastic particles, may not only reduce the nutritional value of the food but also cause physical harm such as gastrointestinal blockages or injuries to the digestive tract. The ingestion of these non-food substances can lead to chronic irritation, inflammation, and in severe cases, surgical interventions if foreign objects cause obstructions or perforations in the gastrointestinal system.

Microbial adulterants pose an immediate health risk by introducing pathogenic organisms into food products. Contamination with bacteria such as Salmonella, Escherichia coli, and Listeria can result in foodborne illnesses characterized by symptoms ranging from mild gastroenteritis to severe systemic infections. In addition, the presence of microbial toxins, such as aflatoxins produced by certain fungi, can lead to long-term health complications including liver cirrhosis and hepatocellular carcinoma. The cumulative impact of these adulterants on health is not limited to immediate toxicity or infection; they also compromise the nutritional integrity of food products and may trigger chronic diseases through persistent inflammatory responses and metabolic disturbances. Consequently, ensuring adherence to stringent food safety standards and regulatory measures is essential to minimise these health risks and protect consumers from the adverse effects of food adulteration.

Uncovering analytical techniques

I'm detailing techniques to detect and prevent adulteration, starting with UV-Vis spectroscopy, FTIR spectroscopy, and HPLC, then moving to GC-MS and NMR for thorough analysis.

6.3.2.1 Analytical Techniques for Adulterant Detection

Detection of adulterants in food products relies on a range of analytical techniques that are designed to accurately identify and quantify unwanted substances. Among these, spectroscopy and chromatography are the most widely employed methods. Spectroscopic techniques, such as ultraviolet-visible (UV-Vis) spectroscopy, infrared (IR) spectroscopy, and Fourier transform infrared (FTIR) spectroscopy, are used to analyse the chemical composition of food samples by measuring the interaction of light with matter. UV-Vis spectroscopy can quickly detect the presence of synthetic dyes and other chemical adulterants by identifying specific absorption peaks, while FTIR spectroscopy offers a molecular fingerprint that can be used to differentiate between authentic ingredients and adulterants based on their unique vibrational transitions. For example, FTIR can detect structural differences between natural and synthetic compounds by comparing characteristic bands corresponding to functional groups such as hydroxyl, carbonyl, and aromatic moieties.

Chromatographic techniques also play a critical role in the detection of food adulterants. High-performance liquid chromatography (HPLC) and gas chromatography coupled with mass spectrometry (GC-MS) are frequently utilised to separate, identify, and quantify complex mixtures of compounds in food matrices. HPLC is particularly effective for analysing non-volatile compounds, such as pesticide residues and synthetic additives, by employing various detectors including UV and fluorescence detectors to provide precise quantitative measurements. Gas chromatography-mass spectrometry, on the other hand, is highly sensitive in detecting volatile and semi-volatile adulterants such as certain organic solvents or adulterants used to mimic flavour profiles. These methods allow for the simultaneous analysis of multiple components in a sample, and the resulting chromatograms provide detailed information about the purity and authenticity of the food product.

Other analytical methods complement spectroscopy and chromatography by offering additional confirmation and greater sensitivity. Techniques such as nuclear magnetic resonance (NMR) spectroscopy are used to elucidate the structural details of suspected adulterants, while inductively coupled plasma mass spectrometry (ICP-MS) can be employed to detect trace amounts of heavy metals that might be present as adulterants. These advanced methods, when integrated into a comprehensive quality assurance program, ensure that food products meet the required safety and purity standards. By combining the rapid screening capabilities of spectroscopic methods with the high resolution and quantitative precision of chromatographic techniques, regulators and manufacturers are able to identify adulteration practices with greater accuracy and take necessary corrective measures to protect public health.

6.3.2.2 Regulatory Measures

Regulatory measures play a critical role in ensuring the safety and authenticity of food products by establishing guidelines and enforcing actions to detect and prevent adulteration. Government agencies and food safety authorities develop comprehensive guidelines that outline the permissible levels of various ingredients, define the acceptable methods of production, and set specific standards for labelling and packaging. These guidelines serve as a framework for manufacturers to ensure that their products meet strict quality criteria. They also provide clear directives on the acceptable practices in food processing and the use of additives, thereby reducing the risk of adulteration. Regular updates to these guidelines are made to reflect new scientific evidence and emerging risks, ensuring that food safety standards remain relevant and effective.

Enforcement actions are an integral part of these regulatory measures. Food safety authorities carry out routine inspections of manufacturing facilities and conduct random sampling of food products from the market to verify compliance with established guidelines. When adulteration is detected or when a product does not meet the required safety standards, enforcement actions may include product recalls, imposition of fines, suspension of production licences, or even legal action against the responsible parties. These actions serve as a deterrent against non-compliance and ensure that corrective measures are implemented swiftly. In addition, regulatory agencies often collaborate with industry bodies and international organisations to share best practices and harmonise standards, thereby strengthening the overall food safety framework. This coordinated approach helps in preventing adulteration, protecting consumer health, and maintaining the integrity of the food supply chain.

6.4.1.1 Nutrient Content Claims

Nutrient content claims on nutraceutical product labels are specific statements that describe the levels of particular nutrients contained in the product, and they must adhere to rigorous standards set by regulatory bodies. These claims provide consumers with important information about the nutritional value of the product, helping them to make informed dietary choices. Standards for expressing nutrient levels typically require that the amount of each nutrient be quantified in relation to the recommended dietary allowances or daily values. For instance, a product may claim to be a "good source" of a nutrient if it provides at least 10–19 percent of the daily value per serving, or "high in" a nutrient if it supplies 20 percent or more of the daily value. Such standards ensure uniformity in labelling, allowing consumers to compare products easily. Regulatory frameworks such as those established by the U.S. Food and Drug Administration (FDA), the European Food Safety Authority (EFSA), or the Food Safety and Standards Authority of India (FSSAI) require that nutrient content claims be substantiated by laboratory analyses and be expressed using specific units—such as milligrams, micrograms, or International Units (IU)—and as a percentage of the recommended daily intake. These specifications are designed to prevent misleading claims and ensure that the labelling accurately reflects the product's nutritional composition.

Furthermore, the guidelines for nutrient content claims also mandate that any claim regarding the presence of a nutrient must be clearly defined and consistent with scientific evidence. For example, if a nutraceutical product claims to be "low in sodium," it must contain sodium at a level that does not exceed the threshold set by regulatory authorities, which is generally around 140 milligrams per serving for foods in the United States. Similarly, claims such as "source of dietary fiber" are based on the product containing a minimum amount per serving, often specified as a percentage of the Daily Value, which in many jurisdictions is standardized at 28 grams per day. This method of quantification ensures that consumers receive accurate information about the nutritional benefits of the product. The requirement to express nutrient levels using these precise standards not only promotes transparency but also helps maintain the integrity of the nutraceutical market by preventing exaggerated or unsubstantiated claims. Overall, the regulatory standards for nutrient content claims play a crucial role in safeguarding public health by ensuring that the nutritional information provided on product labels is reliable, scientifically valid, and easily understandable by consumers.

Navigating health claims

Engaging in health claims on nutraceutical labels involves linking the product to enhanced health outcomes or reduced disease risks. This journey requires thorough scientific substantiation and gaining regulatory nods.

Crafting credible health claims

Regulatory bodies like the FDA, EFSA, and FSSAI mandate health claims be backed by robust scientific evidence and reviewed rigorously to ensure they are not misleading.

6.4.1.2 Health Claims

Health claims on nutraceutical product labels are statements that suggest a beneficial relationship between the product and improved health or reduced risk of specific diseases. These claims must be based on robust scientific evidence and are subject to strict regulatory approval to ensure that they are not misleading to consumers. Scientific substantiation involves the collection of data from well-designed studies, including controlled clinical trials, epidemiological research, and in vitro or in vivo experiments. The evidence must clearly demonstrate that the bioactive components in the product can contribute to a measurable health benefit, such as lowering blood cholesterol levels, reducing inflammation, or improving immune function. For instance, a claim that a product "supports cardiovascular health" must be backed by research showing that its ingredients have been proven to improve parameters such as endothelial function or lipid profiles. In addition to the original research, systematic reviews and meta-analyses are often considered to further validate the health benefits of a product over a broader population.

Regulatory approval for health claims requires that manufacturers submit detailed scientific dossiers to the relevant authorities, such as the Food and Drug Administration (FDA), the European Food Safety Authority (EFSA), or the Food Safety and Standards Authority of India (FSSAI). These agencies review the submitted evidence to ensure that the health claim is supported by credible scientific data and that the claim accurately reflects the effects of the product without exaggeration. The process involves evaluating the quality, consistency, and relevance of the scientific studies, and may include assessments of the product's dosage, bioavailability, and safety profile. Once the evidence is deemed satisfactory, the regulatory agency may grant approval for the health claim, which must then be clearly and accurately presented on the product label. The requirement for scientific substantiation and regulatory approval of health claims helps to protect consumers by ensuring that any claims made on nutraceutical labels are both reliable and based on sound science, thereby maintaining public trust and promoting informed dietary choices.

Clarifying dietary supplement claims

I'm working through dietary supplement claims, noting their distinction from pharmaceutical claims. Substantiation and disclaimers are essential, focusing on supporting health without suggesting disease treatment.

6.4.1.3 Dietary Supplement Claims

Dietary supplement claims refer to statements made on product labels that describe the benefits of the supplement in supporting overall health and specific body functions. These claims are carefully differentiated from pharmaceutical claims, which suggest the ability to diagnose, treat, cure, or prevent specific diseases. In the regulatory framework, dietary supplements are classified as food products rather than drugs, and therefore the claims that can be made are subject to different standards and legal requirements. Manufacturers must ensure that any claim regarding the health benefits of a dietary supplement is truthful, not misleading, and supported by scientific evidence. Regulatory bodies such as the U.S. Food and Drug Administration (FDA) and the Food Safety and Standards Authority of India (FSSAI) mandate that dietary supplement claims must include appropriate disclaimers, for instance, stating that the product is "not intended to diagnose, treat, cure, or prevent any disease."

These legal requirements are designed to prevent consumers from being misled into believing that dietary supplements have the same therapeutic effects as pharmaceuticals. In contrast to pharmaceutical products, which undergo rigorous clinical trials and approval processes, dietary supplements are not required to prove efficacy to the same extent before entering the market. Instead, the focus is on ensuring that the claims are substantiated by reliable scientific data and that the labeling is clear and does not imply unapproved health benefits. The guidelines specify the types of claims that can be made, such as structure/function claims that describe the role of a nutrient or dietary ingredient intended to affect the normal structure or function of the human body. For example, a claim that a supplement "supports immune function" must be backed by evidence from well-designed studies, and the claim must be presented in a manner that avoids any suggestion of disease treatment. By adhering to these legal and regulatory standards, manufacturers maintain transparency and consumer trust while ensuring that dietary supplement claims remain within the boundaries defined by food safety authorities.

Mapping out compliance

OK, let me see. Regulatory agencies and industries are crucial for keeping nutraceuticals compliant with legal and ethical standards. This involves understanding their roles and responsibilities, aiming for a cohesive, detailed response.

Ensuring compliance

Regulatory agencies like FDA, FSSAI, and EFSA enforce standards in production, labelling, and claims to safeguard public health. They guide manufacturers, monitor safety, and educate on best practices.

Ensuring safety and credibility

Regulatory agencies and industry partners clarify allowable ingredient levels, labelling, and claims. This keeps consumers safe, fosters innovation, and guarantees fairness while building trust in the marketplace.

6.4.2.1 Ensuring Compliance

Regulatory agencies play a vital role in ensuring that nutraceutical products adhere to established legal and ethical standards. Agencies such as the U.S. Food and Drug Administration (FDA), the European Food Safety Authority (EFSA), and the Food Safety and Standards Authority of India (FSSAI) set strict guidelines and perform routine inspections to monitor the production, labelling, and marketing of these products. They develop comprehensive regulatory frameworks that require manufacturers to provide detailed scientific evidence for any health or nutrient claims made on product labels. These agencies also conduct periodic audits of manufacturing facilities, verify the accuracy of product testing, and enforce corrective actions whenever non-compliance is identified. By issuing warnings, imposing fines, or ordering product recalls, regulatory bodies protect public health and ensure that the claims made by nutraceutical companies are both truthful and substantiated.

At the same time, the nutraceutical industry bears significant responsibilities to maintain high standards of quality and transparency. Manufacturers must implement robust quality control systems and adhere strictly to Good Manufacturing Practices (GMPs) throughout the production process. This involves maintaining detailed records of production methods, sourcing high-quality raw materials, and routinely testing products to confirm that they meet regulatory standards. In addition, companies are required to ensure that their product labels provide clear, accurate, and comprehensive information, including the amounts of active ingredients and any disclaimers regarding health benefits. The industry is also responsible for staying updated with evolving regulatory requirements and incorporating new scientific evidence into their product formulations and marketing strategies. By engaging in regular internal audits and cooperating with external regulatory reviews, manufacturers not only comply with legal mandates but also build consumer trust and credibility.

Together, the efforts of regulatory agencies and the nutraceutical industry help to create a transparent and accountable marketplace. These joint responsibilities ensure that products are safe for consumption, that health claims are backed by solid scientific evidence, and that ethical practices are maintained throughout the supply chain. This collaborative approach ultimately supports public health, fosters industry innovation, and reinforces consumer confidence in nutraceutical products.

6.4.2.2 Consumer Protection Measures

Consumer protection measures in the realm of nutraceutical products are essential for ensuring that consumers receive accurate and reliable information, and that their health and rights are safeguarded throughout the purchasing process. Regulatory agencies, together with industry bodies, work to enforce standards that mandate transparency in product labelling and advertising, ensuring that all claims made by manufacturers are supported by robust scientific evidence. Transparency involves clear disclosure of all relevant information regarding the product, including the active ingredients, their quantities, potential benefits, and any risks associated with consumption. This allows consumers to make informed choices based on objective data rather than marketing hype.

Accuracy in advertising is a cornerstone of ethical marketing practices. Advertisements for nutraceutical products must present claims in a balanced manner, avoiding exaggeration or misrepresentation of the product's efficacy. This includes the proper use of language, such as stating that a product "supports" or "promotes" health functions rather than claiming it "cures" or "treats" diseases, which are reserved for pharmaceuticals. Regulatory frameworks require that all promotional materials undergo rigorous review to ensure that they do not mislead consumers or create unrealistic expectations. These measures help to prevent the spread of misinformation and protect consumers from potential harm due to unsubstantiated health claims.

Ethical marketing practices further demand that companies engage in fair competition and do not use deceptive tactics to lure consumers. This means avoiding ambiguous terms, hidden disclaimers, or complicated scientific jargon that might confuse the average consumer. Companies are expected to maintain high standards of integrity by providing evidence-based information and by being open about both the benefits and limitations of their products. By adhering to these principles, manufacturers not only comply with legal obligations but also build consumer trust and foster long-term loyalty.

Overall, the implementation of transparency, accuracy in advertising, and ethical marketing practices serves as a critical component of consumer protection. These measures ensure that nutraceutical products are marketed in a responsible manner, that consumers have access to reliable information, and that their health is not compromised by misleading or false claims. This collaborative effort between regulatory authorities and the nutraceutical industry helps to create a trustworthy marketplace where public health is prioritized and consumer rights are rigorously upheld.

6.5.1 Global Regulatory Frameworks

Global regulatory frameworks play a crucial role in ensuring the safety and quality of food products across nations. International agencies and organizations work together to establish guidelines that govern food quality, safety, and nutritional labelling, and these efforts contribute to consistent standards worldwide. These frameworks are essential for facilitating international trade, protecting public health, and promoting transparency in the food industry.

Codex Alimentarius Commission

The Codex Alimentarius Commission is one of the most significant international bodies in food regulation. Established by the Food and Agriculture Organization (FAO) and the World Health Organization (WHO), the Codex sets global standards, guidelines, and codes of practice for food safety and quality. The primary goal of Codex is to protect consumer health and ensure fair practices in food trade by providing a common reference point for food standards. Codex guidelines cover a wide range of topics, including maximum residue limits for pesticides, food additives, contaminants, and nutritional labeling. These standards are developed through a collaborative process that involves experts from various countries, and they are periodically updated to incorporate the latest scientific findings. The Codex Alimentarius also serves as a benchmark for national regulatory agencies, helping them harmonize their own food safety laws with international standards. This harmonization is particularly important for developing countries, as it facilitates access to international markets and builds consumer confidence in exported food products.

European Food Safety Authority (EFSA)

The European Food Safety Authority (EFSA) is the key regulatory body responsible for risk assessment regarding food and feed safety within the European Union. EFSA's work encompasses scientific advice on issues ranging from the safety of food additives to the evaluation of health claims on food products. By providing independent scientific assessments, EFSA helps to inform EU legislation and supports the development of evidence-based policies. EFSA collaborates closely with member states and other international organizations to ensure that food safety practices are consistent across Europe. In addition, EFSA plays an important role in monitoring emerging risks and evaluating new scientific data, thereby continuously updating regulatory measures to protect consumer health. Their assessments also cover nutritional labelling and the evaluation of novel food products, ensuring that all food items available in the market meet strict safety and quality standards. The rigorous scientific evaluations carried out by EFSA enhance consumer trust and contribute to the high safety standards observed in European food markets.

World Health Organization (WHO)

The World Health Organization (WHO) is another vital organization involved in setting global food safety guidelines. While WHO's primary focus is on public health, its work in food safety is essential for preventing foodborne illnesses and ensuring that nutritional guidelines are met. WHO collaborates with international partners to develop strategies and policies that address global food safety challenges. These include the control of foodborne pathogens, management of chemical contaminants, and guidelines on nutritional labelling. WHO's recommendations are often adopted by countries as part of their national food safety policies, and the organization provides technical assistance and training to support capacity building in regions with limited resources. By addressing issues such as food adulteration, microbiological hazards, and environmental contaminants, WHO's initiatives contribute to improving food quality and safety on a global scale. The agency's focus on evidence-based policymaking ensures that food safety standards are scientifically sound and effective in reducing health risks associated with food consumption.

Harmonization of Standards Across Countries

Efforts to harmonize food safety standards internationally are critical in today's globalized marketplace. Harmonization helps eliminate trade barriers, ensures that food products meet uniform safety criteria, and protects consumers regardless of the country of origin. Organizations like Codex Alimentarius, EFSA, and WHO work together to develop universal guidelines that countries can adopt or adapt to fit their regulatory frameworks. This collaborative approach not only supports fair trade but also aids in the rapid response to emerging food safety issues. When standards are harmonized, manufacturers can produce products that are acceptable in multiple markets without the need for significant adjustments. In addition, global harmonization helps to streamline the regulatory approval process for new food products and nutraceuticals, fostering innovation while ensuring consumer safety.

Impact on Global Trade and Public Health

The establishment of international regulatory frameworks and harmonized food safety standards has a significant impact on global trade and public health. By providing a common set of rules, these frameworks facilitate the smooth exchange of food products between countries, helping to reduce disputes and ensure that imported foods meet the same safety criteria as domestically produced items. Furthermore, these standards protect consumers by minimizing the risk of exposure to unsafe or adulterated foods, thus contributing to improved public health outcomes worldwide. The collaborative efforts of global regulatory bodies also help address emerging challenges, such as new contaminants and changing dietary patterns, ensuring that food safety measures remain effective and relevant.

6.5.2 Harmonization Efforts and Standards

Efforts to harmonize food laws on a global scale are essential for ensuring consistent safety and quality standards across international borders, thereby facilitating trade and enhancing consumer protection. One of the cornerstone initiatives in this realm is the Codex Alimentarius, a comprehensive set of standards, guidelines, and codes of practice developed jointly by the Food and Agriculture Organization (FAO) and the World Health Organization (WHO). The Codex Alimentarius serves as a common reference for member countries, outlining safety benchmarks for food additives, contaminants, pesticide residues, and nutritional labelling. These standards not only provide a scientific basis for ensuring food safety but also help to level the playing field in global trade by reducing discrepancies among national regulatory systems.

Codex Alimentarius and Its Role

The Codex Alimentarius represents a significant achievement in the international regulation of food safety. It offers a unified framework that countries can adopt or adapt according to their domestic requirements, thereby promoting regulatory convergence. By establishing internationally recognized limits and guidelines, the Codex ensures that food products meet a minimum level of safety and quality regardless of their origin. This uniformity is particularly beneficial in resolving trade disputes, as it provides a neutral benchmark against which food safety practices can be measured. Furthermore, the Codex framework is continually updated in response to new scientific evidence and emerging food safety challenges, ensuring that the standards remain relevant and effective.

Challenges in Achieving Regulatory Convergence

Despite the benefits, achieving regulatory convergence among diverse national systems poses several challenges. Differences in economic development, cultural practices, and resource availability mean that countries may have varying capacities to implement and enforce stringent food safety standards. Additionally, national regulatory priorities can differ; some countries may prioritize economic growth and market expansion, while others focus more intensively on public health protection. These disparities can lead to inconsistencies in how food safety measures are applied, creating obstacles for international trade and potentially compromising consumer protection in some regions. Harmonizing standards requires extensive collaboration, mutual recognition agreements, and technical assistance to support countries with less developed regulatory infrastructures.

Benefits and Limitations for International Trade and Consumer Protection

The benefits of harmonized standards are significant. For international trade, common food safety standards reduce technical barriers, streamline the regulatory approval process for exports and imports, and enhance consumer confidence by ensuring that products meet a consistent quality benchmark. This harmonization not only facilitates smoother trade flows but also reduces the costs associated with meeting multiple, sometimes conflicting, national regulations. For consumers, harmonized standards provide assurance that the food they purchase, regardless of its origin, adheres to stringent safety criteria, thereby reducing the risk of exposure to contaminants and adulterants.

However, there are limitations to these efforts. One major limitation is the potential for harmonized standards to be too general, which may not address specific regional concerns or unique local food products. In some cases, these global standards may not fully reflect the diverse dietary practices and environmental conditions present in different countries. Additionally, the process of harmonization can be slow, as it requires extensive negotiation, scientific consensus, and mutual trust among nations. Political, economic, and cultural differences may further complicate the adoption of a unified set of regulations, potentially leaving some countries at a disadvantage if they are unable to meet these standards without significant investment in regulatory infrastructure.

6.5.3 Impact on Global Trade and Market Access

Harmonized international food safety standards play a pivotal role in shaping global trade dynamics and market access. By establishing common benchmarks for food quality and safety, these standards help reduce trade barriers and create a more predictable and transparent trading environment. When countries adopt and align with frameworks such as the Codex Alimentarius, exporters and importers benefit from a common understanding of what constitutes safe and acceptable food products. This harmonization minimizes the need for duplicate testing and compliance measures, thereby lowering costs and expediting the clearance of goods across borders. In effect, it facilitates smoother trade flows, enhances competitiveness, and ultimately provides consumers worldwide with access to high-quality food products.

Non-compliance with internationally harmonized standards can have significant negative implications for exporting countries. Products that fail to meet these standards may face rejection at international borders, leading to costly recalls, loss of market share, and damage to a country's reputation as a reliable supplier. Such consequences can hinder economic growth and diminish consumer confidence in the exported food products. Moreover, stringent global standards often require that exporting countries invest in modernizing their food safety systems and regulatory frameworks. While this can be a challenge for countries with limited resources, it also presents an opportunity to improve domestic food safety practices and gain access to larger international markets.

Governments and industries adopt various strategies to align domestic regulations with international expectations. These strategies include updating national food safety laws to reflect the latest scientific developments and international guidelines, investing in capacity building for regulatory agencies, and establishing collaborative programs with international organizations. Governments often engage in bilateral and multilateral agreements to recognize each other's food safety certifications and streamline trade procedures. At the industry level, manufacturers implement robust quality control systems, adhere to Good Manufacturing Practices (GMPs), and participate in voluntary certification schemes such as AGMARK or HACCP. Such initiatives not only ensure compliance with international standards but also enhance product credibility in the global market.

Global cooperation is crucial in maintaining the safety and integrity of the international food supply chain. By working together through international bodies and partnerships, countries can share best practices, provide technical assistance to developing regions, and respond collectively to emerging food safety challenges. This cooperative approach helps in addressing discrepancies between national standards and ensuring that all trading partners adhere to mutually recognized benchmarks. In summary, the impact of harmonized food safety standards on global trade and market access is significant, as they reduce trade barriers, incentivize regulatory improvements, and foster a cooperative international environment that protects public health while promoting economic growth.

6.6.1 Digital Technologies and the Internet of Things (IoT)

Digital technologies, particularly those associated with the Internet of Things (IoT), are transforming food safety monitoring by enabling real-time tracking of environmental conditions throughout the food production and distribution process. IoT devices and sensors can be strategically placed in various stages of the food supply chain—from production facilities and storage units to transportation and retail outlets—to continuously monitor key parameters such as temperature, humidity, and air quality. This continuous data collection allows for immediate detection of deviations from predetermined critical limits, thereby alerting manufacturers and regulators to potential safety breaches before they escalate into major issues.

For example, temperature sensors installed in refrigerated storage units can continuously measure and transmit temperature data to central monitoring systems. If a refrigeration unit fails or if temperatures exceed safe limits, the system triggers an immediate alert, enabling prompt corrective action to prevent spoilage or bacterial growth. Similarly, humidity sensors can detect changes in moisture levels that might promote the growth of mold or other pathogens, while air quality sensors monitor for contaminants and volatile organic compounds that could affect the integrity of food products. The integration of these sensors with digital communication networks facilitates the aggregation of data into centralized databases where it can be analyzed in real time.

Furthermore, the use of IoT devices in food safety monitoring enhances transparency and traceability. Data collected from sensors can be recorded on secure digital ledgers or blockchain platforms, providing an immutable record of environmental conditions during processing and distribution. This traceability is essential not only for quality assurance but also for swift and effective product recalls in case of contamination. By ensuring that every step of the supply chain is monitored, IoT technologies help build consumer trust and meet stringent regulatory standards.

The implementation of these digital technologies also supports predictive analytics. With the accumulation of historical data, manufacturers can identify trends and potential vulnerabilities in their production processes. For instance, repeated temperature fluctuations in a particular storage area may indicate a need for equipment maintenance or process modification. Predictive models can then be developed to forecast potential safety issues, allowing companies to address them proactively.

6.6.2 Blockchain and Supply Chain Transparency

Blockchain technology is increasingly being applied in the food industry to enhance supply chain transparency and ensure the integrity of food products from farm to table. This subsection explores how blockchain systems create immutable, decentralized records of every transaction and movement along the supply chain. Each transaction is recorded in a block that, once verified and added to the blockchain, cannot be altered or deleted. This immutability builds a trusted digital ledger that tracks every step—from the sourcing of raw materials to processing, packaging, and distribution—ensuring complete traceability of food products.

One of the primary benefits of using blockchain technology in the food supply chain is the significant improvement in traceability. With each transaction recorded in real time, any stakeholder, including regulators and consumers, can verify the origin and handling of a food product. In the event of a safety issue or contamination, blockchain facilitates rapid identification of the source and affected batches, enabling faster recall processes and minimizing public health risks. This speed in tracing faulty products is critical during foodborne illness outbreaks, as it allows companies to act swiftly and efficiently, reducing economic losses and preserving consumer trust.

Blockchain also enhances transparency by providing a clear and accessible record of all transactions. This transparency helps to reduce fraud and misrepresentation in food labeling, as every claim regarding origin, quality, and safety is backed by verifiable data stored on the blockchain. For consumers, access to transparent supply chain information can lead to increased confidence in the authenticity and safety of the food they purchase. Retailers and manufacturers benefit as well, since adherence to strict traceability standards can open up new markets that require rigorous food safety certifications.

Moreover, the integration of blockchain technology supports improved collaboration among different stakeholders within the supply chain. Farmers, processors, distributors, and retailers can all contribute to and access the same information, facilitating seamless communication and reducing the risk of errors or discrepancies. This shared platform can also drive innovation in quality control, as data analytics tools can be applied to blockchain records to identify trends, forecast potential safety breaches, and optimize logistics.

6.6.3 Advances in Rapid Testing and Analytical Methods

Recent advancements in rapid testing and analytical methods are transforming the landscape of food safety by enabling quick and accurate detection of contaminants, adulterants, and pathogens throughout the supply chain. One key area of innovation is the development of portable diagnostic devices and biosensors. These technologies utilize various principles such as immunoassays, electrochemical detection, and optical sensing to rapidly analyze food samples on-site. Portable biosensors can detect specific biomarkers or contaminants with high sensitivity, offering results within minutes rather than hours or days. This rapid turnaround is critical for identifying potential safety breaches in real time, thereby reducing the risk of distributing compromised products. The ease of use and scalability of these devices mean they can be integrated into various points along the supply chain, from production and packaging facilities to distribution centers and retail outlets.

In addition to portable devices, next-generation sequencing (NGS) methods have emerged as powerful tools for comprehensive food safety analysis. NGS technologies enable the rapid sequencing of microbial genomes present in food samples, which facilitates the identification of pathogens and the detection of microbial adulterants with unparalleled accuracy. By analyzing the genetic material of a wide array of organisms simultaneously, NGS provides a detailed profile of the microbial community, helping to identify emerging contaminants and track sources of contamination. This level of detailed analysis supports epidemiological investigations and enhances the ability to respond swiftly to foodborne illness outbreaks.

These innovative diagnostic and analytical technologies are increasingly being integrated into routine quality assurance protocols within the food industry. Companies are adopting these methods as part of their standard operating procedures to continuously monitor product quality and safety. The integration of rapid testing devices into digital platforms further enhances their utility, allowing for real-time data collection, automated reporting, and immediate corrective actions when safety parameters are breached. Overall, advances in rapid testing and analytical methods are not only improving the accuracy and speed of contaminant detection but are also contributing to a more proactive approach in ensuring food safety, ultimately protecting public health and maintaining consumer confidence in the food supply chain.

Review Questions

1. Explain the role and jurisdiction of the Food and Drug Administration (FDA) in ensuring the safety and quality of food and nutraceutical products.
2. Discuss the significance of the Food Products Order (FPO) in maintaining quality assurance in food products, including its key requirements and benefits for consumers.
3. What are the specific regulations outlined in the Meat Products Order (MPO), and how do these guidelines help safeguard the quality and safety of meat products?
4. Describe the purpose of the AGMARK certification system and explain how it contributes to the standardization and consumer trust in agricultural produce.
5. Outline the principles of Hazard Analysis Critical Control Point (HACCP) and discuss how the identification of Critical Control Points (CCPs) aids in preventing food safety hazards.
6. Provide practical examples of how HACCP is applied in various food processing sectors to monitor and control potential hazards throughout the production process.
7. Explain the importance of Good Manufacturing Practices (GMPs) in ensuring the quality of food products and nutraceuticals, and discuss the key elements that must be maintained.
8. Discuss the best practices and compliance measures that manufacturers in the food industry should adopt to successfully implement GMPs.
9. Identify the common types of food adulterants, categorizing them into chemical, physical, and microbial adulterants, and provide specific examples of each.
10. Describe the potential health risks associated with food adulteration by discussing specific examples of adulterants and their adverse effects on consumer health.
11. Explain the various analytical techniques used for adulterant detection in foods, such as spectroscopy and chromatography, and discuss the advantages and limitations of these methods.
12. Discuss the regulatory measures, including guidelines and enforcement actions, that are in place to prevent food adulteration and ensure product

safety.

13. Outline the importance of nutrient content claims on nutraceutical product labels and describe the standards and units used to express nutrient levels accurately.
14. Explain the process for substantiating health claims on nutraceutical products, and discuss how regulatory agencies evaluate the scientific evidence behind these claims.
15. Differentiate between dietary supplement claims and pharmaceutical claims, and discuss the legal requirements that govern the claims made on dietary supplement labels.
16. Describe how regulatory agencies, such as the FDA and FSSAI, monitor compliance with food safety standards, and discuss the actions they take when non-compliance is detected.
17. Discuss the role of transparency and accuracy in advertising nutraceutical products, and explain how these practices contribute to consumer protection.
18. Explain the ethical considerations that nutraceutical companies must adhere to when marketing their products, and discuss how these ethical practices help maintain consumer trust.
19. Evaluate the challenges regulatory bodies face in harmonizing food safety standards globally and discuss the impact these challenges may have on international trade.
20. How do legal and ethical frameworks in the food industry promote the development and marketing of safe, high-quality nutraceutical products, and what role does consumer education play in this process?

MCQS

1. **Which agency is primarily responsible for regulating food, drugs, and nutraceutical products in the United States?**
   A. European Food Safety Authority (EFSA)
   B. Food and Drug Administration (FDA)
   C. Food Safety and Standards Authority of India (FSSAI)
   D. World Health Organization (WHO)
   Correct Answer: B
2. **The Food Products Order (FPO) is designed to ensure that food products:** A. Are manufactured at a low cost
   B. Meet quality, purity, and labeling standards
   C. Contain added synthetic nutrients
   D. Are marketed internationally
   Correct Answer: B
3. **The primary purpose of the Meat Products Order (MPO) is to:** A. Regulate dairy products
   B. Establish standards for meat processing and safety
   C. Certify organic produce
   D. Monitor packaging design
   Correct Answer: B
4. **AGMARK certification is used in which country?**
   A. United States
   B. United Kingdom
   C. India
   D. Australia
   Correct Answer: C
5. **What does HACCP stand for?**
   A. Hazard Analysis Critical Control Point
   B. Health and Compliance Control Procedure
   C. Hazard Assessment and Control Protocol
   D. High Assurance of Consumer Protection
   Correct Answer: A
6. **Which of the following is a key principle of HACCP?**
   A. Maximizing production speed
   B. Identifying and controlling critical control points (CCPs)

C. Designing attractive packaging
D. Increasing product flavor intensity
Correct Answer: B

7. **In a HACCP plan, a "critical limit" refers to:**
A. The maximum allowable price of a product
B. A parameter that must be met to ensure food safety at a CCP
C. The minimum shelf life of a food product
D. The recommended daily intake of nutrients
Correct Answer: B

8. **Good Manufacturing Practices (GMPs) are primarily aimed at:**
A. Reducing marketing costs
B. Ensuring the consistency, safety, and quality of production
C. Enhancing the visual appeal of packaging
D. Increasing the speed of distribution
Correct Answer: B

9. **Which element is NOT typically a part of GMP guidelines?**
A. Personnel training
B. Equipment maintenance
C. Detailed documentation
D. Developing advertising slogans
Correct Answer: D

10. **AGMARK certification assures consumers that the agricultural produce has met:** A. Global organic standards
B. Specific quality and purity parameters set by the government
C. Only nutritional content requirements
D. No contamination from pesticides
Correct Answer: B

11. **Which of the following is an example of a chemical adulterant in foods?**
A. Sawdust added to spices
B. Synthetic dyes used to enhance color
C. Sand mixed into powdered products
D. Foreign objects like plastic fragments
Correct Answer: B

12. **Physical adulterants in food may include:**
A. Unauthorized chemical preservatives
B. Non-food materials such as sawdust or stones
C. Excess water added to dilute a product

D. Microbial contaminants

Correct Answer: B

13. **Microbial adulteration in food products refers to:**
    A. The deliberate addition of vitamins
    B. Contamination with harmful bacteria, viruses, or fungi
    C. The use of natural flavor enhancers
    D. Excessive fortification with minerals
    Correct Answer: B
14. **Which health risk is associated with the use of chemical adulterants like Sudan dyes?**
    A. Improved nutritional value
    B. Increased risk of liver damage and cancer
    C. Enhanced flavor
    D. Extended shelf life with no risks
    Correct Answer: B
15. **Which analytical technique is commonly used to detect chemical adulterants in food?**
    A. Spectroscopy
    B. Polymerase Chain Reaction (PCR)
    C. Microscopy
    D. Calorimetry
    Correct Answer: A
16. **High-Performance Liquid Chromatography (HPLC) is used to:**
    A. Increase the weight of a product
    B. Separate and quantify components in a food sample
    C. Change the color of a product
    D. Measure only the water content of a product
    Correct Answer: B
17. **Gas Chromatography-Mass Spectrometry (GC-MS) is particularly useful for:** A. Analyzing heavy metals
    B. Detecting volatile and semi-volatile adulterants
    C. Measuring protein concentrations
    D. Quantifying dietary fiber
    Correct Answer: B
18. **Which of the following is NOT a responsibility of regulatory agencies in food safety?**
    A. Establishing guidelines for food and nutraceutical production
    B. Conducting routine inspections and audits

C. Approving marketing slogans for products

D. Enforcing corrective actions and product recalls

Correct Answer: C

19. **Nutrient content claims on nutraceutical products must be expressed relative to:**

A. The total weight of the package

B. Recommended Daily Values (RDVs) or dietary allowances

C. The cost of the product

D. The volume of the product

Correct Answer: B

20. **Which of the following best describes a health claim on a nutraceutical label?**

A. A claim that the product cures diseases

B. A claim that the product supports a specific physiological function, based on scientific evidence

C. A claim that is not regulated

D. A claim that is solely based on traditional usage

Correct Answer: B

21. **Dietary supplement claims differ from pharmaceutical claims because they:**

A. Are not required to be scientifically substantiated

B. Must not imply that the product can diagnose, treat, cure, or prevent diseases

C. Are subject to the same regulatory process as drugs

D. Focus on cosmetic benefits only

Correct Answer: B

22. **Which regulatory agency is responsible for overseeing food and nutraceutical product standards in India?**

A. FDA

B. EFSA

C. FSSAI

D. WHO

Correct Answer: C

23. **What is the main goal of enforcing Good Manufacturing Practices (GMPs) in food production?**

A. To improve product taste

B. To ensure products are producccd consistently and safely

C. To design better product packaging

D. To decrease production time

Correct Answer: B

24. **What is one common method used by regulatory agencies to ensure compliance with food safety standards?**

    A. Self-reporting by companies

    B. Random inspections and audits

    C. Consumer surveys only

    D. Social media monitoring

    Correct Answer: B

25. **Transparency in nutraceutical advertising is important because it:**

    A. Allows companies to exaggerate health benefits

    B. Ensures consumers receive accurate information about ingredients and health claims

    C. Is optional for companies

    D. Focuses only on visual design

    Correct Answer: B

26. **Which aspect of food safety regulation helps prevent the use of adulterants in food products?**

    A. Strict labeling guidelines

    B. Quality assurance protocols and routine inspections

    C. Increased advertising budgets

    D. Expansion of product variety

    Correct Answer: B

27. **The primary focus of the Food Products Order (FPO) is to:**

    A. Enhance the marketing appeal of food products

    B. Set and enforce quality and purity standards for food items

    C. Increase the shelf life of processed foods

    D. Regulate the pricing of food products

    Correct Answer: B

28. **Which of the following best explains the role of the Meat Products Order (MPO) in food regulation?**

    A. It regulates the nutrient content of vegetables

    B. It establishes safety and quality standards specifically for meat and meat products

    C. It governs the advertising of dairy products

    D. It controls the labeling of fruits

    Correct Answer: B

29. **What does AGMARK certification indicate about an agricultural product?**
    A. That it is imported
    B. That it meets nationally recognized quality and purity standards
    C. That it is free of all pesticides
    D. That it is produced using genetically modified organisms
    Correct Answer: B
30. **In the context of HACCP, what is meant by "risk assessment"?**
    A. Estimating the financial cost of production
    B. Evaluating the likelihood and severity of potential hazards in the food production process
    C. Determining the taste profile of a food product
    D. Setting marketing strategies
    Correct Answer: B
31. **Which of the following is an example of a corrective action in a HACCP system?**
    A. Increasing product pricing
    B. Adjusting a processing parameter when a critical limit is breached
    C. Redesigning the product's packaging
    D. Enhancing the flavor profile of a product
    Correct Answer: B
32. **Which analytical technique is most suitable for detecting non-volatile chemical adulterants in food?**
    A. Gas Chromatography-Mass Spectrometry (GC-MS)
    B. High-Performance Liquid Chromatography (HPLC)
    C. Electron Spin Resonance (ESR)
    D. Infrared Spectroscopy
    Correct Answer: B
33. **Which regulatory measure involves product recalls and fines for non-compliance with food safety standards?**
    A. Voluntary guidelines
    B. Enforcement actions by regulatory agencies
    C. Marketing strategies
    D. Consumer education programs
    Correct Answer: B
34. **What distinguishes nutrient content claims from health claims on nutraceutical labels?**
    A. Nutrient content claims are not regulated

B. Nutrient content claims detail the amount of a nutrient, while health claims describe a relationship between the nutrient and health benefits
C. Health claims can only be made on pharmaceutical drugs
D. There is no difference
Correct Answer: B

35. **Why must dietary supplement claims include disclaimers stating they are not intended to diagnose, treat, cure, or prevent any disease?**
A. To increase consumer confusion
B. To comply with regulatory requirements and differentiate them from pharmaceutical products
C. To reduce production costs
D. To attract more customers
Correct Answer: B

36. **What is the role of internal audits in the context of GMP compliance?**
A. They are used solely for product marketing
B. They help verify that production processes meet established quality standards
C. They replace the need for external regulatory inspections
D. They are optional for all manufacturers
Correct Answer: B

37. **How do Good Manufacturing Practices (GMPs) contribute to consumer safety?**
A. By increasing product prices
B. By ensuring consistent product quality and preventing contamination
C. By reducing the nutritional content of products
D. By solely focusing on product packaging
Correct Answer: B

38. **Which of the following best describes the term "analytical techniques" in the context of adulterant detection?**
A. Methods for enhancing product flavor
B. Methods for identifying and quantifying adulterants in food products
C. Strategies for marketing products
D. Techniques for increasing production speed
Correct Answer: B

39. **What is the primary purpose of consumer protection measures in the nutraceutical industry?**
A. To reduce the cost of products
B. To ensure that consumers receive accurate information and safe

products

C. To promote only synthetic ingredients

D. To increase advertising budgets

Correct Answer: B

40. **How do regulatory agencies enforce compliance with food safety standards?**

    A. Through voluntary self-reporting only

    B. By conducting inspections, audits, and imposing corrective actions such as recalls and fines

    C. By outsourcing the responsibility to manufacturers

    D. By increasing product prices

    Correct Answer: B

41. **Which statement best describes the importance of transparency in nutraceutical advertising?**

    A. It allows companies to hide certain information

    B. It ensures that consumers have access to clear and accurate product information

    C. It is irrelevant to consumer trust

    D. It focuses solely on cost reduction

    Correct Answer: B

42. **What role does consumer education play in the regulatory framework of nutraceuticals?**

    A. It reduces the need for product testing

    B. It helps consumers make informed decisions based on accurate product labels and claims

    C. It is solely the responsibility of manufacturers

    D. It is not considered in food safety regulations

    Correct Answer: B

43. **Which of the following is NOT typically covered by the Food Products Order (FPO)?**

    A. Purity and composition of food items

    B. Quality standards for food processing

    C. Nutritional and labeling requirements

    D. Pricing strategies for food products

    Correct Answer: D

44. **The Meat Products Order (MPO) is primarily concerned with which aspect of meat production?**

    A. Determining marketing strategies

B. Ensuring hygienic processing and quality standards for meat
C. Enhancing the flavor of meat products
D. Increasing the protein content of meat
Correct Answer: B

45. **AGMARK certification is an example of a regulatory measure that ensures:**
A. Compliance with global pharmaceutical standards
B. The quality and purity of agricultural produce
C. That products are marketed internationally without restrictions
D. That food products contain no additives
Correct Answer: B

46. **Which aspect of food safety is directly addressed by HACCP?**
A. Marketing and advertising of food products
B. Identification and control of hazards in the food production process
C. Setting retail prices for food items
D. Designing food packaging
Correct Answer: B

47. **What is a key benefit of using chromatographic techniques in adulterant detection?**
A. They can measure only the color of a product
B. They provide precise separation, identification, and quantification of adulterants
C. They are the least expensive method
D. They require no sample preparation
Correct Answer: B

48. **Which of the following best describes the role of labeling standards in nutraceutical products?**
A. They are used only for decorative purposes
B. They ensure that nutrient content and health claims are accurately represented
C. They are not regulated by any agency
D. They focus solely on price information
Correct Answer: B

49. **How does the integration of Good Manufacturing Practices (GMPs) and HACCP contribute to overall food safety?**
A. By increasing the complexity of production
B. By ensuring that production processes are controlled and hazards are systematically identified and managed

C. By solely focusing on marketing strategies

D. By reducing the need for quality control testing

Correct Answer: B

50. **Which of the following best summarizes the overall purpose of food laws and regulations?**

A. To increase production costs

B. To ensure that food products and nutraceuticals are safe, of high quality, accurately labeled, and free from adulterants

C. To restrict the sale of imported foods only

D. To promote only synthetic nutraceutical products

Correct Answer: B

Glossary

1. **Nutraceuticals:** Food-derived products that provide additional health benefits beyond basic nutrition, often used for disease prevention and health promotion.
2. **Functional Foods:** Foods that naturally contain bioactive compounds providing health benefits beyond basic sustenance.
3. **Dietary Supplements:** Products taken orally that contain vitamins, minerals, herbs, or other bioactive substances intended to supplement the diet.
4. **Phytochemicals:** Naturally occurring bioactive compounds in plants, such as polyphenols, carotenoids, and flavonoids, that contribute to health benefits.
5. **Antioxidants:** Molecules that neutralize free radicals by donating electrons or hydrogen atoms, thereby protecting cells from oxidative damage.
6. **Free Radicals:** Atoms or molecules with one or more unpaired electrons, making them highly reactive and capable of damaging cellular components.
7. **Reactive Oxygen Species (ROS):** Oxygen-derived molecules, including free radicals and non-radical species (e.g., hydrogen peroxide), involved in oxidative processes.
8. **Oxidative Stress:** A state in which the production of free radicals exceeds the body's antioxidant capacity, leading to cellular damage.
9. **Glutathione:** A tripeptide (glutamate, cysteine, glycine) that functions as a major intracellular antioxidant and is involved in detoxification.
10. **Enzymatic Antioxidants:** Proteins such as superoxide dismutase, catalase, and glutathione peroxidase that catalyze reactions to neutralize free radicals.
11. **Synthetic Antioxidants:** Man-made compounds (e.g., BHT, BHA) used to inhibit oxidation in food products and extend shelf life.
12. **HACCP (Hazard Analysis Critical Control Point):** A systematic approach in food production for identifying and controlling potential hazards to ensure safety.
13. **GMP (Good Manufacturing Practices):** Guidelines and regulations ensuring that products are consistently produced and controlled

according to quality standards.

14. **Codex Alimentarius:** A collection of international food standards, guidelines, and codes of practice developed by the FAO and WHO to ensure food safety and fair practices in food trade.
15. **EFSA (European Food Safety Authority):** The European Union agency that provides independent scientific advice on food-related risks.
16. **WHO (World Health Organization):** A global public health agency that, among other roles, helps establish food safety and nutritional guidelines.
17. **FPO (Food Products Order):** Regulatory framework in certain countries ensuring food products meet quality, safety, and labeling standards.
18. **MPO (Meat Products Order):** Regulations specifically governing the quality, processing, and safety of meat and meat products.
19. **AGMARK:** An Indian certification system that verifies the quality and purity of agricultural produce through standardized guidelines.
20. **Free Radical Theory of Ageing:** The hypothesis that cumulative damage from free radicals over time is a major contributor to the ageing process and age-related diseases.
21. **Isoflavones:** A class of phytoestrogens, such as genistein and daidzein, predominantly found in soy products, with estrogen-modulating effects.
22. **Genistein:** A prominent isoflavone found in soy, known for its antioxidant and hormone-modulating properties.
23. **Daidzein:** An isoflavone in soy that, like genistein, exhibits weak estrogenic activity and contributes to various health benefits.
24. **Lignans:** Plant compounds found in seeds and whole grains, metabolized by gut bacteria into enterolignans that have antioxidant and mild estrogenic effects.
25. **Fructo-oligosaccharides (FOS):** Short-chain carbohydrates acting as prebiotics that stimulate the growth of beneficial gut bacteria.
26. **Probiotics:** Live microorganisms that, when administered in adequate amounts, confer a health benefit on the host, often by enhancing gut microbiota balance.
27. **Lactobacillus Species:** A group of beneficial bacteria commonly used as probiotics, known for fermenting carbohydrates into lactic acid.
28. **Carotenoids:** A class of pigments in plants (e.g., beta-carotene, lycopene) with strong antioxidant properties and roles in vision and cellular protection.
29. **α-Carotene:** A carotenoid with provitamin A activity found in orange and red vegetables, contributing to vision and immune health.

30. **β-Carotene:** A well-known provitamin A carotenoid that is converted to retinol in the body, found in carrots and sweet potatoes.
31. **Lycopene:** A red carotenoid pigment, notably abundant in tomatoes, known for its potent antioxidant properties but lacking provitamin A activity.
32. **Xanthophylls:** Oxygenated carotenoids, including lutein and zeaxanthin, that play crucial roles in eye health by protecting retinal tissues.
33. **Lutein:** A xanthophyll that accumulates in the macula, filtering blue light and reducing the risk of age-related macular degeneration.
34. **Chlorophyll-a:** A primary pigment in plants and algae essential for photosynthesis, contributing to the green color and nutrient value of green foods.
35. **Phycocyanin:** A blue pigment-protein complex found in Spirulina, valued for its antioxidant and anti-inflammatory properties.
36. **Ginsenosides:** Bioactive steroidal saponins found in ginseng that are responsible for its adaptogenic and medicinal properties.
37. **Protopanaxadiols:** A subgroup of ginsenosides (e.g., Rb1, Rb2) characterized by their chemical structure and associated with specific pharmacological effects.
38. **Protopanaxatriols:** Another subgroup of ginsenosides (e.g., Rg1, Re) with distinct chemical features and biological activities.
39. **Allicin:** A bioactive sulfur compound in garlic, formed enzymatically from alliin, responsible for garlic's aroma and antimicrobial properties.
40. **Alliin:** The sulfur-containing precursor in garlic that, when activated by alliinase, is converted into allicin.
41. **Diallyl Sulfide:** A sulfur-containing compound derived from garlic, contributing to its antioxidant and antimicrobial effects.
42. **Allyltrisulfide:** A further degradation product of allicin in garlic, known for its potential health benefits and contribution to overall bioactivity.
43. **Glucosinolates:** Sulfur-containing compounds found in cruciferous vegetables (e.g., broccoli) that are converted into bioactive isothiocyanates.
44. **Sulforaphane:** A potent isothiocyanate derived from glucoraphanin in broccoli, known for inducing detoxification enzymes and anticancer properties.
45. **Quercetin:** A flavonoid with strong antioxidant and anti-inflammatory properties, found in many fruits and vegetables.
46. **Kaempferol:** A flavonoid similar to quercetin, present in a variety of

plant foods, that exhibits anti-inflammatory and antioxidant activities.

47. **Rutin:** A flavonoid glycoside derived from quercetin, known for strengthening blood vessels and reducing inflammation.
48. **Naringin:** A flavonoid predominantly found in citrus fruits, noted for its bitter taste and potential to modulate lipid metabolism.
49. **Anthocyanidins:** Flavonoid pigments responsible for the red, purple, and blue colors of many fruits and berries, with antioxidant properties.
50. **Catechins:** A group of flavonoids, abundant in green tea, known for their cardiovascular and metabolic health benefits.
51. **Flavones:** A subclass of flavonoids found in herbs like parsley and celery, contributing to anti-inflammatory and antioxidant activities.
52. **Polyphenols:** A broad category of phytochemicals characterized by multiple phenol structures, known for their antioxidant and health-promoting effects.
53. **Resveratrol:** A stilbenoid polyphenol found in red grapes and berries, known for its cardioprotective, anti-inflammatory, and anti-aging effects.
54. **Tocopherols:** Members of the vitamin E family, fat-soluble antioxidants that protect cell membranes from oxidative damage.
55. **Vitamin E:** A collective term for tocopherols and tocotrienols, essential antioxidants that support immune function and protect lipids.
56. **Vitamin C:** A water-soluble vitamin with potent antioxidant properties, involved in collagen synthesis and immune function.
57. **Malondialdehyde (MDA):** A secondary product of lipid peroxidation used as a biomarker for oxidative stress.
58. **TBARS Assay:** A spectrophotometric method (Thiobarbituric Acid Reactive Substances assay) used to quantify MDA levels in biological samples.
59. **High-Performance Liquid Chromatography (HPLC):** An analytical technique for separating, identifying, and quantifying components in complex mixtures.
60. **Gas Chromatography-Mass Spectrometry (GC-MS):** A method combining gas chromatography and mass spectrometry to detect and quantify volatile and semi-volatile compounds.
61. **Electron Spin Resonance (ESR) Spectroscopy:** A technique that directly detects free radicals by measuring the magnetic properties of unpaired electrons.
62. **ORAC (Oxygen Radical Absorbance Capacity):** An assay that measures the antioxidant capacity of a substance by its ability to quench oxygen

radicals.

63. **Advanced Glycation End-products (AGEs):** Harmful compounds formed when proteins or fats combine with sugars, often enhanced by oxidative stress.
64. **8-OHdG (8-hydroxy-2'-deoxyguanosine):** A biomarker of oxidative damage to DNA, indicating the presence of mutations and stress.
65. **NADPH Oxidase:** An enzyme complex in immune cells that deliberately produces free radicals to destroy pathogens.
66. **Cytochrome P450 Oxidases:** A group of enzymes involved in the metabolism of various substances, which can inadvertently generate free radicals.
67. **Mitochondrial Electron Transport Chain:** A series of protein complexes in mitochondria responsible for ATP production and a major source of ROS due to electron leakage.
68. **Fenton Reaction:** A chemical reaction involving hydrogen peroxide and transition metals (e.g., iron) that produces highly reactive hydroxyl radicals.
69. **Chain Reaction (in Lipid Peroxidation):** A process where the initial free radical attack on lipids leads to the generation of additional radicals, perpetuating cellular damage.
70. **Initiation Phase (Lipid Peroxidation):** The first step in lipid peroxidation where a free radical abstracts a hydrogen atom from a polyunsaturated fatty acid.
71. **Propagation Phase (Lipid Peroxidation):** The stage where lipid radicals react with oxygen to form peroxyl radicals, which further propagate the chain reaction.
72. **Termination Phase (Lipid Peroxidation):** The phase in which free radicals combine to form non-radical, stable products, ending the chain reaction.
73. **Protein Carbonyls:** Oxidation products of proteins that serve as markers for oxidative protein damage.
74. **Glutathione Peroxidase:** An enzyme that reduces hydrogen peroxide and lipid hydroperoxides using glutathione as a substrate.
75. **Catalase:** An enzyme that catalyzes the decomposition of hydrogen peroxide into water and oxygen, protecting cells from oxidative damage.
76. **Superoxide Dismutase (SOD):** An enzyme that converts superoxide anions into hydrogen peroxide and oxygen, mitigating oxidative stress.
77. **Glutathione Reductase:** An enzyme that recycles oxidized glutathione

(GSSG) back into its reduced form (GSH) using NADPH.

78. **Phase I Metabolism:** The initial stage of metabolism involving oxidation, reduction, or hydrolysis reactions that modify bioactive compounds.
79. **Phase II Metabolism:** The subsequent stage of metabolism involving conjugation reactions such as glucuronidation, sulfation, and methylation, which increase water solubility for excretion.
80. **Conjugation Reactions:** Metabolic processes where a compound is linked to another molecule (e.g., glucuronic acid) to facilitate its elimination from the body.
81. **Nanoencapsulation:** A technique that uses nanotechnology to encase bioactive compounds, enhancing their stability and bioavailability.
82. **Liposomes:** Spherical vesicles with lipid bilayers used to deliver bioactive compounds in a controlled manner.
83. **Emulsification:** A process that disperses one liquid into another (e.g., oil in water) to enhance the absorption of lipophilic compounds.
84. **Bioenhancers:** Substances that improve the bioavailability and efficacy of active ingredients in nutraceutical formulations.
85. **Personalized Nutrition:** Tailoring dietary recommendations and nutraceutical interventions based on individual genetic, metabolic, and lifestyle factors.
86. **Nutrigenomics:** The study of how genetic variations affect an individual's response to nutrients and bioactive compounds.
87. **Metabolomics:** The comprehensive study of metabolites in biological systems, providing insights into metabolic responses and nutrient bioavailability.
88. **Proteomics:** The large-scale study of proteins, including their structures and functions, to understand cellular processes and responses to nutraceuticals.
89. **Biosensors:** Analytical devices that combine a biological component with a physicochemical detector to measure specific substances in food or biological samples.
90. **Next-Generation Sequencing (NGS):** Advanced sequencing technology that rapidly analyzes genetic material, useful for detecting microbial contaminants in food safety applications.
91. **Blockchain:** A distributed digital ledger technology that records transactions immutably, used in food supply chains for enhanced traceability and transparency.
92. **Internet of Things (IoT):** A network of connected devices and sensors

that collect and share real-time data, enhancing monitoring in food production and distribution.

93. **Digital Technologies in Food Safety:** Advanced electronic tools and systems used to monitor, control, and document food safety parameters across the supply chain.
94. **Rapid Diagnostic Devices:** Portable and high-speed analytical tools that quickly detect contaminants, adulterants, or pathogens in food products.
95. **Biosensors in Food Safety:** Devices that use biological elements to detect specific contaminants in food, providing real-time monitoring capabilities.
96. **Portable Testing Instruments:** Compact devices designed for on-site analysis of food samples, aiding in quick decision-making during production and distribution.
97. **Quality Assurance (QA):** A systematic process to ensure that products meet defined quality and safety standards throughout production.
98. **Traceability:** The ability to track the history, application, or location of an item through documented records, crucial for food safety and recall management.
99. **Regulatory Compliance:** Adherence to laws, guidelines, and standards established by governing bodies to ensure product safety and quality.
100. **Sustainability in Nutraceutical Production:** Practices that ensure the long-term availability and quality of natural resources while minimizing environmental impact, often incorporated into production and regulatory frameworks

www.ingramcontent.com/pod-product-compliance
Lightning Source LLC
LaVergne TN
LVHW021152160826
845679LV00024B/2090

* 9 7 9 8 8 9 7 2 4 7 4 9 3 *